PICTURE YOURSELF

Learning

Microsoft® Excel® 2010

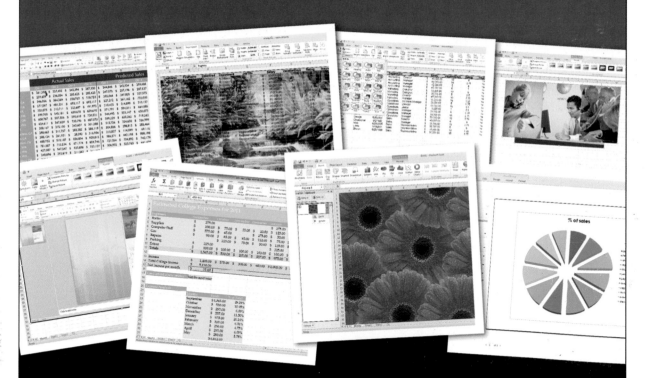

Laurie Ulrich Fuller, Jennifer Fulton, Deidre Hayes, and Jeffery A. Riley

COURSE TECHNOLOGY
CENGAGE Learning™

Picture Yourself Learning Microsoft® Excel® 2010

Laurie Ulrich Fuller, Jennifer Fulton, Deidre Hayes, and Jeffery A. Riley

Publisher and General Manager, Course Technology PTR:
Stacy L. Hiquet

Associate Director of Marketing:
Sarah Panella

Manager of Editorial Services:
Heather Talbot

Marketing Manager:
Jordan Castellani

Acquisitions Editor:
Megan Belanger

Project Editor:
Kezia Endsley

Technical Reviewers:
Keith Davenport, Joyce Nielsen

Copy Editor:
Kezia Endsley

Interior Layout:
Shawn Morningstar

Cover Designer:
Mike Tanamachi

Indexer:
Katherine Stimson

Proofreader:
Brad Crawford

Printed in the United States of America
1 2 3 4 5 6 7 12 11 10

For product information and technology assistance, contact us at

Cengage Learning Customer and Sales Support, 1-800-354-9706

For permission to use material from this text or product, submit all requests online at **cengage.com/permissions**

Further permissions questions can be emailed to **permissionrequest@cengage.com**

Library of Congress Control Number: 2008940752
ISBN-13: 978-1-59863-888-2
ISBN-10: 1-59863-888-2

Course Technology, a part of Cengage Learning
20 Channel Center Street
Boston, MA 02210
USA

Cengage Learning is a leading provider of customized learning solutions with office locations around the globe, including Singapore, the United Kingdom, Australia, Mexico, Brazil, and Japan. Locate your local office at: **international.cengage.com/region**

Cengage Learning products are represented in Canada by Nelson Education, Ltd.

For your lifelong learning solutions, visit **courseptr.com**
Visit our corporate website at **cengage.com**

About the Authors

LAURIE ULRICH FULLER has been using, writing about, and teaching people to use computers for more than 20 years—and has personally trained thousands of people through various colleges, universities, and corporate training centers. She's authored and co-authored more than 25 books on computers, software, and the Internet, beginning with her first books on Microsoft Office in the late 1990s. Her current training focus areas are Microsoft Office and the Adobe Creative Suite, and her most recent books include *Access 2010 for Dummies* and *How to Do Everything with InDesign CS4.* She's the co-author of the *Photoshop Bible* for CS2 and CS3, and produces online and CD-based training in Microsoft Office and Adobe Creative Suite topics, expanding her classroom to include students from all over the world. Laurie also runs her own company, Limehat & Company, which offers training, technical documentation, marketing, design, and promotional services to growing businesses and non-profit organizations. She currently serves on the board of directors for two environmental protection and sustainability organizations in Pennsylvania, where she lives with her husband, mother, and five rescued cats. She invites reader questions about Excel 2010 at help@limehat.com.

JENNIFER FULTON, Senior Partner of Ingenus, LLC and iVillage's former "Computer Coach," is an experienced computer consultant with more than 20 years in the business. Jennifer is a bestselling author of more than 100 computer books for beginner, intermediate, and advanced users, ranging from the self-motivated adult to the college, technical, high school, or middle school student. Jennifer is also a computer trainer for corporate personnel, teaching a variety of classes on Windows, Microsoft Office, PaintShop Pro, Photoshop Elements, and others. In addition, Jennifer has edited and contributed to a number of online college courses.

About the Authors

DEIDRE HAYES spent more than 20 years as a web user experience designer and usability consultant in the corporate environment and has spoken to national audiences on these topics. She oversaw the creation and growth of a successful intranet for a Fortune 500 medical device company and led a team of developers and trainers. Since taking the leap into the freelance world, she has been able to work with a variety of publishers that have given her an opportunity to produce a wide variety of material for readers at all technical levels. When free time allows, she enjoys spending time with her daughter, Alexandra.

JEFFERY A. RILEY, President of Box Twelve Communications, Inc. (www.boxtwelve.com), earned a technical journalism degree from Oregon State University in 1989 and is a former Staff Writer of the *Los Angeles Times.* A 15-year veteran of the Information Technology publishing industry, Jeff has had a hand in—as copy editor, production editor, development editor, acquisitions editor, executive editor, and author— hundreds of books covering IT topics. He is the author of *Introduction to OpenOffice.org* (Prentice Hall) and *2011 Social Media Directory: The Ultimate Guide to Facebook, Twitter, and LinkedIn Resources* (Que Publishing). As president of Box Twelve, he manages the day-to-day operations of a content solutions firm outside Hilton Head, S.C.

Table of Contents

PART III
WORKING WITH GRAPHICS

Introduction

WELCOME TO *Picture Yourself Learning Microsoft Excel 2010*, and the skills and abilities it's about to unleash in you!

Microsoft Excel 2010 is the latest version of what is undoubtedly the world's most popular spreadsheet software. It provides powerful tools for storing and manipulating just about any numerical or text-based data—for accounting, statistics, sales tracking, and scientific analysis—and also gives you effective tools for viewing and accessing the data quickly and conveniently. It's also a great tool for building charts, which take your complex numeric data and convert it to simple, compelling images. Of course, you'll want to use your charts—and perhaps pieces of your worksheets—in your Word and PowerPoint creations, to create a complete set of documents, reports, and presentations that help convey your message to anyone, anywhere. Excel makes that possible, enhancing the power of the entire Office suite.

For all that power, Excel has always been a very user-friendly application, a fact that hasn't changed over the years. There are quite a few tools, however, that bear explaining, which is where this book comes in. For new and self-taught beginning users, this book provides a great set of foundation skills. It then takes readers through more complex and powerful tools, providing comprehensive coverage of a variety of topics that will make this book a must-have for more experienced users as well.

There's "something for everybody" here, so no matter what you imagine when you *Picture Yourself Learning Microsoft Excel 2010*, you'll find what you need to make your imagination a powerful reality.

What You'll Find in This Book

This book is designed to take you from the very basic Excel skills to the more complex features, all at a manageable pace, through the use of visual instruction, clear, informative discussion, logical procedures, and insightful examples. Tips and Notes are plentiful, providing expert advice to go along with the topic at hand, and thus enhancing your understanding.

As a reader, you can take a linear approach, reading the entire book from start to finish, or you can take a more shotgun tactic, looking up just those features you need to use right away. The book can be used effectively either way. We hope, however, that you'll read everything, so that you can confidently say you know how to:

► Open the application and begin using the Excel workspace

► Create your own workbook from scratch

► Add and remove worksheets

► Navigate a workbook with your mouse and keyboard shortcuts

► Save your workbook

► Enter and edit worksheet text and numbers

- ▶ Build your own formulas
- ▶ Understand absolute references and relative addressing
- ▶ Paste formulas to build a series of calculations quickly and uniformly
- ▶ Edit existing formulas
- ▶ Create 3D formulas that combine data from multiple worksheets and workbooks
- ▶ Troubleshoot formula errors
- ▶ Understand and effectively use Excel functions
- ▶ Add and remove columns and rows in a worksheet
- ▶ Apply formatting to make your worksheets and their content more visually appealing
- ▶ Work with Office Themes for a consistent look and feel throughout all your worksheets
- ▶ Add clipart and other images to your worksheets
- ▶ Customize your view of your Excel worksheets and workbooks
- ▶ Use Find and Replace to make corrections and find elusive data
- ▶ Control the order of the records in a list database
- ▶ Generate reports on your data, with built-in calculations
- ▶ Query your database with simple and complex filters

- ▶ Preview, set up, and print your workbooks
- ▶ Customize and control what's included in a printout
- ▶ Scale your printout and control pagination
- ▶ Select the right kind of Excel chart for your needs
- ▶ Format a chart for maximum legibility and visual effectiveness
- ▶ Control who can view and use your workbooks
- ▶ Work with a team to edit a workbook
- ▶ Use Comments and Track Changes to annotate and edit a worksheet
- ▶ Create error messages, warnings, and instructional prompts to help users effectively add data to your worksheets
- ▶ Share your Excel content with Word, PowerPoint, and Access files
- ▶ Build an Excel worksheet from Word and Access tables
- ▶ Export your Excel data in multiple formats for use outside of the Office suite
- ▶ Create customized PivotTable reports that focus on specific areas of your data
- ▶ Build interactive PivotCharts to reflect changing perspectives on your data

Who This Book Is For

Picture Yourself Learning Microsoft Excel 2010 is an effective training and reference book for anyone who is new to Excel, has taught themselves to use portions of the application, or simply wants a great, visual resource to refer to for help in specific areas. The following people will find the book to be of particular benefit:

- ▶ Anyone who needs to create and maintain a budget—whether for a business, a household, a church, a club, or a project

- ▶ Owners of growing businesses who need to track productivity, goals, and business plans

- ▶ Accountants and bookkeepers

- ▶ Human resources and payroll managers who need to keep track of employee data, timesheets, and expense reports

- ▶ Customer service representatives, needing to track calls from and responses to customer inquiries

- ▶ Salespeople and sales support staff who maintain lists of customers, vendors, and products

- ▶ Scientists and researchers who need to store and analyze data derived from tests, surveys, and experiments

- ▶ People who manage non-profit organizations, and need to keep track of donors, volunteers, activities, grants and grant applications, and funding

- ▶ Students who need to keep track of projects and tests

How This Book Is Organized

This book contains 15 chapters, divided into four sections.

Part I, called "Just the Basics," includes the following chapters:

- ▶ **Chapter 1, "Creating a Basic Excel Worksheet"** The foundation skills required to open Excel and get working on your own worksheet, from scratch, are the focus of this chapter. You'll also learn to open existing worksheets and edit their content, as well as add, remove, name, and group your worksheets, and navigate a workbook quickly to speed the data-entry and editing process.

- ▶ **Chapter 2, "Working with Formulas"** In this chapter, you'll learn to build your own formulas from scratch, using cell addresses and your own numbers and values, and controlling order of operations. You'll discover how to paste formulas, and how to edit existing formulas to reflect changes in goals and locations of data within your workbooks. You'll also learn to build 3D formulas that draw data from multiple workbooks and worksheets.

- ▶ **Chapter 3, "Using Excel Functions"** Excel's built-in functions allow you to calculate everything from a simple average to complex statistical analyses. Master the basic functions and tackle the more advanced ones, too—and learn to combine and customize them for your specific needs.

▶ **Chapter 4, "Troubleshooting Formula Errors"** Nobody's perfect, and formulas can be really confusing if you're not sure why they're not working properly. Read this chapter and understand the error messages Excel gives you. You learn to edit your formulas so they give you the results you expect.

▶ **Chapter 5, "Making the Worksheet Look Good"** No matter how accurate and comprehensive your data is, if it's not laid out logically and legibly, nobody will notice the hard work you put into building your worksheets. In this chapter, you'll learn to make your worksheets attractive, consistent, and to draw your users' eyes to the key pieces of information—by adding, removing, and resizing columns and rows, applying color, formatting text and numbers, and using Office Themes and conditional formatting tools.

Part II, called "Handling Larger Workbooks," includes the following chapters:

▶ **Chapter 6, "Managing Large Amounts of Excel Data"** New workbooks start with three worksheets, but you'll find it's easy to add them, and you'll have plenty of reasons to do so—resulting in very large workbooks that you need help managing. Learn to name and group your worksheets, work with and combine worksheets from multiple workbooks, customize your views of your data, and use Find and Replace to search your data to locate and edit specific information.

▶ **Chapter 7, "Sorting Data"** Putting your worksheet data in the right order is key to using it efficiently. If you need to see things alphabetically or numerically—or both—understanding Excel's data sorting tools is essential. In this chapter, you'll also learn to create subtotal reports that include calculations based on your sorted and grouped data, adding dimension and value to your worksheet's content.

▶ **Chapter 8, "Filtering Data"** Finding all the records with something in common or finding the one record you need for any reason could take a long time—if you don't know the tricks to quickly query worksheet data. Learn to use Excel's various filtering tools to show you only the records you need, when you need them.

▶ **Chapter 9, "Preparing to Print"** Need to confine your printout to one page? Want your column letters and row numbers to appear on the print out to make it easier to read? Need page numbers or your name to appear on all the pages of your printout? You can do this and so much more, and this chapter shows you all the ins and outs of managing your print jobs, including preparing and previewing them so there are no surprises when the paper emerges from your printer.

▶ **Chapter 10, "Printing and Other Output Formats"** Once your worksheet's ready to print—all set up and ready to go—you'll want to send it to the right printer and make sure you get just the parts you need and the number of copies you want. You'll also want to know how to share your worksheets and workbooks by e-mail, and this chapter tells you all about that, too.

Part III, called "Working with Graphics," includes the following chapters:

▶ **Chapter 11, "Generating Excel Charts"**
If a picture's worth a thousand words, a chart is worth a million. Taking complex and possibly dull numeric data and turning it into a picture that quickly says, "Sales are up!" or "Productivity is down!" in one simple image is a valuable skill, and you'll acquire it in this chapter. Learn which kind of chart you need for the data you have and the audience you're targeting, the best and quickest ways to build the chart, how to change your chart's type and the data included after the chart already exists, and how to make your chart more visually appealing.

▶ **Chapter 12, "Inserting Illustrations"**
Whether you want to add clipart, photos, a logo, or drawn shapes and lines to your worksheet, this chapter will show you how. You'll learn to dress up your worksheets and draw attention to key data as you resize, move, and crop images, control their stacking order, and use SmartArt to make your worksheets leap off the page or screen and get noticed.

Part IV, called "Using Excel Tools," includes the following chapters:

▶ **Chapter 13 , "Setting Security Options"**
Security is especially important if your worksheets contain salary information, medical data, legally-protected content, or anything you consider sensitive, for any reason. In this chapter, you'll learn to control who can access your Excel worksheets and what they can do to the data if they're allowed to open the workbook in the first place.

▶ **Chapter 14, "Collaborating with Others"**
Although some Excel users may work alone, most worksheets are a collaborative effort. If you need to work with a team to create and maintain your data, this chapter will be an invaluable resource for adding comments to a worksheet, tracking changes so you can tell who edited which cells and what adjustments were made, and for controlling what kind of data can be entered and edited in a worksheet. You'll learn to set up validation rules that help your users understand what kind of data is required in particular cells, and prevent data entry errors before they happen.

▶ **Chapter 15, "Using PivotTables"**
PivotTables are probably the most misunderstood—and most powerful—of Excel's many features, but they're really quite simple to create and customize. In this chapter, you'll learn to select the data to include in the PivotTable, how to structure the PivotTable to show you only the information you need to see, and to add simple calculations—sums, averages, counts—that add dimension to your analysis of the data. You'll also learn to create interactive PivotCharts that reflect the PivotTable data.

Welcome to the book—we hope you enjoy the journey!

Part I
Just the Basics

Creating a Basic

Excel Worksheet

PICTURE YOURSELF HAVING to make a difficult decision. Perhaps you want to buy a new car, or decide which college to attend, or which investment option will result in the biggest return. There are many criteria to consider—some positive and some negative—about each alternative. If only there were a way to compile the data in a way that makes the decision easier. There is...Excel!

Microsoft Excel is the most widely used spreadsheet program in the world. A spreadsheet is a software application that organizes data in rows and columns. Spreadsheets are most commonly used to manipulate numerical data like those used to establish your household budget, calculate profit/loss statements for your business, or determine your GPA.

As good as Excel is at handling numerical data, it can also be used to organize other types of data, including text and formulas. Use the rows and columns in Excel to enter data about your household inventory for your insurance needs, your address book to make sure that birthday cards are sent out on time, or even catalogue your CD collection. Once the data has been stored in Excel, you can sort and filter the data to suit your needs.

Understanding how to create an effective spreadsheet can help you make better decisions. But first, let's start with the basics.

Exploring Excel

TO OPEN EXCEL, choose Start > All Programs > Microsoft Office > Microsoft Excel 2010. When you launch Excel, the application opens a blank document, called a workbook, as illustrated in Figure 1-1. With all of the visual stimuli found in the number of buttons, icons, rows, and columns, even a blank Excel document might appear overwhelming, but take a few minutes to familiarize yourself with all of these elements and you'll be ready to begin entering your own data.

Identifying Screen Elements

A spreadsheet program is a software application that organizes your data into horizontal rows and vertical columns. That portion of Excel is called the worksheet area. Rows are numbered and columns are identified by letters. Above the worksheet area, the Ribbon is a collection of the commands you will use within Excel.

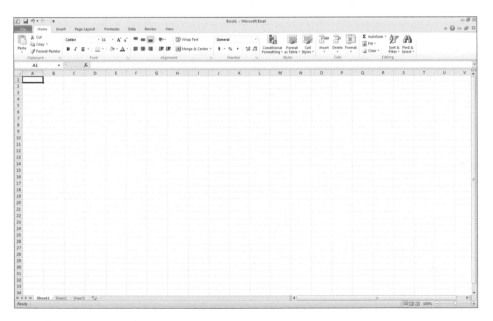

Figure 1-1
The Excel spreadsheet.

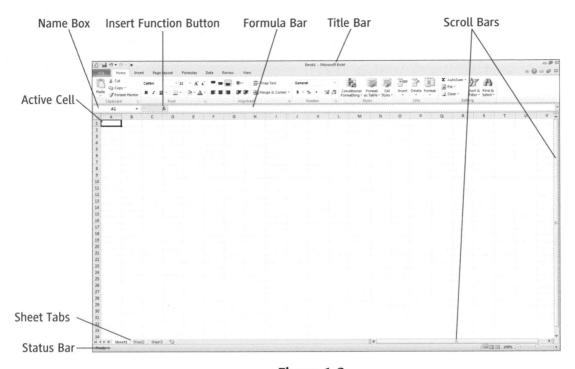

Figure 1-2
Elements of the Excel window.

Apart from the Ribbon, which will be discussed later in this chapter, you will need to be aware of several other elements (see Figure 1-2).

- ▶ **Title bar:** At the top of the application you see a title bar that shows the application name and the file name.

- ▶ **Active cell:** The currently selected cell is called the active cell. The active cell has a thick border around it.

Cell Addresses

Every cell in Excel has an address. The cell address is the column letter and row number associated with a particular cell. Cell A1 is the cell address for the cell that is active when Excel is first opened.

- ▶ **Name box:** Shows the cell address, or name, of the active cell. You can use the range name feature to customize this name. (See "Working with Range Names" later in this chapter.)

- ▶ **Insert Function button:** Opens the Insert Function dialog box. (See Chapter 3, "Using Excel Functions.")

- ▶ **Formula bar:** Displays the contents of the active cell.

- ▶ **Scroll bars:** Excel worksheets have both horizontal and vertical scroll bars.

- ▶ **Sheet tabs:** A new Excel Workbook opens with three worksheets. You can delete unneeded worksheets, or add extra worksheets to suit your needs.

► **Status bar:** At the bottom of the Excel screen is the status bar that provides feedback to you of the current state of your worksheet. The status bar will indicate if the worksheet is ready for data entry, busy calculating, or has identified an error.

Tip

Don't think that Sheet1 is the best name for your worksheet? You can rename the sheet tabs. Double-click the sheet tab name and type a name that better describes your data.

Zeroing in on the Ribbon

First introduced in Microsoft Office 2007, the Ribbon (see Figure 1-3) is common to all Microsoft Office applications. It visually displays all of the most commonly used options needed to perform a particular task. The Ribbon groups these command buttons under functional tabs.

► **Excel program icon:** Clicking on the program icon in the upper-left corner of Excel displays a menu with options for minimizing and closing the application.

► **Quick Access Toolbar:** The Quick Access Toolbar provides access to basic file functions. By default, those functions are Save, Undo, and Redo. However, as demonstrated in Figure 1-4, you can click the Customize Quick Access Toolbar arrow and choose More Commands from the drop-down menu to add the commands that you use most frequently.

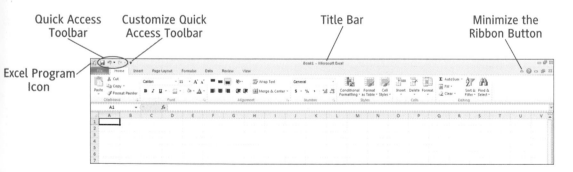

Figure 1-3
Excel's Ribbon is a task-based collection of the commands you can perform in the application.

Figure 1-4
Customize the Quick Access Toolbar to include
the commands that you use most frequently.

▶ **Minimize the Ribbon button:** Click the
Minimize the Ribbon button to remove
all but the Tabs from the Ribbon, as
shown in Figure 1-5. When the Ribbon
is minimized, this button changes to
become the Expand the Ribbon button.
You can temporarily expand the Ribbon
by clicking any of the tabs.

Figure 1-5
Reduce the size of the Ribbon with the
Minimize the Ribbon button.

▶ **Tabs:** Excel command buttons are organized under eight tabs: File, Home, Insert, Page Layout, Formulas, Data, Review, and View. Other tabs appear only when needed. For instance, the Chart Tools tab appears only after you have selected a chart in Excel. Clicking different tabs changes the command options visible on the Ribbon.

▶ **Groups:** Each of the tabs is divided into several collections of related tasks. These collections are called *groups*.

▶ **Dialog Box Launcher:** Some of the groups on the Ribbon include a small arrow icon in the bottom-right corner of the group. This icon is called the Dialog Box Launcher, and clicking it opens a dialog box to refine how the command is applied to your file. Figure 1-6 shows the Insert Chart dialog box launched from the Charts group on the Insert tab.

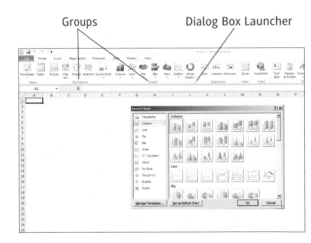

Figure 1-6
The Dialog Box Launcher opens a dialog
box with additional options related to
the command group you selected.

▶ **Galleries:** A Gallery is most often a collection of related formatting options. For instance, in Figure 1-7, clicking the down arrow next to the Themes command button on the Page Layout tab displays a preview of all themes that can be applied to your document. Make a selection from the gallery or click the arrow again to close the gallery. Themes are discussed further in Chapter 5, "Making the Worksheet Look Good."

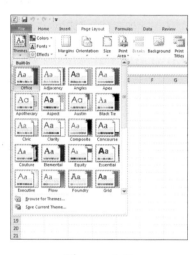

Figure 1-7
The Themes Gallery shows you all themes that can be applied to your document.

Introducing the Backstage View

New to Office 2010 applications is the introduction of a Backstage view of the documents you are working with. The Backstage view is a collection of the commands you use to open a new or existing document. You will also find the commands you might use as you are exiting a document. For instance, commands related to saving, printing, protecting, versioning, and storing properties about your document. None of these commands affect the appearance of the document and affect the whole file, not just a portion of the file. To access Excel's Backstage view, choose the File tab on the Ribbon. Let's take a look at some of the things you can do from this new view.

▶ **Info tab:** Illustrated in Figure 1-8, the Info tab can be used to establish security options for the file, like requiring a password to open the file, or protecting the file from changes to the formatting. You can also record data about your files. You will learn more about these features later in this chapter.

Figure 1-8
Excel 2010's File tab gives you access to the new Backstage view.

Caution

If you close a file in Excel without saving it first, Excel will remind you to save a copy as in previous versions. Excel 2010 goes one step further by automatically saving a copy of your file every 10 minutes while you are working. You will be prompted to open the latest version of that file when you re-open Excel.

▶ **Recent tab:** This tab displays a list of the last 20 documents that were opened in Excel 2010.

▶ **New tab:** Open a new blank spreadsheet, or create a new file based on one of the dozens of templates provided with Excel. Excel gives all new workbooks a default file name (Book1, Book2, and so on) until you replace it.

▶ **Print tab:** Change the page layout, attach headers and footers, select a printer, and specify exactly what you want Excel to print from this tab. You'll learn more about these options in Chapter 10, "Printing and Other Output Formats."

▶ **Save & Send tab:** With the Save & Send tab, you can either send your file as an e-mail attachment, create a PDF version of the file, or save it online, where others can view it with one of the new Office Web applications. You can read more about this tab later in this chapter.

▶ **Help tab:** From this tab, you can access simple solutions to common questions, as well as get information about product support, and links to contact Microsoft directly with your questions or suggestions about Excel. If you are new to Excel, the Getting Started button offers a variety of online tutorials and additional training to accelerate your learning curve. The Options button opens the Excel Options dialog box.

Moving Around the Excel Screen

EACH WORKSHEET IN EXCEL has more than 17 billion individual cells. Luckily, Excel offers several methods using your mouse, your keyboard, and even the Ribbon for moving around them all. Depending on how you use Excel, you may find that you will use all three methods.

Using the Keyboard

Arguably the easiest, but surely the most common, way to move around an Excel worksheet is by using the keyboard. Table 1-1 displays some of the ways you can use the keyboard to move around an Excel workbook.

Table 1-1   Keystroke Movement in Excel

Keystroke	Movement
Arrow keys	Moves one cell at a time in the direction of the arrow
Tab	Moves one cell right
Shift+Tab	Moves one cell left
Enter	Moves one cell down
Shift+Enter	Moves one cell up
Page Up	Moves one full screen up in the current column
Page Down	Moves one full screen down in the current column
Home	Moves to the first cell in column A of the current row
Ctrl+Home	Moves to first cell in the spreadsheet, cell A1
Ctrl+End	Moves to the last cell in the spreadsheet that has any data in it
Alt+Page Down	Moves right one screen in the current row
Alt+Page Up	Moves left one screen in the current row
Ctrl+Arrow key	Moves to the next adjacent cell that contains data, depending on the direction of the arrow
Ctrl+Page Down	Moves to the next worksheet (see Figure 1-9)
Ctrl+Page Up	Moves to the previous worksheet

Active Worksheet

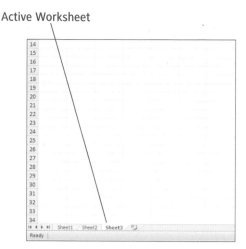

Figure 1-9
Sheet3 is the active worksheet in this Excel workbook.

Tip

If the Ctrl+End keystroke takes you to a blank cell, then Excel remembered something you didn't. This keystroke moves to the intersection of the last row and column that contains data, even if that cell is blank.

Using a Mouse

Any cell that you click on becomes the new active cell. You can use your mouse to select any cell that you can see on the spreadsheet. Use the scroll bars to make more of the worksheet visible. Both the horizontal and vertical scroll bars have arrows at each end (see Figure 1-10) to continue scrolling the worksheet.

Another way to use the mouse within Excel is to toggle between worksheets in your current workbook. New workbooks contain three worksheets, labeled Sheet1, Sheet2, and Sheet3. Clicking any worksheet tab makes that sheet appear on top of the other worksheets as the new active worksheet. Chapter 6, "Managing Large Amounts of Excel Data," will describe how to use multiple worksheets.

Finally, you can use the mouse to select the Name box. If you know the cell address, you can type it into the Name box, press Enter, and move the worksheet directly to that cell.

Scroll Bar Arrows

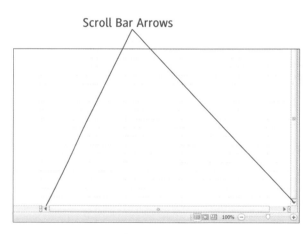

Figure 1-10
The scroll bars allow you to move quickly through an Excel sheet with the mouse.

Tip

If you want to see the last cell in the Excel worksheet, type the cell address XFD1048576 into the Name box and press Enter. Then, press Ctrl+Home to return to the beginning of the worksheet.

Using the Ribbon

You can use the Go To command to activate a specific cell or area of the worksheet. The Ribbon command for executing the Go To command is Home > Editing > Find & Select > Go To. When the Go To dialog box opens, enter the cell address into the Reference box and click the OK button (see Figure 1-11).

Figure 1-11
The Go To dialog box.

Understanding Ribbon Commands

Ribbon commands are easy to follow. The first term (Home) is the tab name, the second term (Editing) is the group name. The last term (Go To) is the command name. If, as in this case, the Ribbon command includes a third term (Find & Select), click the arrow next to the option to open the gallery and find the final command.

Using the Go To command in this manner is exactly the same as typing the cell address in the Name box, however, the Go To command remembers any previous cell addresses that you had entered, which makes returning to specific areas of a worksheet a breeze.

Tip

You can also use a keyboard shortcut to open the Go To dialog box. Press the F5 key, or the Ctrl+G key combination to display this dialog box directly.

Entering Excel Data

ANYTHING YOU CAN TYPE INTO a worksheet's cell can be called data. Whenever you type something into a cell, Excel tries to determine what type of data it is. Excel recognizes three specific types of data: labels (or text), values (or numbers), and formulas (or equations). Formulas are introduced in Chapter 2, "Working with Formulas," so for now you'll spend time learning the differences between labels and values.

Perhaps you are creating a spreadsheet that details the number of days in each month of the year, as in Figure 1-12. The month names are labels, the days are values, and the total number of days is calculated by Excel using a formula.

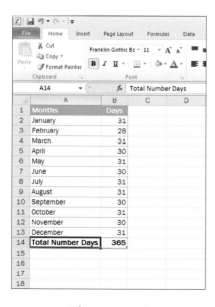

Figure 1-12
A spreadsheet that includes labels, values, and a formula.

Entering Data into a Cell

Regardless of the type of data you want to enter, all data is entered in Excel the same way.

1. Select the cell in which you want to type.

2. Type the information you want into the cell.

3. Press Enter or Tab to accept your data entry and move to the next cell.

Entering Labels

Labels can also be thought of as information about the numerical data in Excel. Excel assumes that any data containing letters is a label and will format it accordingly. Labels are left-aligned in the cell, and cannot be calculated using a formula.

All About Cell Width

By default, the standard width of a cell is 8.43. According to Microsoft, this means that 8.43 characters will fit into the cell. If your label has more than 8.43 characters, Excel automatically extends the data you typed beyond the cell's right border. You will learn how to resize the cells in Chapter 5, "Making the Worksheet Look Good."

Entering Values

A value is any kind of numerical data, or data that can be calculated using a formula. Excel aligns values along the right cell border so that the place value of the data is aligned. Think back to grade school and remember that you learned to line up your ones, tens, and hundreds places to make adding easier. Excel does that for you.

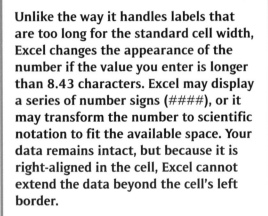

Caution

Unlike the way it handles labels that are too long for the standard cell width, Excel changes the appearance of the number if the value you enter is longer than 8.43 characters. Excel may display a series of number signs (####), or it may transform the number to scientific notation to fit the available space. Your data remains intact, but because it is right-aligned in the cell, Excel cannot extend the data beyond the cell's left border.

Entering Dates

Now let's talk about dates. Excel does not handle dates exactly the same as either labels or values. Even though dates may contain text, dates also have numbers that can be calculated, so they are technically values. As such, dates are aligned along the right cell border.

In order to perform calculations on your dates, behind the scenes Excel must assign a numerical value to all dates. For instance, to Excel January 1, 1900, is assigned a value of 1, meaning that Excel treats this as the first day. Excel handles any date before January 1, 1900, as a label and cannot perform calculations on such dates.

Although this internal calculation does not affect the appearance of dates in your spreadsheet, Excel does have 17 preset date formats, as shown in Figure 1-13, that you can apply to your worksheet. You will learn more about them in Chapter 5, "Making the Worksheet Look Good."

Tip

The following are significant dates in history as recognized by Excel's internal date values.

Date Value	Calendar Date	Event
16,682	September 2, 1945	The end of World War II
27,945	July 4, 1976	America's 200th birthday
36,526	January 1, 2000	Arguably, the beginning of the 21st century

The Same Date Is Entered in Every Row

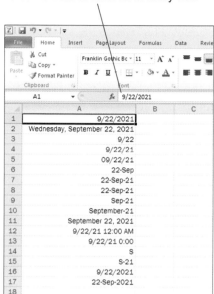

Figure 1-13
Preset date formats in Excel 2010.

Caution

Excel sees dates everywhere. If you are entering invoice number 01-21, Excel assumes you meant January 21 and reformats your number as a date. Refer to Chapter 5, "Making the Worksheet Look Good," to learn how to protect your data from this reformatting.

Using AutoFill

The makers of Excel knew that there are certain types of data that invariably end up inside a spreadsheet: months of the year, days of the week, a series of numbers, and yearly quarters, such as Q1. They found a way to make it easier, and frankly more fun, to enter this type of data—the AutoFill feature.

Follow these steps to use the AutoFill feature in your worksheet.

1. Type the first data item, such as Sunday or January, into the first cell of your series, and press Enter to accept the entry and move to the next cell.

Type Series in Any Order

You do not need to begin your series with the first month of the year, or the first day of the week. Excel will correctly fill the selected cells regardless of your starting point.

2. Left-click on the fill handle, the small black box at the lower-right corner of the active cell, and drag the fill handle across all of the cells you want to fill. You can drag the mouse in any direction.

3. When you release the mouse button, Excel fills in the selected cells with a continuation of your data. Figure 1-14 shows how Excel fills in the cells with a continuation of the months.

Fill Handle

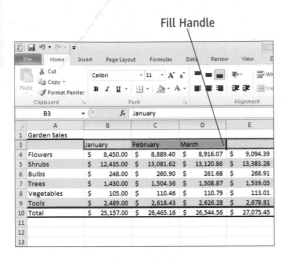

Figure 1-14
Using AutoFill for the months of the year.

4. To AutoFill a series of numbers, you need to enter two data items, not just one. If you enter 1 and 2 in two adjacent cells, select the cells, and then drag the fill handle, Excel will fill the selected cells with 3, 4, 5, and so on. If you enter 2 and 4, Excel will fill the adjacent cells with 6, 8, 10, and so on. Remember to highlight both cells before you drag the fill handle.

You can use also use the AutoFill feature with any sequence that begins with a label and ends with a value, such as Quarter 1 or Inning 1. Excel will leave the label intact and continue the number series. Quarter 1 extends to Quarter 2, Quarter 3, and so on.

AutoFill Repeats Your Data

Apart from the special cases mentioned previously, if you use AutoFill on a single data item, Excel repeats it in the selected cells. For example, if you use AutoFill on a cell with the word *Bunny*, all filled cells contain the word Bunny.

Selecting Cells on a Spreadsheet

NOW THAT YOU KNOW HOW to enter data into a spreadsheet, you will need to know how to select cells. You already know that you can use the mouse to click on a specific cell, the active cell, so you already know a little something about selecting cells on a spreadsheet. However, what do you do if you want to select more than one cell? Selected cells are called cell ranges. A *cell range* can be a single cell, which is also called the active cell, or an entire spreadsheet, and anything in between.

Mouse Pointer Shape

Make sure that the mouse pointer is shaped like a white cross before trying to select cells.

Excel indicates a cell range has been selected by highlighting it, as illustrated in Figure 1-15. As you can see, the selected cells do not have to be adjacent to each other to be selected.

Figure 1-15
Several cell ranges selected in Excel 2010.

Using the Mouse

By far the most common method for selecting cell ranges in Excel is to click one cell and then drag the mouse over the rest of the desired cells.

Try these other methods for selecting cell ranges with the mouse:

▶ Select an entire row by clicking the row number.

▶ Select multiple adjacent rows by dragging the mouse over several row numbers, as shown in Figure 1-16.

▶ Select an entire column by clicking the column number.

▶ Select multiple adjacent columns by dragging the mouse over several column numbers.

▶ Select non-adjacent cells by clicking the first cell, then holding down the Ctrl key while you click each addition cell, or range of cells, you want to include in your selection.

Mouse Pointer Shape, Part II

The mouse pointer will change from a white cross to a black arrow whenever the mouse is positioned over a row or column heading. This change indicates that the action will affect the entire row or column.

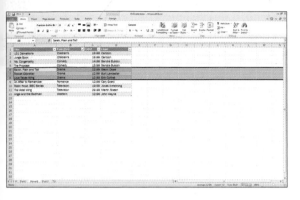

Figure 1-16
Adjacent rows have been selected in this cell range.

Using a Keyboard

Keeping both hands on the keyboard to select cell ranges may save time and productivity. Table 1-2 demonstrates some keyboard shortcuts you can use in Excel 2010.

To select several adjacent columns, you first have to select a cell from each of the desired columns and then use the Ctrl+Spacebar keyboard shortcut. The same is true if you are trying to select multiple rows: first select cells from the required rows, and then use the keyboard shortcut.

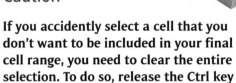

Caution

If you accidently select a cell that you don't want to be included in your final cell range, you need to clear the entire selection. To do so, release the Ctrl key and click any non-selected cell. Then start your selection process again.

Table 1-2   Keyboard Shortcuts for Selecting Cell Ranges

Keystroke	Result
Shift+arrows	Selects multiple cells, in any direction, that are adjacent to your starting point.
Ctrl+Spacebar	Selects the entire column.
Shift+Spacebar	Selects the entire row.

Editing a Worksheet

NO MATTER HOW GOOD WE THINK we are, we all make mistakes. Typos are a given when you are dealing with large amounts of data. So, how do you fix them? Obviously, you can click in any offending cell and retype the entry correctly, but that's not always the fastest method.

If you don't want to have to retype the entry, you can edit the existing entry by following these steps:

1. Double-click the cell, or press F2, to select the cell in Edit mode. The insertion point blinks inside the cell at the end of the entry and the status bar indicates that you are in Edit mode, as shown in Figure 1-17.

2. Use the arrow keys to place the insertion point at the point of the error.

3. Type your changes in the cell. Don't forget to remove the incorrect data. Use Delete to erase the characters to the right of the inscrtion point and use Backspace to remove the characters to the left.

4. Press Enter to accept the changes.

Tip

You can edit the contents of a cell by clicking in the Formula bar and making the change there.

Insertion Point

Edit Mode

Figure 1-17
Making a data entry correction in Excel.

Using Undo and Redo

Picture yourself concentrating really hard on your spreadsheet when someone sneaks up behind you and startles you into clicking on some unknown command button from the Ribbon. You don't have any idea what happened, but you know that it's not right. That's why the Undo command was created.

▶ To correct your last mistake, choose Undo from the Quick Access Toolbar (see Figure 1-18) or press Ctrl+Z.

▶ To correct several mistakes at once, click the Undo down arrow and find the action in the list. Excel will undo all of the actions above the one you are selecting, so choose carefully.

Undo Command   Redo Command

Figure 1-18
Reverse one or more mistakes using the Undo command.

If you undo an action and then decide that you want to restore it after all, choose Redo from the Quick Access Toolbar, or press Ctrl+Y. Unlike the Undo command, the Redo command only restores the last action.

Caution

If you close your worksheet before you caught your mistake, you cannot use the Undo command to reverse the error. Check your work before you close your files.

Inserting and Deleting Cells

You might find yourself in the position of having forgotten crucial data for your spreadsheet. Perhaps you entered January's data and moved right onto March without entering data for February. You can insert a new row or column between the two existing data sets to correct that problem. Figure 1-19 demonstrates this situation.

▶ To insert an entire row, select a row where you want your new row to be. Choose Home > Cells > Insert (arrow) and choose Insert Sheet Rows. Excel inserts a new blank row and shifts the selected row and all rows below it down to make room.

▶ To insert an entire column, select a column where you want your new column to be. Choose Home > Cells > Insert (arrow) and choose Insert Sheet Columns. Excel inserts a new blank column and shifts the selected column and all other columns to the right to make room.

You don't always need to insert an entire row or column. You can also insert a single cell, or range of cells, into your worksheet.

1. Select a cell, or cells, adjacent to where you want to place the new cells.

2. Choose Home > Cells > Insert (arrow) and choose Insert Cells.

3. On the Insert dialog box (see Figure 1-20), choose the option that will place your new cells where you want them to be.

4. Click OK and Excel will shift the existing cells to make room for your new cells.

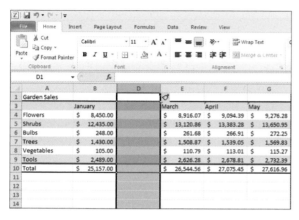

Figure 1-19
Inserting a new column.

Figure 1-20
Choose the option that will place your new cells in the correct location.

Selecting and Inserting Rows

To insert multiple rows or columns, select an equal number of rows or columns first and follow the previous steps. For instance, if you want to insert two columns, you must first select two columns.

Deleting Cells Is Easy

You can delete cells just as easily in Excel. The Ribbon path for deleting cells is Home > Cells > Delete (arrow). Then choose Delete Cells, Delete Sheet Rows, or Delete Sheet Columns to suit your needs.

Moving and Copying Data

YOU'VE LEARNED HOW TO SELECT your data and how to edit it, but that's not enough. You also need to know how to move it. You can do this using either a drag-and-drop method with your mouse, or use the Windows Clipboard to cut and paste your data.

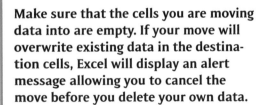

Caution

Make sure that the cells you are moving data into are empty. If your move will overwrite existing data in the destination cells, Excel will display an alert message allowing you to cancel the move before you delete your own data.

Dragging and Dropping Data

You already experimented with dragging the mouse earlier in this chapter as you practiced selecting cells, but drag and drop can also be used to move data from one location on your spreadsheet to another.

1. Select the cells you want to move.

2. Move the mouse pointer to the highlighted border of your selection. The mouse pointer will change into a four-sided arrow.

3. Click and hold while you use the mouse to drag the cells to the new destination (see Figure 1-21) and release the mouse button to accept the change.

Figure 1-21
Moving a cell range using the drag-and-drop method.

Using Cut, Copy, and Paste

Cut and paste are often thought of as the keyboard equivalent of the drag-and-drop method. There are Ribbon command buttons for these options, but once you are more comfortable with their actions, you will probably use the keyboard shortcuts more often.

If you want to use the commands listed in Table 1-3 to move data from one location to a new destination on your spreadsheet:

1. Select the data cells you want to move, following the steps you learned in "Selecting Cells on a Spreadsheet," earlier in this chapter.

2. Press Ctrl+X. The data will be temporarily surrounded by a marquee (which looks ants marching around the cells), as in Figure 1-22.

3. Select the destination cell and press Ctrl+V to move the data.

Tip

If you already entered your data in a row and wished you'd entered it in a column instead (or vice versa), you don't have to delete it and start over. Copy the data and then select the destination cell and choose Home > Clipboard > Paste (arrow). Choose Transpose (see Figure 1-23) and Excel will reformat the data for you.

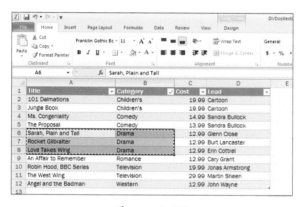

Figure 1-22
A marquee appears around the outside border of the cell range to be cut.

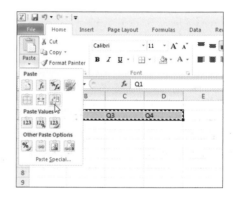

Figure 1-23
The Transpose feature will re-orient your data from rows to columns, or the reverse.

Table 1-3 Basic Keyboard Shortcuts for Cut, Copy, and Paste

Keystroke Shortcut	Ribbon Path	Icon
Ctrl+X	Home > Clipboard > Cut	✂ Cut
Ctrl+C	Home > Clipboard > Copy	📋 Copy ▾
Ctrl+V	Home > Clipboard > Paste	📋 Paste

Working with Range Names

THE LARGER AND MORE COMPLEX your spreadsheets become, the harder it is to remember where the most important data is in the file. If you find yourself searching for the same data again and again, consider assigning a range name to the cells containing that data. By assigning a descriptive name to a single cell or range of cells, you will be able to find that data more quickly.

Naming a Range of Cells

Even though range names are meant to be customized to your requirements, you will still need to follow these simple rules.

▶ **Range names cannot contain spaces.** Use an underscore to take the place of a space. For example, instead of Spring Sales, the range name would be Spring_Sales.

▶ **Range names must begin with a letter, not a number.** For example, use Quarter_3, not 3rd_Quarter.

▶ **Range names cannot be named anything that might be interpreted by Excel to mean an actual cell address.** For example, Q3 is not a good range name because it could be a valid cell address, whereas Quarter3 would make an acceptable range name.

To name a cell or cell range, follow these steps:

1. Select the cell or cell range you want to name.

2. Click the Name box and type the new name for the selected range of cells (see Figure 1-24).

3. Press Enter to accept the change and continue working.

Range Name   Selected Cell

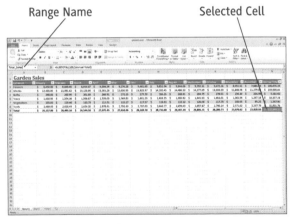

Figure 1-24
Creating a range name in the Name box.

Finding Named Ranges

Excel provides two methods for finding your named ranges in the spreadsheet:

> ▶ Choose Home > Editing > Find & Select > Go To and select your desired name from the list in the Go To dialog box (see Figure 1-25).

> ▶ Click the down arrow in the Name box of the worksheet and select your desired name from the list.

In either case, Excel immediately highlights the selected cells, just as if you had selected them manually.

Figure 1-25
Using the Go To command to find a named range.

Using the Name Manager

You've learned how to add new named ranges using the Name box of your spreadsheet, but Excel also provides a Name Manager feature from the Ribbon. This tool offers you a way to edit and delete existing named ranges, as well as create new ones.

To edit or delete an existing name, choose Formulas > Defined Names > Name Manager from the Ribbon. Excel will display the Name Manager dialog box shown in Figure 1-26. Select the range name that you want to edit or delete and click the appropriate button.

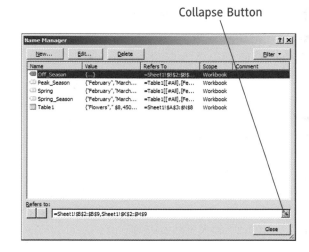

Figure 1-26
Use the Name Manager to add, edit, or delete range names.

To add a new name using the Name Manager:

1. Click the New button and enter a range name in the Name box.

2. Click the Collapse button, shown in Figure 1-27, and use your mouse to select the cells in your range.

3. Click the Collapse button again to return to the full-sized New Name dialog box and click OK when you are finished.

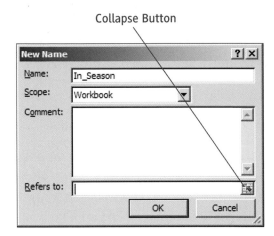

Collapse Button

Figure 1-27
Adding a new range name using the Name Manager.

Understanding Data Validation

YOUR WORKSHEET WORKS FOR YOU only if the data entered is valuable. Typos and carelessness can ruin your data. Imagine that you were paid solely on commission and the payroll manager made a mistake when she entered your largest sale of the year. Your wallet would be directly affected by a data entry error.

Excel provides a Data Validation feature that can help protect the data in your worksheet. Data validation helps restrict the kind of data that is entered into a specific cell, or range of cells. Data can be restricted in the following ways:

- ► **Values:** You can specify that whole numbers or decimals be used, and you can choose minimum and maximum values. For instance, a realtor's commission may be restricted to a maximum of .07, or 7%, of the sales price.

- ► **Dates and Times:** You can require a specific date, or specify that the dates fall within a certain range. For example, only dates within the current year are valid.

- ► **Text:** You can specify that the data in these fields is a specific length. For example, telephone numbers are 10 digits long if you include the area code and do not include the dashes.

- ► **Lists:** You can create a list in another area of the worksheet and then require that all entries in the validated cell be one of the items in that list.

Accepting Blank Cells

In addition to these validation options, you can also decide whether to accept blank cells in your data. Click to deselect the Ignore Blank option when you are creating your validation to prevent your spreadsheet users from leaving blanks in the data.

Applying Data Validation

Follow these steps to apply data validation to a range of cells:

1. Select the cells you want Excel to validate.

2. Choose Data > Data Tools > Data Validation to open the Data Validation dialog box as shown in Figure 1-28.

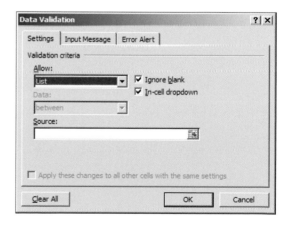

Figure 1-28
The Data Validation dialog box has three tabs.

3. On the Settings tab, open the Allow drop-down menu and choose which type of validation you want to apply.

4. If needed, open the Data drop-down menu to refine your validation criteria. If you entered criteria in the Data box, you may also need to specify the requirements in the Minimum and Maximum boxes.

5. If you choose List in the Allow drop-down menu, you have the option of entering all of the values for the list in a named range somewhere else in your spreadsheet. Make sure the In-cell drop-down option on the Settings tab is checked so that Excel will display the list of acceptable data entry items in the cell when users select that cell.

6. Consider adding a message to alert users of the data validation requirements before they begin entering data. On the Input Message tab, type a message title in the Title box and type your message in the Input Message box. The users will see a pop-up message with a bold text title, shown in Figure 1-29, as soon as the cell has been selected.

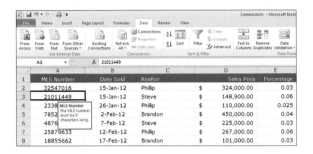

Figure 1-29
The input message is displayed whenever the cell is selected.

7. Excel displays a default error message when data entered into a cell cannot be validated. You can specify the text on the message to remind users exactly what the rules are for a particular cell. From the Error Alert tab (see Figure 1-30), type a title for the message in the Title box, and type your message in the Error Message box.

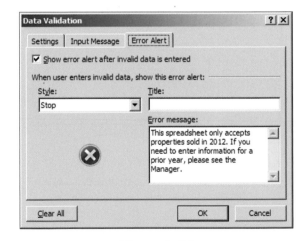

Figure 1-30
The Error Alert tab on the Data Validation dialog box.

8. Choose one of the following error message styles from the Style drop-down menu.

Style	Purpose
Stop	Prevents users from entering any invalid data. Displays an error message with Retry or Cancel options. Stop is the most restrictive error message.
Warning	Warns users that they have entered invalid data, but does not prevent them from doing so. Displays an error message with Yes (to accept the invalid entry), No (to edit the invalid entry), or Cancel (to remove the invalid data) options.
Information	Informs users that they have entered invalid data, but does not prevent them from doing so. Displays an error message with OK (to accept the invalid entry) or Cancel (to remove the invalid entry). Information is the most flexible error message.

9. Click OK to close the Data Validation dialog box.

Removing Data Validation

To remove data validation from a selected cell or cell range, choose Data > Data Tools > Data Validation. Click the Clear All button in the Data Validation dialog box and click OK to accept the change.

Using Data Validation

Excel provides two other useful data validation features. The first shows you all of the cells in your spreadsheet that have validation restrictions. The second shows you all of the cells that contain invalid data.

► Choose Home > Editing > Find & Select > Data Validation. All cells with any kind of validation restrictions will be highlighted, as if you had selected them with the mouse.

► Choose Data > Data Tools > Data Validation (arrow). Choose Circle Invalid Data. Excel will place a red circle (see Figure 1-31) around any cells that contain invalid data. Choose Data Validation (arrow) and then Clear Validation Circles to remove the red circles.

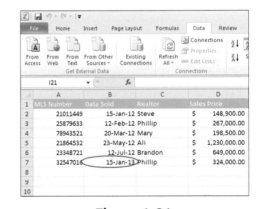

Figure 1-31
Excel shows you which cells contain validation errors.

Saving a Worksheet

PICTURE YOURSELF WORKING for hours to create the perfect worksheet and then your neighborhood or office complex suffers a power outage and all of your hard work is lost. Well, that might have happened in the past, but Excel has gone a long way to dispel that disheartening experience with its AutoSave feature. Every 10 minutes, Excel will save a copy of your file. In this way, even in the event of a power failure, you can be sure that you will never lose more than 10 minutes' worth of work.

But don't rely solely on the AutoSave feature. Get into the habit of saving your file shortly after you begin working on it. You will be able to replace the temporary Book1 file name with a more descriptive name and store the file in an appropriate location on your computer or network.

Tip

If you need to share your file with friends who have not yet upgraded to Excel 2010, you should change the file type. Click the Save As Type down arrow and select Excel 97-2003 Workbook. Other options for sharing your files are discussed in Chapter 14, "Collaborating with Others."

Saving the First Time

The first time you save your file, choose File > Save As from the Ribbon. Excel displays the Save As dialog box, as shown in Figure 1-32. From the Save As dialog box, enter the following information about your document.

▶ **File name:** Feel free to be as descriptive as you want, within reason. You have 255 characters, including spaces, to name your files.

▶ **Location:** Use the Save In folder or the favorite links area to find the perfect location in which to store this file.

▶ **Save As Type:** Excel Workbook, as shown in Figure 1-32, is the default file type in Excel 2010 files.

Save Thumbnail Option   Tags Box   Title Box

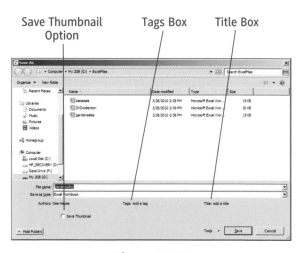

Figure 1-32
The Save As dialog box in Excel 2010.

Creating a Basic Excel Worksheet · **Chapter 1**

Adding the following information about your file is optional. However, Excel stores this data with your document so that you can use any or all of it if you need to use the Search box to find a file you misplaced.

▶ **Save Thumbnail:** Select this option and Excel will store a thumbnail image, or miniature picture, of your file next to the file name. In this way, the thumbnail acts as a preview of your file to help you recognize it when you are ready to re-open the file (see Figure 1-33).

▶ **Tags:** Click the Tags box to add any words that you might associate with your file. For instance, a spreadsheet to track the family budget might include the tag "budget" or "financial".

▶ **Title:** Click the Title box to add a title. This might be important if you used abbreviations in your file name. Suppose your file name was FY2012. You might choose to add Fiscal Year 2012 to the Title box.

Tip

You will only need to use the File > Save As command once. Once you have specified the file name and location that you want associated with your document, you can press Ctrl+S, or choose File > Save from the Ribbon, to save a copy of your document at any time. However, use the File > Save As command again any time you need to move or rename the file.

Closing and Exiting Excel

When you are ready to stop work for the day, there are several ways to exit an Office application.

▶ Choose File > Exit from the Ribbon.

▶ Choose Alt+F4 from the keyboard.

▶ Click the Close button in the upper-right corner of the Excel application window.

▶ Click the Excel program icon > Close command in the upper-left corner of the Excel application window.

Figure 1-33
A thumbnail image of your file appears next to the file name in the folders.

Working with

Formulas

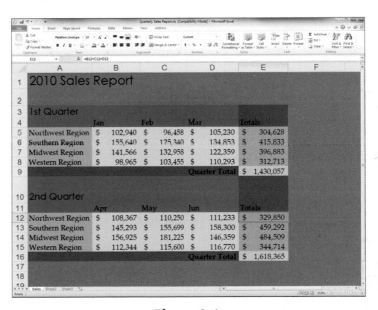

EXCEL CAN HELP YOU DO a lot of things with your data—sort it, organize it, and analyze it. These abilities are fun and useful, but I'm guessing that after putting all that data into an Excel worksheet, the first thing you will probably want to do is to perform mathematical calculations on it. For example, after entering the Northwest Region sales totals for April, May, and June (see Figure 2-1), you might want to add them all up so you can see how well they did in the second quarter. Excel calls such calculations *formulas*.

Figure 2-1
Excel formulas let you perform any number of calculations on your data.

But let's face it: nobody particularly likes math, especially complex math that involves several calculations, each dependent on the last result being correct. For example, after calculating the Second Quarter sales total for the Northwest Region, you might want to add that total to the Second Quarter totals for the Midwest, Western, and Southern Regions so you can see how well the company is doing overall. If you were calculating this by hand (or even with a calculator), and you made a mistake in calculating the Northwest Region's sales total, then the company total would be wrong as well. With Excel, you can easily create one total and then reference that total in another formula, without having to reenter the formula for calculating the first total all over again.

If you make changes to your data, Excel automatically recalculates your formulas. For example, if you change the May sales total for the Northwest Region from $110,250 to $112,750, then the second quarter sales total changes automatically from $329,850 to $332,350 (for example). Excel can handle anything from simple calculations, such as adding two numbers together, to complex calculations, such as adding only the May sales values from each salesperson and dividing by the total number of salespeople to calculate the average sales amount for May.

Creating Formulas

TO CREATE A FORMULA, you type it into a cell. After you press Enter, the result of the calculation is displayed (rather than the formula itself). If you click the cell, the formula you typed appears in the Formula bar (see Figure 2-2). All formulas begin with an equals (=) sign, and typically include a reference to one or more cells. The values in the referenced cells are used when calculating the formula result. These cell values can be static (meaning they don't change) or the result of another formula. For example, in cell E12, you might enter a formula that adds monthly sales for the Northwest Region to calculate the Second Quarter sales total. In cell E16, you might enter a different formula that references the value in cell E12, adding it to the Second Quarter totals for the other regions. If you have to change the Northwest Region's May sales amount later on, the total in cells E12 and E16 are automatically recalculated for you.

Formula Bar   Actual Formula   Result

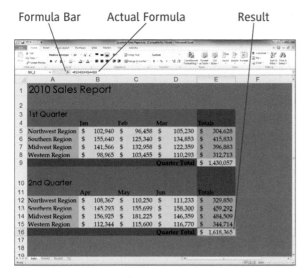

Figure 2-2
While the result of a formula appears in the active cell, the formula itself appears in the Formula bar.

Formula Versus Result

In Figure 2-2, notice that the formula = E12+E13+E14+E15 appears in the Formula bar, but that the result, $1,618,365, appears in cell E16.

Tip

Excel comes with many built-in formulas (such as rounding to the nearest dollar or finding the maximum value in a group of numbers). The built-in formulas are called *functions***, and they make it easier for you to perform calculations on your data without actually typing the corresponding mathematical formula into a cell. See Chapter 3, "Using Excel Functions," for more information.**

Using Mathematical Operators

As you learned earlier, all formulas begin with an equals (=) sign. Besides the equals sign, a formula typically includes one or more cell addresses that reference the values in those cells, and one or more *mathematical operators*, that tell Excel to add, subtract, multiply, divide, or to do something else with those values. Here are some common operators you should know:

▶ **Addition**   +

▶ **Subtraction**   –

▶ **Multiplication**   *

▶ **Division**   /

▶ **Exponentiation**   ^

Using Exponential Operations

An example of an exponential operation is 2^3. To indicate exponential calculations in a formula, use ^ as in C4^2, which tells Excel to take the value in cell C4 squared.

In addition to cell addresses and mathematical operators, formulas can also contain *constants*, which is just a fancy name for a number, such as 32, 2.75, or 5%. Yes, although you should not use dollar signs ($) or commas when entering a constant into a formula, if you prefer, you can use a % sign to enter a percentage such as 25% rather than using its decimal form (.25).

Creating a Simple Formula

Simple formulas include only one mathematical operator, such as subtraction (−). For example, suppose you own a gourmet food service that sells pre-packaged gourmet foods. Cell B12 contains the number of black bean taquitos you had in stock at the beginning of August, and cell C12 contains the number of black bean taquitos left at the end of August. In order to calculate how many taquitos you sold during August, you subtract the value in cell C12 from B12. Follow these steps:

1. Click the cell in which you want the result of the formula to appear.

2. Type an equals (=) sign.

3. Click the cell you want to reference in the formula, or type its address. For example, click cell B12. Excel places a colored box around cell B12; in the Formula bar, the cell address B12 appears in this same color (see Figure 2-3). You can type a value (such as .25) instead of a cell address if you like.

The color of the cell reference in the formula matches the border surrounding the actual cell

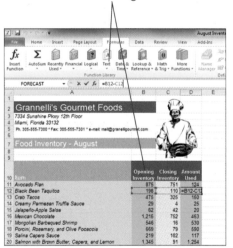

Figure 2-3
Cells referenced in a formula are surrounded by a colored box that matches the cell address in the formula itself.

4. Type an operator to indicate the type of calculation you want Excel to perform. For example, type + (addition), − (subtraction), * (multiplication), or / (division).

5. Click the next cell you want to reference in the formula, or type its address. For example, click cell C12. Excel places a differently colored box around this new cell, and uses that same color for the cell address shown in the Formula bar. You can type a value (such as 1.35) instead of referencing a cell if you want; for example, you might type =D25*.07 to calculate a 7% sales tax on an invoice total.

6. Press Enter to complete the formula. The result of the calculation appears in the cell you selected in Step 1.

Tip

If you start typing a formula but no longer want to enter it, press Esc or click the Cancel button on the Formula bar (the X).

A formula does not need to contain cell references, as you know. In fact, a formula can contain only constants if you want, thus having Excel act like a sort of calculator. For example, you might type =387*.0024 in a cell. After you press Enter, Excel provides the answer, just like any other calculator: 0.9288.

Using Range Names in Formulas

In Chapter 1, "Creating a Basic Excel Worksheet," you learned how to name a cell or range of cells with a *range name.* If you plan on referring to a special cell in several formulas, you can give it a name such as Gross_Pay. Then, to calculate the Social Security tax (which is currently 6.2%), you could use this formula: =Gross_Pay*.062.

To calculate the amount of 401(k) withholding (assuming the employee wants to save 4% of his pay), you could use the formula =Gross_Pay*.04. To quickly name a cell, click it, type a range name in the Name box at the left end of the Formula bar (see Figure 2-4), and then press Enter.

Name Box   Range Name

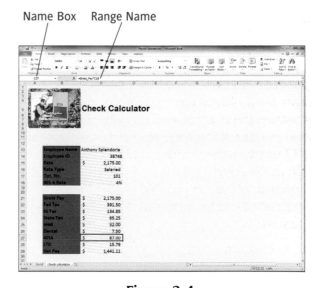

Figure 2-4
Use named ranges in your formulas to make it easier to reference the right cells.

Creating a Compound Formula

A compound formula contains more than one mathematical operator. For example, suppose that you want to calculate the amount of black bean taquitos sold in August, but it's a little more complicated than simply knowing how many taquitos you had at the beginning and end of the month. You need to account for deliveries during the month, and any returns for damaged packaging/spoiled food. In order to calculate the actual number of taquitos you had available for sale, you take the opening inventory, add any deliveries, and subtract the returns. From this new balance, you subtract the closing inventory (the number of taquitos left over at the end of the month) to calculate the number of taquitos sold. Your formula to calculate the total taquitos available might look like this: =B12+C12–D12 (assuming B12 contains the number of taquitos on-hand at the beginning of August, C12 contains the number of taquitos delivered during the month, and D12 contains the number of taquitos returned). Follow these steps to create your own compound formula:

1. Click the cell in which you want the result of the formula to appear. In this example, click cell E11.

2. Type an equals (=) sign.

3. Click the cell you want to reference in the formula, or type its address. You can type a value (such as .25) instead of a cell address if you like. For example, type =B11.

4. Type an operator such as + (addition), – (subtraction), * (multiplication), or / (division) to indicate the type of calculation you want Excel to perform. The formula now looks like this: =B11+.

5. Click or type the address of the next cell you want to reference in the formula, or type a value. For example, click cell C11.

6. Type another operator such as + (addition), – (subtraction), * (multiplication), or / (division) to indicate the next type of calculation you want Excel to perform. For example, type +. The formula now looks like this: =B11+C11.

7. Click or type the address of the next cell you want to reference in the formula, or type a value. For example, click cell D11.

8. Repeat Steps 6 and 7 as needed to complete the formula. The formula now looks like this: =B11+C11–D11.

9. Press Enter. The result of the calculation appears in the cell you selected in Step 1, as shown in Figure 2-5.

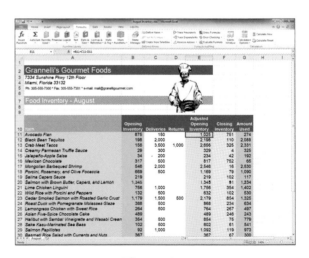

Figure 2-5
Compound formulas contain multiple mathematical operators.

Tip

You do not have to create long, compli-cated formulas to solve common problems, such as adding up a long column of numbers. Excel provides a *function* (built-in formula) just for that, and it's called SUM. You learn about functions in Chapter 3, "Using Excel Functions."

Considering the Order of Operations

When you create compound formulas (formulas that utilize more than one mathematical operator), you need to stop and consider the order in which Excel solves that formula. You see, Excel doesn't solve a formula by moving from the left to the right, calculating as it goes. Nope, Excel performs the operations in a formula in a particular order:

▶ Exponential operations and operations within parentheses

▶ Multiplication and division

▶ Addition and subtraction

Order of Operations

When a formula uses both multiplication and division, Excel decides which operation to perform by moving left to right through the formula.

Let's consider the following formula: =C2+B8*4–D10, and the values C2=50, B8=3, and D10=14.

▶ Excel first takes B8*4, which is 12.

▶ Next, since addition and subtraction are both calculated at roughly the same time, Excel moves left to right to complete its calculations.

▶ Thus, Excel takes C2 and adds the result of B8*4, which is 50+12, or 62.

▶ Finally, Excel takes this result and subtracts D10, or 14, resulting in a final total: 48.

If you don't consider Excel's order of operations, you can run into problems with your formulas. For example, suppose you are trying to find the average sales amount per salesperson, using this week's sales totals. If you use a formula such as =A2+B2+C2/3, you'll get the wrong answer because Excel will start by taking C2/3, and then add that result to A2 and B2. To tell Excel to add the sales totals first, use parentheses like this: =(A2+B2+C2)/3. Excel performs the calculations in parentheses first, and then it moves on to multiplication/division and addition/subtraction.

Using Parentheses to Control the Order of Operations

You can use as many parentheses as you want in a formula. Excel performs the calculation within the left-most parentheses first, and then performs the calculation within the next set of parentheses moving to the right. For example, consider the formula =(A2–B2)–4*(C2/D2), and the values A2=32, B2=20, C2=10, and D2=5. Excel first takes A2 minus B2, or 32–20=12. Next, Excel takes C2 divided by D2 since it is also in parentheses, to get 10/5=2. Excel performs the multiplication next, taking 4 times the result of C2/D2 (which is 2) to get 8. Finally, Excel subtracts 8 from the result of A2 minus B2 (which is 12) to get 4 as the final answer.

You can nest parentheses within parentheses if needed. Consider this formula: =((A2–B2)–4)*(C2/D2). Excel performs the calculation in the innermost parentheses, subtracting B2 from A2, to get 12. Next, Excel works outward to the next set of parentheses, and subtracts 4 from 12 to get 8. Excel then takes C2 divided by D2 since it is also in parentheses, to get 2. Excel performs the multiplication last, taking 8 times 2 to get 16 as the final result.

You can plug these same values into a worksheet and play with the formula, changing the order of operations to something else in order to analyze the results.

Editing Formulas

EXCEL DOES NOT LET you enter formulas that make no sense, such as trying to divide something by zero. Such formulas are flagged as errors. You learn how to identify and fix these errors in Chapter 4, "Troubleshooting Formula Errors." Still, it's easy to make errors on your own, by accidentally referencing the wrong cell, or forgetting to use parentheses to control the order of operations. Luckily, editing a formula is similar to editing other data in a worksheet.

Follow these steps:

1. Click the cell that contains the formula. Remember, this cell displays the formula result, and not the formula, in the cell. However, after you click the cell, the formula appears in the Formula bar.

2. Click within the Formula bar, or press F2 to begin editing. Cells referenced in the formula are surrounded by colored borders, as shown in Figure 2-6.

Referenced Cells

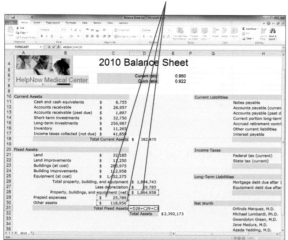

Figure 2-6
Cells referenced in a formula are surrounded by
colored borders that you can use to edit the formula.

3. You can edit a formula in one of two ways:

- **Drag the border around a referenced cell and drop it on another cell to change the cell reference in the formula.**

- **Edit the formula by first moving the insertion point, either by clicking within the formula or by pressing the left and right arrow keys.** Press the Backspace key to delete characters to the left of the insertion point; press the Delete key to delete characters to the right. Type additional characters as needed to correct the formula.

4. Press Enter to save your changes.

Tip

To edit a formula quickly, double-click the result cell. The formula appears in the cell where you can edit it, rather than moving the mouse pointer all the way up to the Formula bar. When you double-click a cell, the insertion point is placed within the formula so you can immediately begin editing right in the cell.

Controlling Recalculation

WHEN YOU PRESS ENTER after typing in a formula, Excel automatically calculates the result. If you change the values in any of the referenced cells, Excel recalculates the result using the new values. This automatic recalculation is one of the things that make Excel so powerful. For example, you could enter the starting budget amounts for your department, and continue to make changes to those values until you come up with a budget total that's both realistic and within company limits.

If you have a lot of formulas in your budget worksheet however, you might not want to have to wait for constant recalculations as you play around with your budget amounts. To prevent automatic recalculation, change to Manual mode by clicking the Calculation Options button on the Formulas tab, and selecting Manual from the menu that appears (see Figure 2-7). After changing to manual, click either the Calculate Sheet button on the Formulas tab (to recalculate formulas in the current worksheet) or Calculate Now (to recalculate formulas in all open workbooks).

Recalculate Entire Workbook   Recalculate Current Worksheet

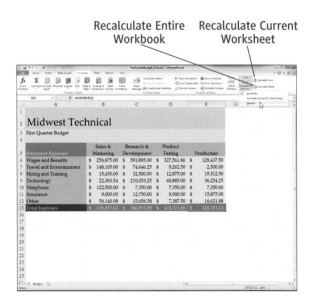

Figure 2-7
Control when formula results are calculated.

Some Features Affect All Open Workbooks

When you change the calculation method, you affect all open workbooks. For example, if you click the Calculation Options button on the Formulas tab and select Manual, then all open workbooks will wait until you tell them to recalculate by clicking the Calculate Sheet or Calculate Now button, or until you change the setting back to Automatic calculation.

Copying Formulas

ANOTHER THING THAT'S COOL about Excel's formulas is how easy it is to reuse them. For example, after you carefully type in a formula that calculates the number of black bean taquitos available for sale during August, taking into account any deliveries or returns during the month, you don't want to repeat the process with the next item in your inventory. Luckily, Excel allows you to copy formulas, automatically adjusting the cell references for you. For example, if you copy that formula for black bean taquitos to the jalapeño-apple salsa row, the cell references are automatically adjusted so you calculate the adjusted opening inventory for salsa and not taquitos. In Figure 2-8, the formula in cell E12, which calculates the adjusted opening inventory for taquitos, is =B12+C12−D12. When copied to cell E15 (the salsa row), the formula is adjusted so that it uses similar cells in row 15 instead: =B15+C15−D15.

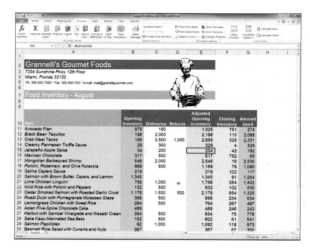

Figure 2-8
When formulas are copied, cell references are automatically adjusted to reflect the formula's new location.

Copying with AutoFill

Typically, you will want to copy formulas to nearby cells so they can use similar data. For example, in Figure 2-9, you might type the formula for September total expenses in cell B11, and then copy that formula across row 11 to the other month columns. The simplest way to copy formulas to adjacent cells is to use AutoFill. With AutoFill, you simply drag from the source cell to copy its data to adjacent cells. In this case, you will copy a formula from one cell to nearby cells, simply by dragging over them with something called the AutoFill handle.

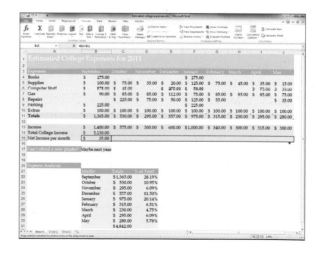

Figure 2-9
Use AutoFill to copy formulas to adjacent cells.

Follow these steps:

1. Click the cell containing the formula you want to copy. For example, you might click in cell B15. After you click, a dark border appears around the cell, indicating that it's the active cell.

2. Move the mouse pointer to the lower-right corner of the active cell. The mouse pointer changes to a cross.

3. Drag the AutoFill handle (the cross) down the column or across the row to copy the formula to adjacent cells. For example, you might drag the AutoFill handle across row 15 to copy the September Net Income formula shown in Figure 2-9 across the row to the other months.

4. Release the mouse button to copy the formula. Again, the cell references in the original formula are adjusted to reflect the new column/row to which the formula is copied. For example, if cell B15 contains the formula =B13–B11, and you copy it to cell B16 (one row down), then the formula is changed to =B14–B12 (the row part of the cell addresses is changed by one row). If you copy that same formula to cell C15 (one column over), then the formula is changed to =C13–C11 (the column part of the cell addresses is changed by one column).

Be Sure You Know What You Want to Copy

If your copied formulas contain errors, it may be because cell addresses changed that maybe shouldn't have. If you do not want a cell address to change when you copy it, you can change the cell address from a relative reference to an absolute one. See the upcoming section "Creating an Absolute or Mixed Formula Reference" for help.

Sometimes, you don't actually want to copy the formula, but its result, to another part of the worksheet. See the section "Copying Values Instead of Formulas" for more info.

Copying with Copy and Paste

AutoFill is perfect to use if you want to copy formulas to adjacent cells. But what do you do if the cells are not next to each other? Using the Copy and Paste commands, you can copy a formula anywhere in your worksheet—even from one worksheet or workbook to another. Follow these steps:

1. Click the cell containing the formula you want to copy. A dark border appears around the cell, indicating that it's the active cell.

2. Click the Copy button on the Home tab to copy the formula, or press Ctrl+C. A dashed "marching ants" border appears around the formula cell, as shown in Figure 2-10.

Click to paste copied data

Click to copy selected cell(s)

A solid border surrounds
the cells into which the
formula will be pasted

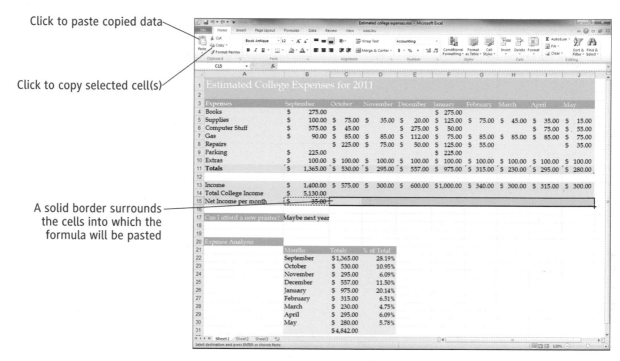

Figure 2-10
Marching ants surround the cell(s) to be copied.

3. Click the cell to which you want to copy the formula. If you want to copy the formula to multiple adjacent cells, you can drag over them; to copy the formula to a series of non-adjacent cells, click the first cell, press and hold Ctrl, and click each additional cell. Each cell you select is highlighted.

4. Click the Paste button on the Home tab or press Ctrl+V to copy the formula to the selected cell(s). The cell references in the original formula are adjusted to reflect the new column/row to which the formula is copied.

Tip

The "ants" continue to march around the original formula cell until you either type something into a cell, or make some other edits to the worksheet. The marquee is telling you that you can select additional cells and click Paste to copy the formula to that new selection. If you do not need to copy the formula to other cells and you want to dismiss the marching ants marquee immediately, simply press Esc.

Copying Values Instead of Formulas

Formulas adjust automatically when you copy them, but that may not be always what you want. For example, suppose a worksheet contains last year's household budget versus actual expense results, and you want to copy those values elsewhere in the worksheet so you can plug in estimated amounts for this year and analyze the new results using the formulas you've already created. Follow these steps:

1. Select the cell(s) containing the formula(s) whose value(s) you want to copy. A dark border appears around selected cells.

2. Click the Copy button on the Home tab or press Ctrl+C. The dark border changes to a dashed "marching ants" border.

3. Select the cell(s) to which you want to copy the formula result(s).

4. Click the arrow on the Paste button on the Home tab. On the palette menu that appears (see Figure 2-11), select exactly what you want to copy:

   - **Values:** Pastes the formula result

   - **Values & Number Formatting:** Pastes the formula result and its number format

   - **Values & Source Formatting:** Pastes the formula result, its number format, and its cell formats

Figure 2-11
Excel offers various options for pasting the results of your formulas.

Tip

Notice in Figure 2-11 that as you slide the mouse pointer over the palette menu of Paste choices (the mouse pointer currently rests on the Values & Source Formatting choice) the result of that choice is previewed on the worksheet in the range F9:I21. The preview feature, which works with all sorts of formatting choices, allows you to preview your paste options.

Creating an Absolute or Mixed Formula Reference

NORMALLY WHEN YOU COPY a formula, the cell addresses in the original formula are adjusted to reflect the new location. For example, if you copy the formula =B8*2.25 from cell B10 to cell C10, the formula automatically changes to =C8*2.25 to reflect the new column to which the formula has been copied.

Sometimes, this automatic adjustment is not what you want to happen. For example, in Figure 2-12, cell C31 contains the total of the monthly college expenses. To determine the percentage of the total expenses that September represents, you might type the formula =C22/C31 in cell D22. However, if you then copy this formula down the column, you'll soon discover a problem. For example, when you copy the formula to cell D23, it changes to =C23/C32 (the rows in the cell addresses are adjusted by one row down). However, as you can see in Figure 2-12, cell C32 is empty, so not only will the formula result be wrong, you'll get an error because Excel doesn't like it when you try to divide by zero.

Error Messages

When you create a formula that results in certain errors, such as trying to divide some number by zero, Excel displays an error message in the cell instead of the formula result. To learn more about such errors and how to fix them, see Chapter 4, "Troubleshooting Formula Errors."

Figure 2-12
Sometimes you don't want Excel to automatically adjust cell references when formulas are copied.

In this example, what you want to do is to have all the copied formulas refer to cell C31 (which contains the total college expenses) when you copy the formula from cell D22 (which computes the percentage of the total college expenses incurred in September) to the other monthly cells (D23:D30). To do that, you must make the cell address C31 *absolute* (non-changeable) rather than *relative* (changeable).

Creating an Absolute Formula Reference

To make a cell reference in a formula absolute, add a $ (dollar sign) before the letter and the number that make up the cell address. For example, the formula for cell D22 in this example should read =C22/$C$31 to indicate that cell C31 is an absolute cell address. As you can see in Figure 2-13, when the formula is copied from cell D22 to cell D23, the first cell address in the formula is adjusted for the new row (C22 is changed to C23), but the second cell address is not changed at all ($C$31 stays $C$31) resulting in the formula =C23/$C$31.

Follow these steps to type a formula that uses absolute cell addressing:

1. Click the cell in which you want the result of the formula to appear. In the example shown in Figure 2-13, you would click cell D22.

2. Type an equals (=) sign.

3. Click the cell you want to reference in the formula, or type its address. For example, click cell C22. To make the cell address absolute, you can type the dollar signs when typing the cell address, or you can press F4 after typing the cell address to make that address absolute. Since you don't want to make cell C22 absolute in this example, continue to Step 4.

4. Type an operator such as + (addition), − (subtraction), * (multiplication), or / (division) to indicate the type of calculation you want Excel to perform. For example, type / to indicate division.

5. Click or type the address of the next cell you want to reference in the formula. For example, type the cell address $C$31, or click cell C31 and press F4 to change the formula to =C22/$C$31 automatically.

6. Repeat Steps 4 and 5 as needed to complete the formula.

7. Press Enter to complete the formula. The result appears in the cell.

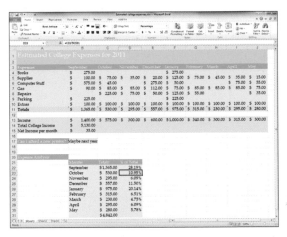

Figure 2-13
To prevent Excel from adjusting a cell address when a formula is copied, make that cell address absolute.

Absolute Cell References

Both simple and compound formulas can contain absolute (or, as you learn in the next section, mixed) cell references.

8. Copy the formula to other cells, such as cell D23. Any absolute cell addresses used in the formula are not adjusted. In Figure 2-13, you can see that the formula is changed to =C23/$C$31 when copied to cell D23 from cell D22.

Creating a Mixed Formula Reference

Sometimes you do not want to refer to an absolute cell address, but a mixed one, in which only part of the cell address (the column letter or the row number) is absolute. Typically, you use mixed references when you want to copy a single formula across a wide range. For example, consider the sales worksheet shown in Figure 2-14.

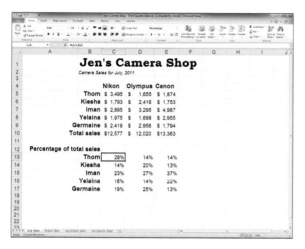

Figure 2-14
Use a mixed reference to copy a formula
throughout a range.

The formula in cell C13 calculates Thom's contribution to the total Nikon sales in July. After entering this one formula, you can copy it to the range C13:E17 to compute other averages you want.

Here's how it works: the formula in cell C13 is =C5/C$10. The cell address C$10 is a mixed address; the row number 10 is absolute, but the column letter C is not. When you copy this formula to cell C14 (one row down), it becomes =C6/C$10. This formula takes the Nikon sales amount for Kiesha and divides it by the total sales for Nikon cameras and accessories in cell C10 to compute her contribution to the total Nikon sales. When you copy the formula to cell D13, it becomes =D5/D$10 (the column part of the second cell reference changes but not the row). This formula takes the Olympus sales amount for Thom and divides it by the total sales for Olympus cameras/accessories in cell D10 to determine Thom's contribution to that total. Thus, you can enter one formula in cell C13, and because it uses a mixed reference, easily copy that formula throughout a range to instantly create the formulas you need.

Follow these steps to type a formula that uses mixed cell addressing:

1. Click the cell in which you want the result of the formula to appear. In the example shown in Figure 2-14, you would click cell C13.

2. Type an equals (=) sign.

3. Click the cell you want to reference in the formula, or type its address. For example, click cell C5. To make the cell address a mixed reference, you can type the dollar sign in front of either the column letter or the row number when typing the cell address, or you can type the regular cell address and press F4 two or three times to cycle through various versions of the address: regular cell address, absolute address, mixed cell reference with an absolute row, or mixed cell reference with an absolute column. Since you don't want to make cell C5 absolute in this example, continue to Step 4.

4. Type an operator such as + (addition), – (subtraction), * (multiplication), or / (division) to indicate the type of calculation you want Excel to perform. For example, type / to indicate division.

5. Click or type the address of the next cell you want to reference in the formula. For example, type the cell address C$10, or click cell C10 and press F4 twice to change the formula to =C5/C$10 automatically.

6. Repeat Steps 4 and 5 as needed to complete the formula.

7. Press Enter to complete the formula. The result appears in the cell.

8. Copy the formula to other cells, such as to the range C13:E17. Any mixed cell addresses used in the formula are only partially adjusted. For example, the formula in cell C13 is =C5/C$10, and when it's copied to cell E17, it is changed to =E9/E$10.

49

$$2 \times 2 = y \quad (tgx)' = \sec^2 x \quad y'' \quad ctg x = 1$$

$$\int dx = x + c \quad c^2 = a^2 + 6^2 \quad \log a \quad 1 = \emptyset \quad \log_x \quad a = 1$$

$$L: \begin{cases} x = x_1 + lt \\ y = y_1 + mt \\ z = z_1 + nt \end{cases} \quad y = \sqrt{e^{3x+1}} \quad C^1 = \emptyset \quad \ell = \lim_{k \to \infty} \left| \frac{a_k}{a_{k+1}} \right|$$

$$\log_x \quad 1 = \emptyset \quad \Delta = \det A$$

$$|AB| = \sqrt{88} \quad P = \frac{e^{a-\delta}}{1 + e^{a-\delta}} \quad \lim_{x \to 0} \frac{1}{|x|} = \infty$$

$$(\int dx)' = F(x) \quad y = x + \sqrt{x^3} \quad a \geq 0 \quad a = 0 \quad a < 0 \quad \lim_{k \to \infty} U_k = 0$$

$$x_0 = 1 \quad \int_a^b f(x)\,dx = y$$

$$(\cos x)' = -\sin x \quad \sin^3 x = 3\sin x - \sin 3x \quad \sqrt[4]{ab} = \frac{\sqrt[4]{a} \cdot \sqrt[4]{6}}{}$$

$$\frac{4}{3}\pi R^3 \quad J = \begin{vmatrix} x'_p & x'_\theta & x'_\varphi \\ y'_p & y'_\theta & y'_\varphi \\ z'_p & z'_\theta & z'_\varphi \end{vmatrix} \quad f'(x) = \lim_{\Delta x \to 0} \frac{f(x-\Delta x) - f(x)}{\Delta x} \quad \sqrt[2u]{a^{2u}} = |a|$$

$$A = \begin{bmatrix} a_{11} a_{12} & a_{1n} \\ a_{21} a_{22} \cdots a_{2u} \\ a_{u1} a_{u2} \cdots a_{nn} \end{bmatrix} \quad U_1 + U_2 + U_3 + \cdots + U_k = \sum_{k=1}^{n} U_k \quad tg x = \frac{\sin x}{\cos x}$$

$$\int dF(x) = F(x) + C \quad a^x \cdot a^y = a^{x+y}$$

$$S = \begin{cases} x = p\cos\varphi \cdot \sin\theta \\ y = p\sin\varphi \cdot \sin\theta \\ z = p\cos\theta \\ dV = p^2 \sin\theta\, dp\, d\theta\, d\varphi \end{cases} \quad a^{\log_a b} = b$$

$$\lim_{x \to \infty} \left(1 + \frac{1}{x}\right)^x = e$$

$$+ z = y \quad \frac{x^2}{a^2} = \frac{y^2}{6^2} \quad S = \int \frac{7x}{ax+1} \quad |A| = \sum_{i=1}^{n} b_i A_{ij} \quad \sin^2 x + \cos^2 x = 1$$

$$\lim_{x \to a} c = c \quad y = a + \frac{7x}{ax+1} \quad \int e^u\, du = e^u + C \quad \int a^x\, dx = \frac{a^x}{\ln a} + C$$

$$\pi = 3,141592654 \quad S = \frac{1}{2} a h_2$$

Using Excel

Functions

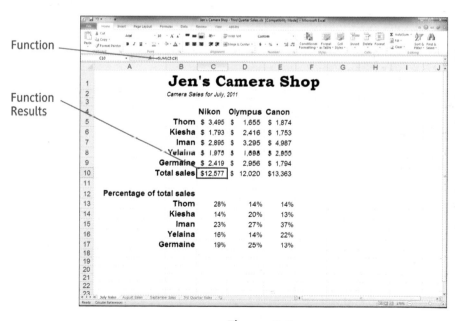

FORMULAS ARE TOUGH ENOUGH to enter correctly into an Excel worksheet, which is why Excel provides built-in formulas called *functions* that you can use to quickly enter common formulas. Functions are ready-made formulas that perform a series of operations on a specified range of cells. For example, suppose you want to calculate the sum of the values in the range C5:C9, as shown in Figure 3-1.

Function

Function Results

Figure 3-1
A quick way to total a range of cells
is to use the SUM function.

Considering Form versus Function

IF YOU USED A FORMULA, you might enter =C5+C6+C7+C8+C9 in cell C10 to display the total of those cells. Although entering this formula is not particularly difficult, it is tedious. Instead of typing such a formula, you can use the SUM function to get the same results much more quickly. As you can see in Figure 3-1, the function =SUM(C5:C9) is entered into cell C10 to compute the total you need.

You learn to enter a function properly in the next section, "Understanding Function Syntax." For now, let's concentrate on the basics. Again, a function is a pre-programmed formula. You feed a function some data, such as a range of cells, and it spits out an answer, such as the total of the values in those cells. What kind of data, you ask? Not to worry: when you enter a function, Excel provides you with a wizard that assists you in filling in the blanks so you won't fail to provide the function with some needed data.

Obviously, the SUM function is pretty simple, and something you might be able to do without in situations where you are adding the contents of only three or four cells. But try adding up a long column or a range of cells using a regular formula, and you will soon tire of typing all those plus signs between cell addresses. In addition to the SUM function, Excel provides many other functions, grouped into various categories such as Financial, Lookup & Reference, and Math & Trig.

For example, there's a PMT function you can use to calculate monthly payments on a loan. You feed the PMT function an interest rate, total number of payments over the life of the loan, and the loan amount, and presto! The PMT function calculates the amount due each month.

And the fun doesn't end there: using the PMT function, you could compare the interest rates on various loans of particular amounts, and purchase prices of several homes in your area, and quickly identify which home is the best deal for you. If you had to work manually, computing these same payment amounts would be difficult and time-consuming, and by the time you figured things out, somebody else might have already bought the home of your dreams.

Understanding Function Syntax

EVERY FUNCTION HAS THE SAME basic elements:

- ▶ First, just like a formula, a function starts with an equals sign =.

- ▶ Next comes the function name, such as SUM, which tells Excel which calculation should be performed.

Tip

The function name is not case-sensitive, which means you could type SUM or sum in this example. However, after you enter the formula, Excel changes the function name to uppercase automatically.

- ▶ The next thing is an open parenthesis, (, which shows Excel that what follows is the data the function needs to work, such as a range of cells to add.

- ▶ After the opening parenthesis come the values you feed the function, which are called *arguments*. Arguments appear in parentheses. For example, to tell SUM what range of cells you want to add, you type that range in parentheses, like this: (C5:C9). The argument for a function is often a range of cells, but it can be other things, such as an actual value (or a cell with a value in it), a range name (such as AprilSales), a date or time, or an expression (formula) such as .0725/12.

- ▶ Some functions allow you to enter multiple arguments; other functions require them (as in the PMT function mentioned earlier, which requires you to feed it the interest rate, number of payments, and the total loan amount). Regardless of whether an argument is required, separate each argument with a comma.

Tip

Text is another type of argument you might use with certain functions. When entering a bit of text as an argument, be sure to enclose that text in quotation marks. For example, if you wanted to add Chicago in front of the year shown in a particular cell, you could use the CONCATENATE function (as discussed later in this lesson), and feed it the text string "Chicago" (in quotations of course) as one of its arguments.

- ▶ Finally, to show you are done entering arguments, you type a closing parenthesis, like this:).

For example, you might type the function =SUM(G12:J26) in a cell to add the values in the range, G12:J26. To enter a function into a cell, you can either type it manually, or use the Function wizard, as you'll see later in this lesson.

Creating a Total with the SUM Function

AS YOU MIGHT GATHER from the examples so far, SUM is by far the most popular function. In fact, you will most likely use the SUM function in just about every workbook you create.

The SUM function is used to total the values in a range of cells. In fact, you can enter as many ranges as you want as arguments to the SUM function, as long as you remember to separate those arguments with commas. For example, take a look at the payroll worksheet shown in Figure 3-2. In order to calculate the net pay, you must take an employee's gross pay, minus a bunch of deductions. The first set of deductions is for taxes, which for the first employee are found in the range I8:K8. Next comes the medical deduction in cell M8, and then the 401(k) and long-term disability deductions in the range O8:P8. So when you enter all these arguments, the SUM function becomes =SUM(I8:K8,M8,O8:P8), with each of the three arguments (a range, a single cell address, and then another range) separated by commas. Notice in Figure 3-2, the actual formula is =H8-SUM(I8:K8,M8,O8:P8), which takes the gross pay minus all the deductions totaled up to calculate the net pay.

Like all Excel formulas, when you change the values in the cells referenced by the SUM function, the result automatically changes. This makes SUM an even more powerful tool when used in a worksheet where the values change often, such as a budget worksheet.

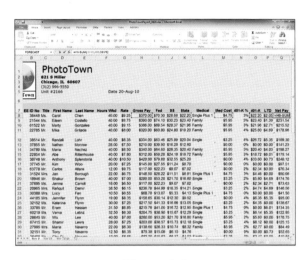

Figure 3-2
The SUM function allows you to enter multiple ranges to be summed.

Probably because the SUM function is so popular, Excel provides you with several ways in which you might enter it. For example, you might enter the SUM function manually, by typing in its formula. You might decide to enter the SUM function with the aid of a wizard, or you might use something called the AutoSum button to enter it quickly into a cell. You learn all these methods in this section.

The SUM Function, Or Any Function!

Because the SUM function is so popular, it is used in the following sections as an example for how to enter functions. As you learn how to enter the SUM function manually or with the help of the wizard, keep in mind that this same process may be used to enter any function you like. Later in this chapter, you learn about the most popular functions and the arguments they require so you can enter those functions properly, regardless of the method you choose.

Entering a SUM Function Manually

If you like entering functions by hand, Excel provides Formula AutoComplete to help you complete function formulas faster. Follow these steps:

1. Click in the cell where you want the result of the SUM function to appear.

2. Type the equals sign (–).

3. Type **SUM**.

4. Type an opening parenthesis if needed. If you selected SUM from the Formula AutoComplete list as shown in Figure 3-3, and then pressed Tab, then the opening parenthesis is added for you.

Tip

With Formula AutoComplete, you type = and then begin typing a few letters of the function (such as S or SU), and a drop-down menu appears with choices that match what you've typed. The list of choices narrows as you continue to type more letters. Whenever you see the function you want, you can select it from the list by highlighting it with the up or down arrow keys and then pressing Tab (not Enter). By the way, when a function is highlighted in the list, a ScreenTip appears, explaining the purpose of that function. After making a selection from the list, you'll be prompted to enter the appropriate arguments for that function.

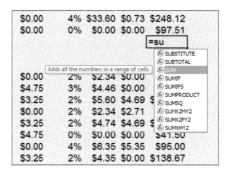

Figure 3-3
Select the function you want to use from the Formula AutoComplete list.

5. Type the first argument. In case you've forgotten that SUM is waiting for you to type the range you want summed, just take a look at the ScreenTip that now appears below the result cell, as shown in Figure 3-4. As you enter each argument for a function, it appears in bold in this ScreenTip so you can always keep track of exactly which argument you are entering. In this case, you can type a range address as the second argument, or drag over the range to select it. Remember that a range address can be a single cell address, or a group of contiguous cells.

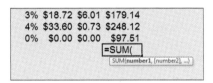

Figure 3-4
Formula AutoComplete prompts you to enter the correct arguments for a function.

6. If you want to enter a second argument (another range to sum), type a comma, and then type the second range address or drag to select the range. As soon as you type the comma, the second argument is bolded in the ScreenTip. Notice in Figure 3-4 that some of the SUM arguments appear in square brackets, as in [number2]. The square brackets indicate that an argument is optional, which means that you do not need to enter it if you don't want to. Which in this case, means that you do not need to enter more than a single range to sum for the SUM function to work. If an argument is not displayed in square brackets, it is required.

7. Repeat Step 6 to add as many ranges to the SUM function as you like.

8. When you're through entering arguments, type the closing parenthesis and press Enter. The selected ranges are summed, and the result appears in the cell you selected in Step 1.

Tip

You can also skip the typing business and press Enter or Tab to let Excel add that closing parenthesis for you.

For example, you might type =SUM(A1:A40, C1:C40) to add the values in the ranges A1 through A40 and C1 through C40.

Entering a SUM Function with the Function Wizard

You can enter a function, even the SUM function, by typing it into a cell, or by using the Function wizard. Granted, with a function as simple as SUM, you probably won't bother using something as handholding as a wizard. Still, it's useful to know how to use the Function wizard to enter any function, even SUM. Follow these steps:

1. Click in the cell where you want the result of the SUM function to appear.

Finding the Right Function

One of the things the Insert Function dialog box does for you is help you locate the function you need. If you already have a good idea of the kind of function you want, you can click the button for the appropriate category on the Formulas tab. For example, if you know you're looking for a text function, click the Text button on the Formulas tab. A list of text functions appears. In this case, we're trying to add the values in a range of cells, so click the Math & Trig button on the Formulas bar instead. As you highlight a function in the list (such as the SUM function), a ScreenTip appears, describing the function. Click to insert the function and bring up the Function wizard. Skip to Step 4 to continue.

Tip

To enter a function you've entered into a worksheet recently, click the Recently Used button on the Formulas bar and select it from those listed.

2. Click the Insert Function button, located at the left end of the Formula bar, as shown in Figure 3-5. The Insert Function dialog box appears (see Figure 3-5).

3. To locate the function you need, type a short description of it in the Search For a Function text box and click Go. For example, to locate a function that adds a bunch of cells, type **add** in the Search For a Function box and click Go.

   Instead of typing a description, you can select a category such as Math & Trig to narrow the list of functions. Open the Or Select a Category list and select the category into which you think your mystery function falls. To enter a function you've used in the worksheet recently, choose Most Recently Used from the Or Select a Category list.

   Regardless of which method you choose here, a list of matching functions appears in the Select a Function box, as seen in Figure 3-5.

Insert Function
Button

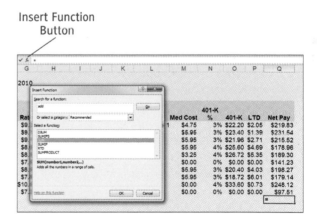

Figure 3-5
Use the Function wizard to insert a function.

4. Select one of the functions listed in the Select a Function box. A description of the function, and its syntax, appears just below this box. We want to use the SUM function, so select it from the functions listed.

5. Click OK to insert the selected function. The Function wizard appears (see Figure 3-6).

6. Now it's time to feed the function the information it needs to perform its calculation. You feed this information to the function through its arguments. Required arguments appear in bold in the Function wizard; optional arguments (if any) appear in regular text. Here you can see that the SUM function requires only one argument—a range of cells to add.

With some functions, such as the SUM function, Excel will often guess the cells you want to use as the argument. In this case, it guessed that I wanted to use the range Q8:Q17 because that range of cells was just above the result cell. Still, as often as Excel gets it right, it sometimes guesses wrong. If that has happened to you, or if Excel hasn't taken a guess, click inside the first argument box, which in this case, is labeled Number1. A description of the argument appears in the bottom of the Function wizard. This helps you to enter appropriate values into each of the argument boxes. Type the argument value. For example, type the range address Q8:Q17.

As you enter the arguments, the value of that argument is displayed to the right of the text box. By "value," I don't necessarily mean the amount—if you enter a range, you will see the values for each cell in the range listed to the right. If you enter a single cell address, you'll see its value. If you enter a text string, you'll see the text listed to the right, and so on.

Required Argument   Argument Description   Collapse Button   Function Result

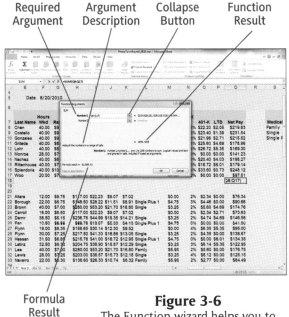

Formula Result

Figure 3-6
The Function wizard helps you to enter arguments for a function.

Using Help for Arguments

If you need help understanding the arguments for a particular function, click the Help button located in the upper-right corner of the dialog box.

Also, as you enter arguments for a function, Excel calculates the current result and displays it just below the last argument. At the bottom of the dialog box, Excel displays the result of the entire formula, which might be different. For example, consider the formula shown in Figure 3-7, in which the function, SUM, is only part of the formula. In that example, I am trying to calculate the net pay for an employee's paycheck. So the formula takes the value in cell I8 (the gross pay) and subtracts the total of all the deductions (which is calculated using SUM). So, in the Function wizard, the result shown under the last argument (150.171) is the total of all the deductions. At the bottom of the dialog box, the result of the formula (the next pay) is displayed: $219.83.

7. To enter another argument, click in the second argument box, and then type its value. In this case, you can click the second argument box and enter another range for SUM to add up. Repeat this step to enter more arguments.

8. Click OK to enter the function.

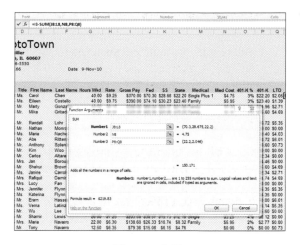

Figure 3-7
A function can be only part of a formula.

Selecting and Entering Data

A simpler way to enter a range address into an argument box is to select it. To do that, click the Collapse button at the right end of the argument box (see Figure 3-6). The Function wizard collapses to show only the argument box. This collapsing business essentially gets the wizard out of the way so you can get down to selecting the range you want to use. Anyway, go ahead and drag over the cells in the range you wish to select. To expand the wizard again, click the Expand (formerly Collapse) button.

Entering a SUM Function with the AutoSum Button

Again, entering a SUM function into a worksheet is a pretty popular thing to do—so popular in fact, that Excel provides you with a shortcut way in which to enter it: the AutoSum button. So instead of tediously entering a formula such as =C3+D3+E3+F3+G3, you can use the AutoSum button to use the SUM function instead: =SUM(C3:G3). Here's how:

1. Click in the cell where you want the result of the SUM function to appear. As you learn in Step 3, AutoSum works best if you put your result cell adjacent to the cells you want to sum.

2. Click the AutoSum button on the Home tab, as shown in Figure 3-8.

3. As soon as you click the AutoSum button, it takes a guess as to which adjacent cells you might want to sum, and it highlights those cells with a marching ants border (see Figure 3-8). If you don't like this guess (which you won't, if your result cell is not located right next to the cells you want to sum), just drag over the range you really want to sum to select it.

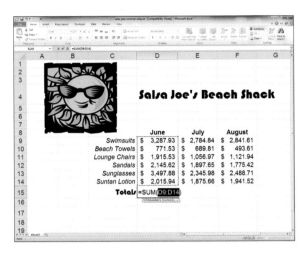

Figure 3-8
The AutoSum button allows you to enter the SUM function quickly.

4. To sum more than one range, type a comma and drag over an additional range to select it.

5. Press Enter or Tab to complete the formula. The result of the SUM function appears in the result cell.

Tip

If the result cell is not right next to the cells you want to use in the SUM function, you might want to beat Excel to the punch and select the cells to add first by clicking the AutoSum button. Excel will not try to guess which range you want to sum, but will instead simply display the selected range as the first argument.

Tip

Before entering a second argument for the SUM function, make sure that the cursor is positioned at the end of the first range address. If you manually selected the first range, the cursor is already in the right spot; if you like Excel's guess, keep it and simply click at the end of that range address in the Formula bar. Then type your comma and add the second range address.

Using AutoSum to Enter Other Functions

The AutoSum button is not a single purpose gadget—nope, it can be used to enter a variety of very common functions into your worksheet. Here's a brief description of each one— you learn more about each of these functions later in this chapter:

► **AVERAGE:** Calculates the average of a group of cells

► **COUNT:** Counts the number of cells in a range that contain values, whether it's text, a number, or something else

► **MIN:** Displays the minimum value in a range

► **MAX:** Displays the maximum value in a range

To enter any one of these functions using the AutoSum button, follow these steps:

1. Click in the cell where you want the result of the function to appear. Again, keep in mind that Excel is better capable of guessing the range to use if you put your result cell adjacent to the cells you want to use with the function. If you don't want to do that, select the range to use, and click the AutoSum button to prevent Excel from wasting your time with a wrong guess.

2. Click the arrow on the AutoSum button on the Home tab. A menu appears, as shown in Figure 3-9.

Figure 3-9
The AutoSum button allows you to enter other functions besides SUM.

3. Select the function you want to use from those listed. For example, click Count Numbers.

4. The function you selected is inserted into the result cell. Unless you preselected a range, AutoSum makes a guess as to which adjacent cells you want to use, highlighting those cells with a marching ants border (see Figure 3-8). If you don't like this guess, drag over the range you really want to use to select it.

5. To enter another argument, type a comma and drag over an additional range to select it.

6. Press Enter to complete the formula. The result of the selected function appears in the result cell.

Calculating Results Without Entering a Formula

SOMETIMES, YOU DON'T WANT to add another formula into an already complicated worksheet. No, sometimes, all you want to do is to perform a quick sum to check some values, or to find the maximum sales amount in a given range. Turns out you can quickly calculate the average and sum of a selected range. You can also count the number of cells in that range with something in them. Just select any range, and instantly, Excel calculates the AVERAGE, COUNT, and SUM, and displays these results on the Status bar, as shown in Figure 3-10.

You are not limited to displaying only the Average, Sum, and Count on the Status bar; you can display additional (or different) automatic results on the Status bar as you see fit. Right-click the Status bar to display a menu, as shown in Figure 3-11.

Halfway down the menu, you'll see a selection of display options: Average (equivalent to the AVERAGE function, which computes the average of the selected range), Count (equivalent to the COUNTA function, which counts the cells with some kind of data—non-blank), Numerical Count (equivalent to the COUNT function which counts the cells with numbers), Minimum (equivalent to the MINIMUM function, which finds the minimum value in a range), Maximum (equivalent to the MAXIMUM function, which finds the maximum value in a range), and Sum (equivalent to the SUM function, which totals the values in a range). Select the functions you want to display (these functions appear with a checkmark in front of them on the menu).

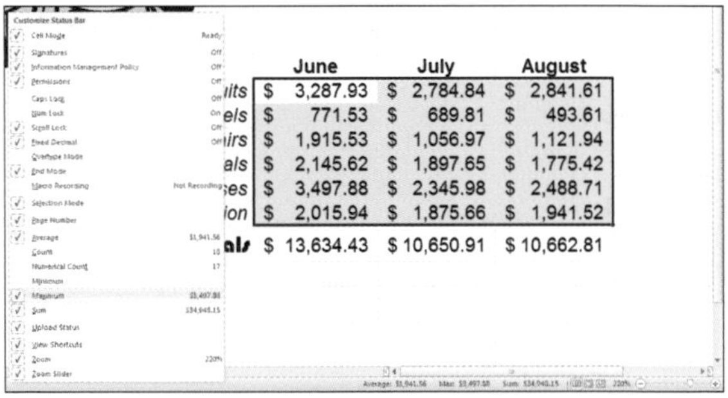

Figure 3-11
Select the functions you want to display on the Status bar.

Excel displays the AVERAGE, SUM, and COUNT of the selected range

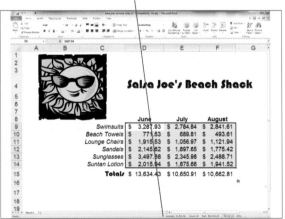

Figure 3-10
Excel can perform some calculations for you automatically.

Nesting Functions

YOU LEARNED EARLIER THAT you can include a function in a larger formula, like this formula, which uses the SUM function: =C12–SUM(A2:C10). You can also use a formula as an argument for a function, such as the PMT function, which calculates the monthly payment for a loan: =PMT(.08/12,60,–12570).

As they say, that's not all! You can also use another function as an argument for the current function. Now you might be thinking, functions make me dizzy. Why would I ever want to nest one function inside another? A popular reason is to round the result. You learn more about the ROUND function later in this chapter, but for now all you need to know is that it rounds a value (which is its first argument) to a given number of decimal places (its second argument).

Consider the formula shown in Figure 3-12. It uses the ROUND function to round the average of the predicted sales for Quarter 2 to the nearest whole dollar. Notice that the first argument, what to round, is the function, AVERAGE. The second argument, 0, tells the ROUND function which decimal point to round to.

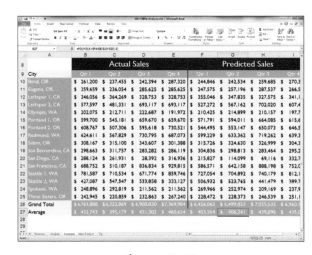

Figure 3-12
Nest one function inside another when needed.

To nest one function in another, follow these steps:

1. Click in the cell where you want the result of the formula to appear.

2. Type the equals sign (=).

3. Begin entering the main function, either by typing its name and an opening parenthesis, clicking the Insert Function button and selecting the function, or selecting the function from the AutoSum list. For example, type **=ROUND(**.

4. Enter the arguments for the main function, separated by commas. If the argument is a function itself, type the function name (such as AVERAGE) and the function's arguments, enclosed in parentheses. For example, you could type =ROUND(AVERAGE(A2:G4).

5. After entering the arguments for the main function and for any nested functions, type the closing parenthesis and press Enter. For example, your completed formula might look like this: =ROUND(AVERAGE(A2:G4),2). The result of your formula appears in the result cell selected in Step 1.

Order of Operations

Remember that Excel solves a formula by performing the innermost calculations first, and then moving outwards. So the main function in this case is the one you want performed *last*, after the other function has been calculated. To round the result of a function, you want ROUND performed last, so it's treated as the main function and entered first into the formula.

Tip

Probably the most common mistake when nesting functions is to forget the closing parenthesis for the function, whether it's the main function or a nested one. Excel typically catches such mistakes and makes a guess as to where you want the closing parenthesis to go, so you won't usually get an error when you forget one. However, keep in mind that this is only a guess, and in my experience, it's often a wrong one. So be sure to check your formula to make sure the parentheses are where they should be, or you might get an incorrect result.

Using Other Functions

EXCEL COMES WITH MANY FUNCTIONS, not just SUM. You have already learned about a few of them, such as ROUND and AVERAGE. Because there are so many, Excel groups all of its functions into specific categories, on the theory that this will make it easier for you to find them when needed. For the most part, these categories go a pretty long way in helping you quickly find the function you are looking for. The trick is to get to know what the categories mean, and the best way to do that is to introduce you to the prominent players in each category.

Buttons for each of the function categories are located on the Formulas tab, as shown in Figure 3-13. Click one of these buttons to display a list of functions in that category, and then select the function you want from the list. For example, click the Math & Trig button on the Formulas tab and select the SQRT (square root) function. The function is inserted into the result cell, and the Function wizard appears to guide you through the process of entering the appropriate arguments for that function. After doing that, click OK in the wizard to complete your formula.

Figure 3-13
Use the buttons on the Formulas tab
to enter any function you want.

As I introduce you to the most popular functions in each category, I describe the arguments you need to use. Now, you might have noticed by now that Excel names its arguments—for example, for the SUM function, it uses names like Number1, Number2, and so on. In this section, I might use a different name that I find more descriptive, such as Range1, Range2, so don't let the names confuse you.

Tip

The functions you've used recently are listed on the Recently Used menu. Click the Recently Used button on the Formulas tab, and select a function you've used recently from those listed on the menu that appears.

Use the ScreenTips

As you hover the cursor over a function category list, a ScreenTip appears, describing the purpose of that function. (See Figure 3-13.)

Using the Financial Functions

The Financial functions are used by accountants and the like, to perform common tasks such as calculating the accrued interest on a security, depreciation on an asset, future value of an asset, or the monthly payment on a loan. Because most of the Financial functions are used by financial experts who understand them, I won't dwell on too many. There are a few Financial functions, however, that just about anyone might use, and in this section, I explain more about them.

PMT

The PMT function can be used in three ways—to calculate the monthly payment on a loan, the interest rate you might earn on an investment, or the monthly deposit needed in order to reach some future total deposit amount. You feed the PMT function various information such as loan amount, interest rate, number of payments, and so on, depending on the result you're looking for. Let's take a closer look.

To use the PMT function to calculate a loan, use the following syntax:

```
=PMT(Rate,NumberofPayments,LoanAmt)
```

For example, suppose you are looking at buying a used car for somewhere between $10,000 and $12,000. You've found several loans and you want to compare them (see Figure 3-14). The first loan amounts have already been calculated, so you'll enter the formula in cell C8 for the second loan, which is for six years at 7.25%.

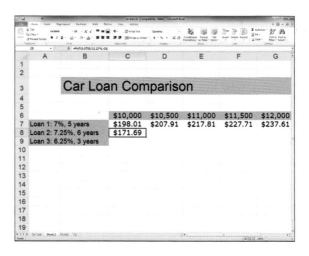

Figure 3-14
Use the PMT function to calculate loan payments.

Type =**PMT(.0725/12,6*12,−10000)** and press Enter. It's important that all the arguments are based on the same interval. The first argument is the interest rate, which needs to be converted to its monthly equivalent. So you need to divide the yearly interest rate of 7.25% (which is .0725 in decimal form) by 12 to calculate the interest rate per month. The next argument is the number of monthly payments. Because the loan is for six years, you take 6 times 12 to calculate the number of months. The last argument is the present value of the loan, which for cell C8 is $10,000. Notice that the loan amount is entered as a negative. You don't have to do that, but if you don't, the PMT function returns a negative value because of the way the function performs its calculation. Although a negative payment amount might be pleasing to you, it probably won't be acceptable to your bank. So be sure to enter the loan amount as a negative value.

Copying Formulas Across Rows

You could type the formula =PMT(.0725/12,6*12,–C8) and then copy it across the row to calculate the monthly payment for the various loan amounts you are considering.

Skip an Argument with a Comma

Notice that you type two commas after 15, which is the second argument, NumberofPayments. The extra comma is to indicate that you are not entering the third argument for the PMT function, which is CurrentValue. You skip this argument because it's not needed for this type of calculation.

Another reason you might use the PMT function is to calculate the interest you might earn on an investment, such as a CD (Certificate of Deposit). Use the following syntax:

```
=PMT(Rate,NumberofPayments,CurrentValue)
```

For example, to calculate the annual interest you might earn on a CD with an interest of 3.75%, five-year term, and an investment of $5,000, you type =PMT(.0375,5,–5000). Because you are cal-culating the annual interest, you don't have to divide the interest rate by 12. If the interest rate is calculated quarterly however, you'll need to adjust the formula: =PMT(.0375/4,5*4,–5000).

The final reason to use the PMT function is to calculate the amount you need to invest now, if you want to reach some future amount over time. Use the following syntax:

```
=PMT(Rate,NumberofPayments,,FutureValue)
```

For example, suppose you want to invest money annually in a CD that pays 6% in order to save $50,000 by the end of its term, which is 15 years. Type =PMT(.06,15,,–50000).

FV and PV

Two other useful Financial functions are FV and PV, which find the future or present value of an investment, given a specific interest rate and an amount to be invested each period. Use the following syntax:

```
=FV(Rate,NumberofPayments,PmtAmt,PresentValue,
    Type)
```

```
=PV(Rate,NumberofPayments,PmtAmt,FutureValue,
    Type)
```

Like the PMT function, all of these values need to be roughly equivalent, so if you are making quarterly payments, you need to divide the annual interest rate by four. In addition, like the PMT function, you need to enter the future or present value as a negative if you want to get a positive result.

The final argument for both functions, Type, tells Excel when the payment is made: use a 1 if you pay at the beginning of the month, and a 0 if you pay at the end (you can also omit this value and 0 is assumed). So let's determine how much you'll have at the end of five years, if you invest $100 per month at 4%. Type this formula: =FV(.04/12,5*12,–100). Hmmmm. It looks like at the end of five years, you'll have $6,629.90. Not bad!

So what's it worth to you in spending power, right now, to make those $100 payments each month? Try this formula: =PV(.04/12,5*12,−100). Well, looks like all that money is worth $5,429.91 right now. But keep in mind that you only have to part with $100 of it each month. That thought should keep the pain level down, along with the thought that after five years, you'll have earned almost $1,200! Now that's worth a little pain.

Using Logical Functions

Logical functions are used to display text or a value, or to perform some calculation, *only if some condition is true.* If the condition is not true, some alternate text or value is displayed, or some other calculation is performed. For example, you could tell Excel to compare the value in cell G10 with the value in H10, and if G10 is greater, to perform the calculation G10*.05. If G10 is not greater than H10, you could tell Excel to perform the calculation H10*.05 instead. The most common Logical function is the IF function, which has several variants.

IF

The syntax for the IF function is =IF(Condition,ActionIfTrue,ActionIfFalse). The first argument, Condition, is a logical test, which is essentially a comparison. If the comparison is true, the action listed as the second argument is taken. If the comparison is not true, the action listed as the third argument is taken.

To create a logical test or condition, you can use any of the following operators:

- ► = Equal
- ► <> Not equal
- ► > Greater than
- ► < Less than
- ► >= Greater than or equal to
- ► <= Less than or equal to

For example, to test whether A2 is larger than B2, use the condition A2>B2. Now, suppose a teacher wants to use the IF function to determine whether a student has failed her class. Assuming the first student's grade is in cell C4, she could type =IF(C4>64,"Pass","Fail") in cell D4. If the first student's grade is 65 or greater, then the word Pass will appear in cell D4. Otherwise, the word Fail appears. The teacher could then copy this formula down column D to display either Pass or Fail for each student.

Tip

You can nest one IF function within another if you want to test for multiple conditions. Suppose for example, that in order to pass the course, the student must get at least a 65% average on his/her homework, and at least 72% on the final test. Assuming that the homework average is in cell B4, and the final test score is in C4, the teacher could type the following into cell D4 to indicate whether the first student passed or failed, and why: =IF(B4>64,IF(C4>71,"Pass","Failed Final"),"Failed Homework").

SUMIF and SUMIFS

Although technically listed as a Math & Trig function, SUMIF acts like a Logical function so it's listed here. Use SUMIF to add a group of cells only if some condition is true. The syntax for the SUMIF function is as follows:

```
=SUMIF(RangeToCheck,"Condition",RangeToSum)
```

For example, consider the worksheet shown in Figure 3-15. In order to compute the total of all sales in the Eastern region, this formula is entered in cell I6: =SUMIF(C5:C17,"Eastern",E5:E17). Basically, this formula looks at each cell in the range C5:C17, and for the ones that contain the word Eastern, it adds the value in the corresponding cell in column E.

The last argument in the SUMIF function is optional, which means that if you want to compare values in a range and add those same values if some condition is true, you can leave this last argument out. For example (using the worksheet shown in Figure 3-15), suppose you want to add all the values in the range E5:E17 that are over $3 million. You could type =SUMIF(E5:E17, ">3000000").

Tip

The Condition argument in the SUMIF and SUMIFS functions must be entered in quotations, as in "Eastern" and ">10".

The SUMIFS function is similar to SUMIF, except that it allows you to enter multiple conditions to identify the cells you want to add. The syntax for the SUMIFS function is as follows:

```
=SUMIFS(RangeToSum,RangeToCheck,"Condition",
  RangeToCheck2,"Condition2",...and so on)
```

Looking at the worksheet in Figure 3-15, suppose you want to add up all the sales over $1 million for the Eastern region only. In cell I12, you could type =SUMIFS(E5:E17,C5:C17,"Eastern", E5:E17,">1000000").

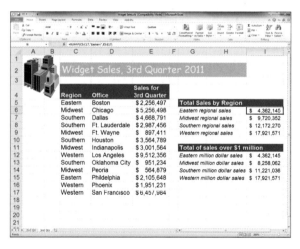

Figure 3-15
Use SUMIF to add selected cells.

COUNTIF and COUNTIFS

The COUNTIF and COUNTIFS functions work similarly to SUMIF and SUMIFS, except that they count the cells that meet the given condition, rather than add them. Also, although COUNTIF and COUNTIFS are Statistical functions, they are similar to Logical functions so I describe them here. To insert them into a worksheet, click the More Functions button on the Formulas tab, select Statistical, and then select either COUNTIF or COUNTIFS from the menu that appears.

The syntax for the COUNTIF function is =COUNTIF(RangeToCount,"Condition").

The syntax for the COUNTIFS function is =COUNTIFS(RangeToCount,"Condition",RangeTo Count2,"Condition2",...and so on).

Tip

Also like SUMIF, the Condition argument in the COUNTIF and COUNTIFS functions must be entered in quotations.

For example, suppose you have a list of potential clients for your new printing business. You want to properly staff your sales force so that they can pay a visit to each these potential clients and close that sale. To do that, you need to count the number of clients in various parts of the city, based on ZIP code. Assuming that the ZIP codes are listed in the range G2:G200, you could type =COUNTIF(G2:F200,"78112") to count all the potential clients in ZIP code 78112.

If you want to count all the potential clients in the ZIP codes 78112 and 83046, you could use the COUNTIFS function instead: =COUNTIFS (G2:G200,"78112", G2:G200,"83046").

Using Text Functions

Not surprisingly, Text functions are used to manipulate text. You use Text functions most often in database worksheets—worksheets that contain a list of names and addresses, inventory items, or statistical data. These functions help you manipulate the text to display what you want. Text functions can also be used on numbers that are entered as text such as a house number, Social Security number, ZIP code, part number, and such.

CONCATENATE

The CONCATENATE function takes the text in several cells and combines it to form a new text string. Take a look at the worksheet shown in Figure 3-16.

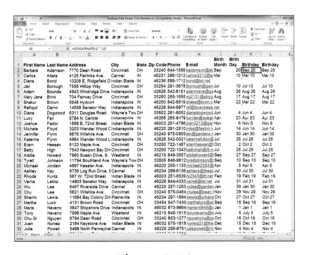

Figure 3-16
Use CONCATENATE to add text strings together.

As you can see in this garden club member database, the month a member was born appears in column H, whereas the birthday appears in column I. Having the birth month and birthday separated into two columns enables you to sort the database as needed. For example, it's easy to produce a list of everyone with April birthdays, by either sorting or filtering the Birth Month column. Let's suppose though, that you want to import this list into an e-mail program so you can send out meeting reminders, garden events, and the like. Since you also want to congratulate members on their birthday, you want that information as well. The only problem is, your e-mail program does not have separate fields for Birth Month and Birth Day. Instead, it has one field called Birthday. Using the CONCATENATE function, this problem is easily taken care of.

The syntax is
`=CONCATENATE(Text,Text2,Text3,...and so on)`

As the argument, you can either type the address of a cell that contains text (text or numbers treated as text), or a text string (enclosed in quotations). To solve the problem here, in cell K2, type =CONCATENATE(I2, " ",J2). The result, shown in cell K2, is a text string that combines the member's birth month and day, with a space in between: "Sep 20". Now, since your e-mail program won't be able to make much sense of the formula, you simply copy the result in column K to column L, using the Paste Value command so that you paste the result and not the formula. At that point, it's safe to remove columns I–K and keep only column L for importing into your e-mail program.

LEFT and RIGHT

The LEFT function is used to extract a certain number of characters from a text string, starting at the left. The RIGHT function works similarly, except it extracts characters starting from the right. Let's take a look at one reason why you might need to do this extracting business. Suppose you're in charge of inventory at a large computer store that caters to corporate customers. You're moving to a new computerized inventory system, and you need to generate product numbers that take advantage of its capabilities to sort and filter. You've decided to change the inventory numbers slightly, by adding a store code (extracted from the current store name) in front of the last portion of the current product number.

The syntax for the LEFT function is
`=LEFT(TextCell,NumberOfCharacters)`

The syntax for the RIGHT function is
`=RIGHT(TextCell,NumberOfCharacters)`

Consider the worksheet shown in Figure 3-17. Assume you want to take the first two letters of the store name (such as "Ca" for the Carmel store) and add the last four digits of the current product number. To add these two strings together into a new string, you'll use our friend, the CONCATENATE function. As you can see, to create the new inventory number in cell D8, you need to use three functions: =CONCATENATE (LEFT(A8,2),RIGHT(B8,4)). The LEFT function extracts the first two characters from the store name (in this case, "Ca"), whereas the RIGHT function extracts the last four digits of the current model number (in this case, "1245"). Finally, the CONCATENATE function puts them together to form a single text string, Ca1245. Copy this formula down column D, and voila! You have your new inventory numbers, easy as pie.

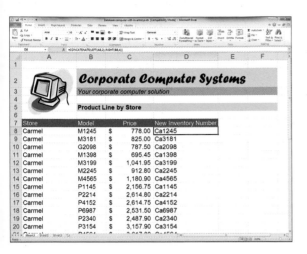

Figure 3-17
Use Excel's LEFT and RIGHT functions
to create a new inventory number.

You Can Use the & Sign to Concatenate

You can also perform this same task with the following formula: =LEFT(A8,2)&RIGHT(B8,4). The & sign essentially performs the same task as the CONCATENATE function, combining the results of the LEFT and RIGHT functions into a single text string.

TEXT and VALUE

The TEXT function converts a number into equivalent text. The syntax is =TEXT(Number, "Format"). The Number argument is pretty easy to understand—it's either the address of a cell containing a number, or a formula that results in a number. The Format argument is any valid number or date format. If you open the Format Cells dialog box (by clicking the Dialog Box Launcher in the Number group on the Home tab) and select Custom, you'll find many examples of valid formats. Here are some samples:

Format	Number	Result
#,##0.00	29874	29,874.00
$#,###	29874	$29,874
0.00%	.0257	2.57%
m/d/yy	May 14, 2010	5/14/10
mmm-yy	May 14, 2010	May-10

Tip

The Format argument must be enclosed in quotations, as in =TEXT(G4,"m/d/yy").

Suppose you run a construction business, and you have a worksheet that everyone in your department is supposed to update as soon as a particular job is completed, listing the total cost of that job, the number of weeks it took to complete, and the approximate level of customer satisfaction. You use this worksheet to create a list of recent referrals for new clients, so it's pretty important that it's updated often.

You want to display the date at the top of the worksheet, but you also want to make it clear what that date means by preceding it with the text, "Updated on". As you can see in the worksheet shown in Figure 3-18, the formula you need is ="Updated on " &TEXT(TODAY(),"m/d/yy"). The TODAY function, which is described in the section "Using Date and Time Functions," is a simple function that displays today's date. The date is updated every time the worksheet is recalculated. So if you open the workbook at some later date, this date is automatically changed to reflect the current date. If today's date was already displayed elsewhere in the worksheet, you could simply reference that cell in the formula like this: ="Updated on " &TEXT(B3,"m/d/yy").

Figure 3-18
Use TEXT to change a number into text.

The VALUE function is the opposite of TEXT, converting a text string that looks like a number into an actual value that can be calculated just like any other number. The syntax is =VALUE(Text).

Using Date and Time Functions

The Date and Time functions help you display dates or times in the worksheet without actually entering them. For example, there are functions for entering the current date or the current date and time. There are other functions you can use to add or subtract dates—for example, you might want to subtract the start date of a job from its end date in order to calculate how long the job took. Only work on weekdays? No problem; there's a date function that counts the number of weekdays only between two dates.

Dates Are Stored As Numbers

Excel stores all dates as numbers so that you can perform date calculations, such as subtracting one date from another. The date, January 1, 1900, is equal to 1, whereas June 3, 2001, is equal to 37,045. Subtract the two and you get 37,044 days.

TODAY

The TODAY function does not have any arguments. You simply type =TODAY() into a cell, press Enter, and the current date appears. You can then apply any date format you want to display the date the way you like. Every time the worksheet is recalculated, TODAY updates the date in the cell automatically.

Recalculating Your Formulas

In Chapter 2, "Working with Formulas," you learned how to control when Excel recalculates a workbook. By default, Excel recalculates a workbook automatically, whenever you open or save it. In addition, Excel normally recalculates formulas every time a cell to which it refers changes. When Excel recalculates a workbook, it updates the results of all formulas, including the TODAY and NOW functions. To force recalculation at any time, click the Calculate Now button on the Formulas tab.

NOW

The NOW function is similar to TODAY except that it displays the current date and time. Like the TODAY function, the NOW function does not have any arguments. You type =NOW() into a cell, and the current date and time are displayed. When the worksheet is recalculated, the date and time are updated.

DAY, MONTH, and YEAR

The DAY, MONTH, and YEAR functions work similarly. Each has only one argument, Date, and each extracts something from that date—the day, the month, or the year. The syntax is

```
=DAY(Date)
```

```
=MONTH(Date)
```

```
=YEAR(Date)
```

For example, suppose you have a worksheet that lists your employees, and you want to determine how many years each employee will be with you come the end of the year. You've decided to take the year each person was hired, and subtract it from 2011 to calculate the number of years each employee has been working for you, come 12/31/2011. Assuming the first employee's hire date is in cell I10, you use this formula: 2011−YEAR(I10). The result is a date, which appears rather confusing. Simply format the cell using General format, and a value such as 12 appears.

Tip

Keep in mind that a formula such as =MONTH(G4)−MONTH(F4) literally takes the month number of the date in cell G4 minus the month number of the date in cell F4. This may not be what you want. For example, suppose G4 contains the date 10/15/10, and cell F4 contains the date 5/21/10. Take 10−5 and you get 5 months, although clearly 5 months has not passed from 5/21/10 to 10/15/10. A better formula might be =(G4−F4)/365.25*12, which subtracts the two dates to compute the number of days between them, and then divides that total by 365.25 to calculate the number of years, which is then multiplied by 12 to get the number of months. Of course, you're going to end up with a fraction of a month, so use ROUNDDOWN: =ROUNDDOWN((G4−F4)/365.25*12).

NETWORKDAYS

The NETWORKDAYS function calculates the number of workdays between two dates. By workdays, I mean Monday–Friday, minus any obvious holidays such as Christmas and New Year's. The syntax is:

```
=NETWORKDAYS(StartDate,EndDate,Holidays)
```

The last argument, Holidays, is optional, but it allows you a way to specify the holidays your office uses, such as Martin Luther King Day, Veterans Day, and so on. The argument is a range, such as M2:M12, that contains the dates you want treated as holidays. So for example, if you had a worksheet that listed the starting and ending date of a job, you could calculate the number of workdays it took to complete that job with a formula like this: =NETWORKDAYS(C2,D2).

DATE

The DATE function allows you to compose a date, using each of its three arguments: Year, Month, and Day. The syntax is:

```
=DATE(Year,Month,Day)
```

The DATE function is useful in situations where the month, day, and year of a date are stored in separate cells, as they might be in a large database. For example, if you had a membership database for your parents' association that listed everyone's birth month in one column and birth day in another, you could use the DATE function to compose their actual birthday this year, assuming the birth months are in column G and the birth days are in column I: =DATE(YEAR(TODAY()),G2,I2).

Understanding the Time Arguments

The Year argument should be a four-digit one, so Excel knows for sure what century you're talking about (1911 vs. 2011). The Month and Day arguments can be negative. If Month is negative, Excel subtracts that many months, plus one, from the year specified to determine what month you mean. For example, if you enter =DATE(2001,–2,13), then the result is 10/13/00 (three months from the beginning of 2001). If Day is negative, Excel subtracts that many days, plus one, from the beginning of the month specified. For example, =DATE(2010,8,–15) results in 7/16/10 (16 days from August 1).

Another example is to compute a date so many years, months, or days from some other date. For example, suppose an employee review is due three months from an employee's hire date. You could add 180 (3*30) to the hire date, but that's not exactly accurate, as some months have 31 days and one of them has 28 or 29 depending on the year. No, all you want to do is to take a date like 2/15/10 and add three months to get 5/15/10. So you use the DATE function and a few old friends to add three months to the hire date, which let's say is stored in cell E4: =DATE(YEAR(E4),MONTH(E4)+3,DAY(E4)). Obviously, this formula, with a small tweak, would work easily in situations where you need to add or subtract so many years from a date, like this example, which adds 25 years to a date: =DATE(YEAR(E4)+25,MONTH(E4),DAY(E4)). To add or subtract days, you can be more straightforward: =E4+15.

Using Lookup and Reference Functions

The Lookup and Reference functions are used to locate data in a large database of information, such as an employee or inventory database. The two most common of these functions include VLOOKUP and HLOOKUP.

VLOOKUP and HLOOKUP

Both VLOOKUP and HLOOKUP are used to look up information in a database. The VLOOKUP function looks up the data vertically down a particular column, whereas HLOOKUP looks up data horizontally across a particular row. Here is the syntax:

```
=VLOOKUP(ItemToFind,Range,ColumnNumber,Type)
```

```
=HLOOKUP(ItemToFind,Range,RowNumber,Type)
```

The ItemToFind is a cell address, formula, or the actual value you are trying to find in the database, such as a particular employee. This item must be contained in the first column/row of the Range you specify. So, if you're looking up an employee using his ID, the ID needs to be the first column or row of your database Range.

The Range, by the way, needs to include the column/row that contains the labels or everything will be thrown off. The ColumnNumber/RowNumber is the column/row where the data you're trying to look up is stored. For example, if you're trying to look up an employee's phone number, and that phone number is in column 5 of the Range, you would use 5 as your ColumnNumber argument.

Finally, the Type is optional, but if you omit it, Excel assumes "True," which means that your database is sorted by the ItemToFind column/row, and that you will accept an answer that's close but not over if the actual item can't be found. For example, suppose you are looking up an employee by his ID, and that the Range is sorted by ID, from lowest to highest. If you tell Excel to look up ID number 417 and there isn't one, Excel will look up the closest ID that isn't over 417 (such as say, 415) and give you the results for that person. If you set Type to False, Excel will only provide an answer if an exact match is found. Also, if you set Type to False, Excel does not assume that the Range is sorted by ID (to continue this example).

Consider the worksheet shown in Figure 3-19, which shows an employee database for PhotoTown. Because the database is set up vertically, with the labels across the top of each column, you need to use VLOOKUP to look up an employee's emergency phone number when needed. You've planned the worksheet so that you can enter the employee's name in cell I4, and his/her phone number appears in cell I5. Type =VLOOKUP(I4,C7:H37,6,FALSE). Cell I4 has the value to look up, which in this case is the employee's name. The range C7:H37 has the data—note that column C contains the employee names.

Remember that the thing you are looking up (the employee's name in this example) must be contained in the first column/row. The number 6 tells Excel to look up data in the sixth column of the Range for the matching employee. The sixth column in this case is the Emergency Phone Number column, which is exactly what we want.

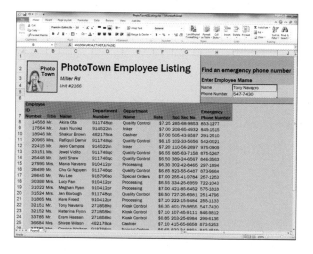

Figure 3-19
Look up data in a large database of information using VLOOKUP or HLOOKUP.

Using Mathematical Functions

You already know some mathematical operations for use in formulas (+, −, *, /, and ^), but what about the Mathematical functions? Which ones might you find the most useful for analysis of data? Well, you are already pretty familiar with one Mathematical function, SUM, which is used to add a group of cells. Let's take a look at some others.

INT

Need to round a result down to the nearest integer? Then the INT function is for you. The syntax is =INT(Number). Now typically, you won't enter an actual number as the argument for the INT function, because I'm guessing you could probably round it down to the nearest integer in your head. Instead, you will probably enter a cell address, like this: =INT(G4). Assuming G4 contains the value 102.31, the result is 102. If G4 contains the value, 102.72, the result is still 102 since INT always rounds *down*.

You can also nest a formula or a function with INT if you like. For example, consider the formula =INT(SUM(G10:J32)). It tells Excel to total the values in the range G10:J32, and then round them down to the nearest integer. Consider this formula: =INT(A2/40). It tells Excel to take the value in cell A2, divide it by 40, and then round the result down to the nearest integer.

ROUND

The ROUND function adjusts a value to a specific number of digits. Now, there are several reasons why you might want to round the results of your formulas, such as to stop your worksheets from driving you crazy. Let me explain.

When a cell is formatted to a specified number of decimal places, the display of that value is the only thing affected. The actual value in the cell is still used in all calculations. For example, if a cell contains the value 13.45687, and you decide to display only the first two decimal places, the value 13.46 will display in the cell, but the value 13.45687 will be used in all calculations, including totals, which is where the "driving you crazy" part comes in. Take a good look at the worksheet shown in Figure 3-20.

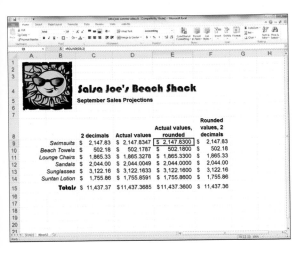

Figure 3-20
Your totals can drive you crazy if you forget to round.

In this worksheet, you can see the actual values (column D), and the values that appear in the worksheet if you apply a two-decimal format to those numbers (column C). Let's pretend for a second that your worksheet only shows Column C—Column D is there only so you can see what's going on. If you do some quick math, you will see that the September Sales Projections in Column C look as if they have been added incorrectly, since 2147.83+502.18+1865.33+ 2044.00+3122.16+1755.86 equals 11,437.36 and not 11,437.37.

So, here's the lesson you need to learn: if you plan on displaying a limited number of decimal places in your worksheet and not whole numbers, you might want to use the ROUND function to adjust each value so that the displayed value is equal to the actual value used in calculations.

Let's take a look at the worksheet if you round the values, and then add them. As you can see in Column E, the actual values, which are displayed with four decimal places, have been rounded to the nearest penny. So even when you display the values using only two decimal places (as shown in Column F), the total is correct. Of course, if you are interested in every digit of the calculated sales projections, you should display them fully so that your totals will look correct.

To round a value to the nearest specified decimal place, use this syntax: =ROUND(Number,Digits). For example, to round the value in cell G21 to the nearest penny, type =ROUND(G21,2). To round to the nearest whole number, type =ROUND(G21,0). To round to the left of the decimal point, use a negative number. For example, to round to the nearest hundred, type =ROUND(G21,−2).

Using ROUNDUP and ROUNDDOWN

Rather than rounding to the nearest specified digit, you can force Excel to round up by using the ROUNDUP function instead. Use the ROUNDDOWN function to force Excel to round down. Both ROUNDUP and ROUNDDOWN work the same way as ROUND, with two arguments, Number and Digits.

Using Other Functions

On the Formulas tab, Excel groups other functions that while perhaps less popular, are still very useful. In fact, you may find yourself using the Statistical functions quite often, although perhaps you will not often insert them using the Formulas tab. Most likely, you will insert the following Statistical functions using the AutoSum button, explained earlier in this chapter:

▶ **=AVERAGE(Range1,Range2,...and so on):** The AVERAGE function calculates the mean (average) of the values in the given Range(s).

▶ **=COUNT(Range1,Range2,...and so on):** The COUNT function counts the cells in the given Range(s) containing numbers (cells that are blank cells or contain text are ignored).

▶ **=MIN(Range1,Range2,...and so on):** The MIN function finds the lowest value in the given Range(s).

▶ **=MAX(Range1,Range2,...and so on):** The MAX function finds the highest value in the given Range(s).

There are a few related functions that you might be interested in, such as the COUNTA function, which counts the number of non-blank cells (numbers and text cells are counted) in the given ranges. The syntax is:

`=COUNTA(Range1,Range2,...and so on)`

The COUNTBLANK function is similar, except that it counts the number of blank (empty) cells in the given ranges. The syntax is:

`=COUNTBLANK(Range1,Range2,...and so on)`

Troubleshooting

Formula Errors

T'S THE NATURE OF COMPUTING to encounter errors. In fact, that's one reason for using a computer for complex tasks—so that it can check your work for errors and let you know when you've created one. Of course, nothing's perfect, not even a computer, and so you cannot depend on Excel to flag every error for you. For example, you might have referenced the wrong cell in a formula. The formula is valid, but displays the wrong result because it is using the wrong values.

In such cases, Excel provides you with other ways in which you can double-check your work and eliminate errors. For example, you might display the formulas in a worksheet so you can easily double-check them in order ensure that they were entered correctly. In addition, Excel provides you with tools for locating formulas with incorrect syntax, tracing formulas back to their source(s), and observing changes to results when values are changed.

Displaying Formulas in a Worksheet

AS YOU KNOW, FORMULAS DO NOT normally display in the worksheet. Instead, the results of formulas appear in the result cells. If you click a result cell, the formula appears in the Formula bar—but that means in order to check a formula, you have to first find and then click its result cell and look in the Formula bar. A rather tedious process, especially if your worksheet has a lot of formulas.

Luckily, Excel allows you to display formulas instead of results when needed. With formulas displayed, it's easier to double-check each one to ensure that it was entered correctly, which is particularly helpful when the formulas in your worksheet are long or complex.

Tip

With formulas displayed, you can print them if you like, and then use the printout to double-check formulas.

Displaying formulas in a worksheet is an all-or-nothing thing, which means that once you display formulas, they remain displayed in that worksheet until you turn the feature off. By the way, this is a worksheet-level feature, so if you want to display formulas in all the worksheets in a workbook, you need to repeat these steps for each worksheet.

Follow these steps to display formulas:

1. Change to the worksheet containing the formulas you want to display. To change from one worksheet to another, click the worksheet's tab, located along the bottom of the Excel window.

2. Click the Formulas tab.

3. Click the Show Formulas button, located in the Formula Auditing group. Cells are automatically expanded to display formulas fully, as shown in Figure 4-1.

Cells referred to by the result cell are highlighted   Show Formulas Button   Result Cell

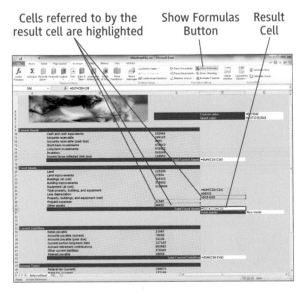

Figure 4-1
One way to check formulas is to display them in the worksheet.

Expanding Cells

Don't freak out when Excel expands the result cells in order to display your formulas. Although the worksheet may look a bit odd, result cells will return to their normal size when you turn off the display of formulas.

As a reminder, while you are poking around the worksheet checking formulas, keep in mind that if you click a result cell, the cells referred to in that formula are highlighted by colored boxes that match the same cell addresses in the worksheet (see Figure 4-1). Remember as well that you can drag a colored box and drop it on a new cell to change a cell reference used in the formula.

To hide formulas once again, click the Show Formulas button on the Format tab to turn it off.

Tip

To quickly display or hide formulas in the current worksheet, press Ctrl+` (the accent key to the left of the 1 key—it also has a tilde ~ on it).

Understanding How Excel Handles Formula Errors

GRANTED, EXCEL CAN'T READ your mind. So it can't know that you meant to subtract the July Expenses from July Revenues. Thus, it won't bop you on the head when you accidentally subtract June's Expenses from July Revenues instead. Still, there are some errors Excel knows are errors, such as dividing by zero. Excel helps you to identify most of these errors when they occur by displaying an error message such as #DIV/0 in the result cell of the formula containing the error. For other errors such as forgetting to type a closing parenthesis, Excel may flash a dialog box at you indicating the mistake (and offering you a chance right then to fix it),

and not display an error message in the cell. All of these errors are described in detail in the section "Understanding Formula Error Messages."

Because some formula errors do not cause an error message to display in the result cell, you may want Excel to help you identify errors in another way—through an instant, "Hey, that's an error!" flagging thing, or with a "Let's check the worksheet for errors now, one at a time, just like a spelling checker" sort of thing. You learn both methods in the section "Checking for Errors Automatically One at a Time."

Understanding Formula Error Messages

Excel has a list of specific formula errors that it will flag if you make them, by displaying a message in the result cell. All of these error messages start with a pound sign #, as you will soon see.

####

If this error appears in a cell, Excel is not telling you that a formula contains an error. Instead, it's simply letting you know that this particular cell contains data that's wider than the cell. In most cases, all you have to do is widen the column to correct the problem and eliminate the error message.

Tip

To quickly widen a column to just the right width, move the cursor to the right edge of the column. Double-click this right edge, and the column automatically expands to fit the widest entry in that column.

#VALUE!

When this error message appears, Excel is telling you that you are trying to use the wrong type of data for your formula. For example, the formula might use a function that requires a text argument, and you've pointed it to a cell that contains a number. Or the function might be looking for a single cell argument, and you entered a range. In any case, to eliminate the error, edit the formula so that it uses the type of data the function is looking for.

#DIV/0!

When you see this error message, the formula is attempting to divide some number by zero. For example, in the formula =A5/B5, if B5 is zero or empty, the result will be the #DIV/0! error. Typically, this error occurs not because you actually wanted to divide by zero, but because the cell you are referring to is currently empty. You can just live with the error flashing you in the face until you enter values in the worksheet, or you can tell Excel to ignore this particular error by changing your options (as explained in the section "Telling Excel Which Errors to Flag"). But if you share this workbook with someone else, and Excel is not set up to ignore this error, the error will display in the result cell—perhaps causing confusion for your colleague. One way to ignore this error is to use the IF function, like this: =IF(B5=0,"",A5/B5).

Using the IF Function

To learn more about the IF function, see Chapter 2, "Working with Formulas," for help.

#NAME?

This error message is telling you that Excel doesn't recognize some kind of text you have used in a formula. Typically, this means you have either misspelled a range name or referred to a non-existent range name. Or perhaps you misspelled a function name, forgot to put a text string in quotations, or left out the colon in a range address (A2:G10).

#N/A

This means that the value you want to use in a formula isn't there. This does not mean you are referring to a blank cell—instead, it means that you've tried to look up data in a table, and the value you are trying to find isn't there. For example, if you type =VLOOKUP("Alice",B7:E44,3) and "Alice" is not in the first column of the table, Excel displays the error #N/A. You might also get the #N/A error if you accidentally leave out a required argument for a function, or attempt to use invalid data as an argument (such as entering a range address when the function is expecting a single cell address).

> ## More About VLOOKUP
>
> If you want to learn more about the VLOOKUP function, see Chapter 2, "Working with Formulas," for help.

#REF!

The #REF! error is telling you that a cell reference used in a formula is invalid. This typically happens right after you paste new cells (using the Insert Copied Cells command) over the top of the cells referenced in the formula, pushing those cells down or right. It may also happen if you use the Delete Cells command, which has the reverse effect.

#NUM!

You see this error when you use a non-numeric argument in a function that is looking for a value. The #NUM error also appears when the formula is a number too large or too small for Excel to represent.

#NULL!

Basically, this error is telling you that you left out the comma when specifying more than one range in a function. For example, if you type =SUM(A1:A6 C1:C6), you get the #NULL error. Curiously enough, if the ranges intersect in some way, as in =SUM(A1:C6 B3:B10) and you use a space, Excel thinks that you want it to add only the cells in both ranges (B3:B6), and so you don't get an error.

Circular Reference

A circular reference does not result in an error message that appears in the result cell. But Excel does send up a few flags when it occurs.

First off, a *circular reference* is caused when a formula references itself. For example, suppose you type =SUM(B2:B10) in cell B10. You are telling Excel to add all the values in the range B2:B10, including the total you are creating in cell B10, which of course changes that total, which changes the total again, and so on, in an endless circular loop.

When you accidentally create a circular reference, an error message appears on the status bar similar to: "Circular Reference:F12". If you open a workbook that contains a circular reference, you will see a warning telling you that the workbook contains one or more circular references.

Avoiding Common Formula Errors

There are other errors you might make when entering a formula, and those errors may not result in an error message such as DIV/0! being displayed in a cell. Here is a list of things you should be careful of when typing a formula:

▶ **Make sure you type equals sign (=) at the start of every formula.** If you don't, Excel typically thinks that what you've typed is text, and displays it in the cell without calculating anything. For example, if you type AVERAGE(B4:B7), you'll see that text, and not a result. Some formulas, when you forget the equals sign (=), are interpreted as a date: if you type 3/8 instead of =3/8, you get March 8 instead of 0.375.

▶ **Don't forget to match up all your parentheses.** If you forget a closing parenthesis, Excel will warn you of the problem and may attempt to "fix" your formula by adding a closing parenthesis. This guess may not be what you wanted. The only way to know for sure is to carefully check the formula and add the parenthesis where it belongs.

▶ **If you need to enter a date in a formula, make sure you use a four-digit year.** If you don't, Excel may assume you mean a year from the 20th century instead of the 21st. For example, if you enter =YEAR("02/20/25"), Excel assumes you mean 02/20/1925, rather than 02/20/2025.

▶ **Formulas that are inconsistent with formulas in surrounding cells are interpreted as a possible error.** For example, if A10 contains the formula =(A2–A8)/A9 and you enter =(B2–B8)/(B9*2.75) in B10 and =(C2–C8)/C9 in C10, Excel notices the inconsistency and assumes cell B10 has an error because it's different.

▶ **Formulas that omit adjacent cells may also be flagged as errors.** For example, if you type the formula =AVERAGE(C3:C10) in cell C14, it will be flagged as a possible error if cells C11, C12, and C13 contain data which perhaps should be included in the formula.

▶ **When using functions, make sure you enter all required arguments and that you refer to cells that contain the kind of data the function is looking for.** Also, when entering a number as an argument, do not include any formatting such as commas (,) and dollar signs ($), as in $12,387. You can, on the other hand, use % to enter a percentage in a formula, as in 2%.

▶ **If you turn on worksheet protection (which you'll learn about in Chapter 13, "Setting Security Options"), all cells in the worksheet are typically protected against changes.** Still, you can selectively "unprotect" the cells you want to allow others to enter data into. Even so, if you unprotect a cell with a formula, Excel will see that as a possible error, because it's unusual that you would want to allow anyone to change a formula in a worksheet you're protecting against unwanted changes.

▶ **Referring to cells on another worksheet or in a different workbook within a formula is a tricky business.** For example, ='April'!H43–10 tells Excel to take the value in cell H43 on the worksheet called April, and subtract 10 from it. However, if you forget to put the name of the worksheet in single quotations (not double-quotations), or if you leave out the exclamation point (!) after the sheet name, Excel will flag the formula as an error because it won't know what you're referring to. The simplest way to avoid such errors is to click the cell you want, even if that means switching workbooks to click the right cell.

Telling Excel Which Errors to Flag

YOU HAVE LEARNED A LOT about the types of errors Excel typically flags, and why it flags them as errors. You may prefer to not have certain errors flagged as such, especially if you use workbooks in which they would not be considered actual errors.

Flagging Errors

Errors are flagged with a triangle marker if you set up Excel to do that (see the section "Telling Excel to Flag Result Cells with an Error" for help). Regardless, if a formula is considered to be in error, Excel can point it out to you during an error check (see the section, "Checking for Errors Automatically One at a Time"). The errors that Excel flags with a marker or during an error check are partially determined by the "rules" you select by following the steps given here.

To tell Excel which errors you want it to watch out for, follow these steps:

1. Click the File tab to display Backstage.

2. Select Options from the list on the left. The Excel Options dialog box appears.

3. Select Formulas from the list on the left. The Formula options appear on the right, as shown in Figure 4-2.

Select the Errors Excel
Should Watch For

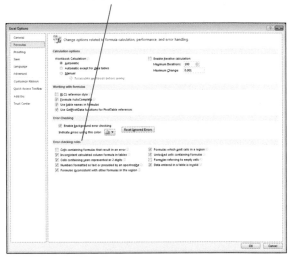

Figure 4-2
Tell Excel which errors you want it to look for.

Just What Is a Calculated Column?

To understand what a calculated column is, you have to first understand tables. Tables are created from organized rows and columns when you format them as a table (using the Format as Tables button on the Home tab or the Table button on the Insert tab). Once formatted as a table, you can quickly filter your data (limit its display to selected types, such as all rows with a Sales value over $1,000) or sort it. You can also create a calculated column by typing a formula in one cell of that column, and letting Excel copy it down the rest of the column for you automatically. After that, if you change the copied formula in any cell in that column, Excel once again copies the new formula throughout the column. Of course, when Excel does that, it displays the Paste Options button, which allows you to prevent this automatic copying business. At that point, one formula in the calculated column will be different from all the others, and it will be flagged as an error unless you tell Excel differently. In addition, because of the one inconsistent formula, any changes to the consistent formulas in that column will not be automatically copied down the column.

4. In the Error Checking Rules section, select the check boxes for the errors you want Excel to flag if they occur (deselect any you do not want):

   - **Cells Containing Formulas That Result In An Error:** Controls whether the # error messages such as #VALUE! and #NAME? are ignored.

   - **Inconsistent Calculated Column Formula In Tables:** Controls whether an inconsistency in a calculated column is treated as an error.

   - **Cells Containing Years Represented As 2 Digits:** Controls whether a date with a two digit year (such as 3/10/11), when used in a formula, is flagged as an error.

   - **Formulas Inconsistent with Other Formulas in the Region:** Controls whether Formula A is flagged as an error if adjacent cells contain similar formulas that are different from Formula A.

   - **Formulas Which Omit Cells in a Region:** Controls whether a formula that omits cells near a range used in the formula (assuming these nearby cells contain data) is flagged as an error.

   - **Formulas Referring to Empty Cells:** Controls whether formulas that include empty cells as arguments are flagged as errors. You already know about dividing by zero (an empty cell), and how that is flagged with #DIV/0! message. But other errors can occur when blank cells are used, such as =AVERAGE(H12:J24), in which the average would be different if an empty cell were included.

   - **Data Entered in a Table Is Invalid:** Controls whether invalid data (as defined by the Data Validation command) is flagged as an error when entered into a table.

5. Click OK.

Telling Excel to Flag Result Cells with an Error

EXCEL CAN BE SET UP TO flag a formula's result cell if it contains an error, with a small green triangle in its upper-left corner in order to let you know that there's a problem. You might think that displaying an error message such as #NUM! *and* flagging a cell with a green flag is a bit much, but that little green flag makes it easier to correct such errors, as you will see in a moment.

Green flags do not appear on error cells unless you tell Excel that you want them to display. To tell Excel to flag formulas with errors, follow these steps:

1. Click the File tab to display Backstage.

2. Select Options from the list on the left. The Excel Options dialog box appears.

3. Select Formulas from the list on the left. The Formula options appear on the right, as shown in Figure 4-3.

4. Select the Enable Background Error Checking option.

5. (Optional) If you want, select the color you want Excel to use for its error triangles (the triangles that appear in the upper-left corner of error cells). Normally, Excel uses green, but you can choose a different color if you want. Just click the Indicate Errors Using This Color button to open a palette of colors.

Set Options that Enable Excel to Flag Errors

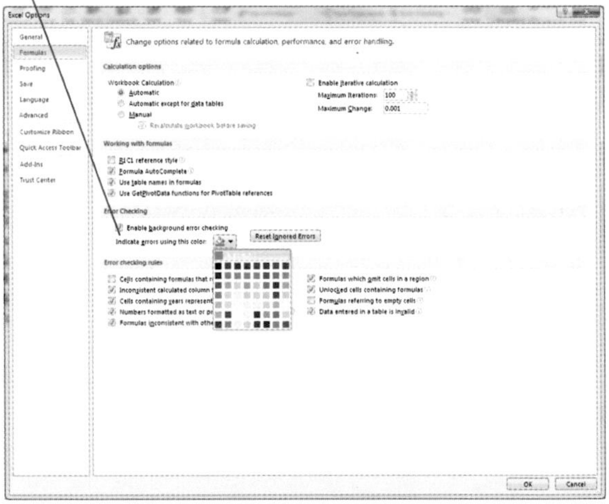

Figure 4-3
Cells referenced in a formula are surrounded by a colored box that matches the cell address in the formula itself.

6. Click OK. Excel immediately marks any error cells with a small triangle of the color you selected.

Once cells are flagged, you can use the flag to help you fix them. Follow these steps:

1. Click a flagged cell. An Error Checking button appears to the left, as shown in Figure 4-4. If you move the mouse pointer over this button, a description of the type of error appears in a ScreenTip.

Error Checking Button   Formulas with Errors Are Flagged

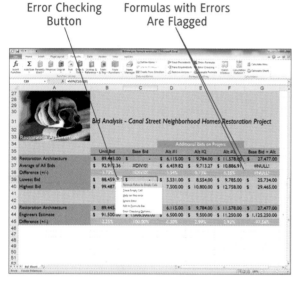

Figure 4-4
Use its flag to correct a formula's error.

Tip

To reset a worksheet so that previously ignored errors are no longer ignored, click the File tab to display Backstage and select Options from the list on the left. The Excel Options dialog box appears. Click Formulas from the list on the left to display the Formula options. In the Error Checking section, click the Reset Ignored Errors button and click OK.

2. Click the Error Checking button. A menu of options to correct the error appears.

3. Select an option from the menu. These options vary, but here's a brief description of some of the common options:

   - **Help on this Error:** Displays the Help page related to this particular formula error, so you can get additional help with resolving it.

   - **Trace Error:** Displays arrows that point to the cells referred to in the formula. To learn more about tracing a formula, see the section "Identifying Formula Precedents and Dependents."

   - **Ignore Error:** Removes the flag from the result cell, and ignores the error in any future searches unless you reset the worksheet.

   - **Edit in Formula Bar:** Moves the cursor to the Formula bar so you can edit the formula and correct it.

   - **Error Checking Options:** Displays the Excel Options dialog box so you can change Excel's error checking options.

4. Fix the error.

5. Repeat Steps 1–4 to fix other errors in the worksheet.

Checking for Errors Automatically One at a Time

EXCEL FLAGS MOST ERRORS with a message such as #NULL! Or #NA, and if you like, it can even add a small triangle to the upper corner of an error cell. You can then go hunting through a worksheet looking for these messages and little flags (if shown) and correct formula errors one by one.

Another way in which you can check a worksheet for errors (whether or not you display error flags) is to have Excel point the errors out to you, one at a time, like a spelling checker. Follow these steps:

1. Click the Error Checking button on the Formulas tab. The Error Checking dialog box highlights the first cell with an error, as shown in Figure 4-5.

2. On the left side of the Error Checking dialog box, the address of the cell with the error is listed, along with its formula. Just below that is a description of the error. Click one of the buttons on the right side of the Error Checking dialog box. The buttons change a bit, depending on the type of error, but here's a list of the ones you'll most likely see:

   - **Trace Error:** Displays arrows that point to the cells referred to in the formula. To learn more about tracing a formula, see the section "Identifying Formula Precedents and Dependents."

Error Cell   Select an Option to Fix the Error

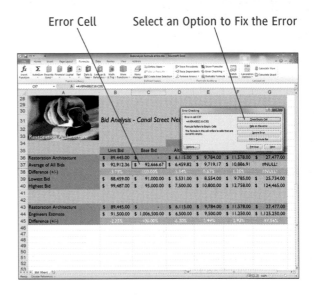

Figure 4-5
Cells referenced in a formula are surrounded by a colored box that matches the cell address in the formula itself.

   - **Help on this Error:** Display the Help page related to this particular formula error so you can get additional help with resolving it.

   - **Ignore Error:** Removes the flag from the result cell and ignores the error in any future searches unless you reset the worksheet.

   - **Edit in Formula Bar:** Moves the cursor to the Formula bar so you can edit the formula and correct it.

Tip

After you click Ignore Error, that error is ignored by Excel from now on, regardless of the method you use to check the worksheet. You can reset a worksheet so that previously ignored errors are no longer ignored, by clicking the File tab to display Backstage, selecting Options from the list on the left, selecting Formulas from the list on the left, and clicking the Reset Ignored Errors button. Click OK to close the dialog box.

- **Show Calculation Steps:** For complex formulas, Excel offers this option, which displays the Evaluate Formula dialog box. See the section "Evaluating a Formula" for help.

- **Options:** The Options button appears on the left in the Error Checking dialog box. Click it to display the Excel Options dialog box so you can change Excel's error checking options.

3. Fix the error with the formula.

4. Click Next to display the next error. Click Previous at any time to display a previous error.

5. Repeat Steps 3 and 4 to find and repair all errors in the worksheet.

Tip

When you find an error in a formula, one way in which you might need to correct it is to change the cell(s) that the formula references. For example, you might need to change the formula =SUM(D2:D10) so that it reads =SUM(D2:D12). When you click a cell with a formula, and then click in the Formula bar, the cells referenced by the formula are outlined with colored borders. You can drag these colored borders and drop them on different cells, in order to change the cells used in the formula. You can also resize a colored border to make the formula reference more or fewer cells in that range.

Using the Watch Window

If you are trying to find a problem with formulas in a large worksheet, using the Watch Window may help. With the Watch Window, you can watch as values change in selected cells—whether or not those cells are currently displayed onscreen. So with the Watch Window, you're not stuck scrolling up and down in a large worksheet, or jumping back and forth between sheets as you check values and fix problems—the Watch Window can display critical cells for you so you can see how your edits affect them.

Using the Watch Window

The Watch Window allows you to view cells located in the current worksheet, other sheets in the current workbook, or in a different workbook that's currently open.

Follow these steps to use the Watch Window:

1. Click the Watch Window button on the Formulas tab. The Watch Window task pane appears, as shown in Figure 4-6.

Tip

You can dock the Watch task pane along any side of the workbook window, or float it in the middle. To dock the Watch task pane, drag it by its title bar toward the side of the workbook window, until it automatically expands and locks in place. To float the Watch window again, drag it by its title bar away from its docked position until the Watch Window snaps back into its smaller window shape, as shown in Figure 4-6. Drop the task pane wherever you like in the Excel window.

2. Click the Add Watch button, located at the top of the task pane. The Add Watch dialog box appears (see Figure 4-6).

3. In the Add Watch box, type the address of the cell or range you want to watch, or simply select the cell/range in the worksheet.

4. Click Add. The cell or range of cells you selected is added to the Watch list. Notice in the Watch Window, that the address of the selected cell(s) is listed, along with their corresponding values. If the cell(s) contains a formula, it is listed as well.

5. Make changes to the worksheet. If your changes affected any of the watched cells, those new values appear in the Watch Window.

Add Watch Button · Delete Watch Button · The Watch Window shows you the current value and formula in each cell on the Watch list

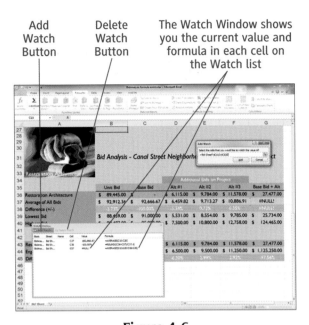

Figure 4-6
Watch as values change as you edit your worksheet formulas and data.

6. To close the Watch Window, click the Watch Window button on the Formulas tab again, or click its Close button.

Removing Cells from the Watch List

The cells you are watching remain listed in the Watch list, even after you close the Watch Window. So if you click the Watch Window button at a later time, you can reexamine the values in those same cells. To remove a cell from the Watch list, select it in the listing and click the Delete Watch button, located at the top of the Watch Window.

Evaluating a Formula

Another way in which you can determine the problem with a formula is to evaluate it. Evaluating is especially helpful when trying to troubleshoot complex formulas with lots of parentheses, because evaluating allows you to review exactly how Excel is solving each step of the formula. As you evaluate a formula, Excel solves the formula's first step and displays that intermediate result. When you're ready, Excel continues, solving the next step, and so on, until the formula is solved and the final result is displayed.

Follow these steps to evaluate a formula:

1. Click a cell containing a formula.

2. Click the Evaluate Formula button on the Formulas tab. The Evaluate Formula window appears, as shown in Figure 4-7.

Actual Formula   Evaluation of Formula

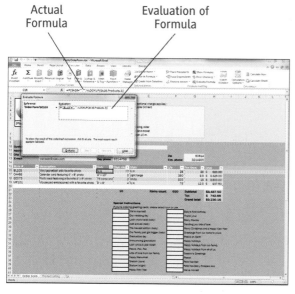

Figure 4-7
Evaluate a complex formula step by step.

3. Click the Evaluate button. Excel solves the first step in the formula, which is underlined. In this case, the formula is =IF($A16="","",VLOOKUP($A16,Products,3)). Excel is moving left to right in this formula, so it looks up the value in cell A16 in preparation for comparing whether A16 equals "" (blank). So after you click Evaluate, in the Evaluation box, Excel displays IF(BL105="","",VLOOKUP($A16,Products,3)).

Tip

If the underlined reference in the formula is a reference to another formula, you can jump to that other formula and evaluate it step by step by clicking the Step In button. Click Step Out after evaluating this second formula, to return to the first formula to finish its evaluation.

4. Click the Evaluate button again to solve the next step in the formula. See Figure 4-8. In this next step, the formula appears as IF(FALSE,"",VLOOKUP(($A16,Products,3)) because the value in cell A16 is not blank.

Figure 4-8
After you click Evaluate again, Excel solves the next step in the formula.

5. Continue to click the Evaluate button until each step of the formula is solved.

6. After evaluating the formula, click Restart (see Figure 4-9) to evaluate it again from the beginning, or click Close to close the Evaluate Formula window.

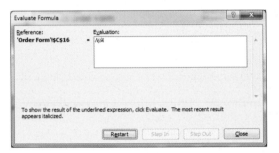

Figure 4-9
Continue to evaluate the formula until you reach the final result.

Identifying Formula Precedents and Dependents

The value of a cell rarely depends on just what is entered into it. Often, a cell contains a formula, and its value depends on the values of the cells referenced in that formula. In addition, the cell and its result might be referenced in yet another cell.

If you want to see how the value of one cell might affect others, you can trace its dependents using the Trace Dependents button. A *dependent* is a cell whose value depends on the value in another cell. For example, suppose cell G10 contains the formula B2/G9. If you traced the dependents of cell B2, Excel would point to cell G10 with a blue arrow, because the value in G10 depends on the value in cell B2.

You can trace a cell's precedents as well. A *precedent* is a cell referred to by the formula in the current cell. For example, if you traced the precedents of cell G10, Excel would point to cells B2 and G9, because they are referenced in its formula.

Dependents/Precedents in Other Worksheets

Dependents and precedents may not be cells in the current worksheet; they may be located in another worksheet or workbook. In any case, Excel can help you to identify the cells that relate to the current cell.

Follow these steps to trace a cell's dependents (cells whose value depend on the value of the current cell):

1. Click the cell whose dependents you want to trace.

2. Click the Trace Dependents button on the Formulas tab. Blue arrow(s) point from the selected cell to cells that depend on the current cell's value, as shown in Figure 4-10.

3. To trace dependency further, click the Trace Dependents button again. Arrows point from the dependent cells identified in Step 2, to any cell(s) that depend on their value.

4. Repeat Step 3 to trace dependents back as far as you want to go. When there are no more dependents, Excel beeps to tell you so.

Starting Cell · Arrows Trace Dependent Cells

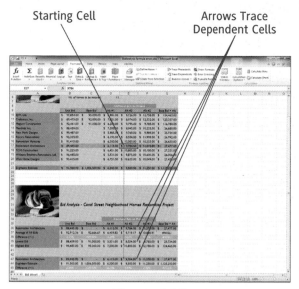

Figure 4-10
Arrows point to dependent cell(s).

Understanding Excel's Tracing Icons

Sometimes Excel uses a red arrow to trace dependents/precedents. The red arrows tell you that a dependent or precedent cell contains an error. In addition, sometimes you may see an arrow pointing to a small worksheet icon. This icon tells you that the dependent/precedent cell is located on another worksheet or workbook.

Tip

To clear the arrows from the screen, click the Remove Arrows button on the Formulas tab.

Follow these steps instead, if you want to trace a cell's precedents (cells whose value affects the value of the current cell). You do not need to clear any previously displayed arrows if you don't want to.

1. Click the cell whose precedents you want to trace.

2. Click the Trace Precedents button on the Formulas tab. Blue arrow(s) point from the selected cell to any cells referenced by the formula in that cell, as shown in Figure 4-11.

Arrows Trace Precedent Cells · Starting Cell

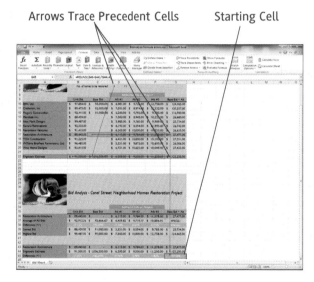

Figure 4-11
Arrows point to precedent cell(s).

3. To trace precedency further, click the Trace Precedent button again. Arrows point from the original precedent cells identified in Step 2, to any cell(s) upon which their values depend.

4. Repeat Step 3 to trace precedents back as far as you want to go. When there are no more precedents, Excel beeps to tell you so.

Tip

You can selectively clear the arrows from the screen by clicking the arrow on the Remove Arrows button on the Formulas tab, and selecting either Remove Precedent Arrows or Remove Dependent Arrows from the menu that appears. Both of these options remove precedent/dependent arrows one level at a time—so repeat the command to remove the next level and so on. By the way, if you select Remove Arrows from this menu, all arrows are removed instantly.

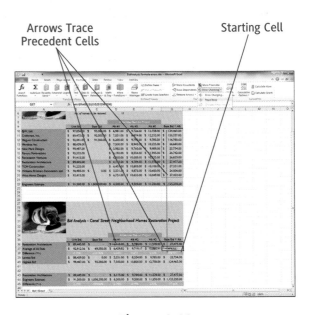

Figure 4-12
Arrows point to precedent cell(s) of an error cell.

Tracing an Error

When a formula contains an error that Excel recognizes, it often displays an error message in the result cell, such as #NULL! Once you know that a formula contains a recognizable error, you can quickly trace its precedents to see where the error value may be coming from. Follow these steps:

1. Click the cell that contains an error message you want to trace.

2. Click the arrow on the Error Checking button on the Formulas tab. Blue arrow(s) point from the selected cell to any cells referenced by the formula in that cell, as shown in Figure 4-12.

Tip

You can also click the Error Checking button that appears when you click in the error cell, and select Trace Error from the menu that appears, in order to quickly trace the formula's precedents.

Controlling Whether Errors Print

WHEN ERRORS EXISTING in a worksheet, Excel often displays error messages in result cells (such as #DIV/0!) instead of some kind of result. If you are printing your worksheet, you may prefer to display a blank cell rather than an irritating message. If so, follow these steps to prevent error messages from appearing in your printout:

1. Click the Page Layout tab.

2. Click the Dialog Box Launcher in the Page Setup group. The Page Setup dialog box appears, as shown in Figure 4-13.

Figure 4-13
Choose what to display in place of error messages in result cells.

3. Click the Sheet tab.

4. Click the down arrow on the Cell Errors As drop-down menu to open it, and choose what you would like to display in place of the error messages that normally appear in result cells with errors. You can display a blank (empty) cell, dashes, or the text, #N/A.

5. Click OK. The worksheet does not change, but what appears when you print will.

6. To print the worksheet, click the File tab to display Backstage.

7. Select Print from the list on the left. The Print options appear on the right.

8. After setting your print options, click Print to print the worksheet.

Making the Worksheet

Look Good

PICTURE YOURSELF TAKING A WORKSHEET FILLED with numbers and text—mind-numbing amounts of it—and turning it into a visually-appealing report with borders and shaded columns to delineate the conceptual or literal sections of the data, color and font formatting applied to draw viewers' attention to important details, and the kind of polish that gets your work noticed (in a good way). Got that image in your mind? Great. Now let's make it happen, using Excel 2010's simple, yet powerful, formatting tools.

Adjusting Columns and Rows

ONE OF THE EASIEST AND MOST effective ways to make sure your worksheet is legible and simple to view is to make sure there's enough room for your data. Cramped columns and rows make it hard to read your worksheet content, so give everything enough elbowroom. As shown in Figure 5-1, where you see two worksheets with identical information side by side, it's easy to see which one is easier to absorb by someone viewing the data.

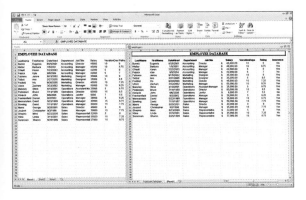

Figure 5-1
The worksheet on the left is cramped and crowded.
Its companion on the right is spread out
just enough so that everything is easy to read.

Of course, you don't want to spread everything out too much, because for worksheets that will be printed, this can waste paper and make reading the printed data too difficult, with columns and rows that fall on all the unnecessary additional pages. Your goal is to provide enough room for the data to be legible, in print or onscreen.

Changing Column Width

To change column width—making the column wider or narrower, whichever is appropriate— here are your options:

> ▶ **Double-click.** Take your mouse and point to the seam, as shown in Figure 5-2, between the column letters at the top of the column you want to widen and the one to its right. When your mouse pointer turns to a two-headed arrow, double-click. The column is automatically adjusted to the width of the widest entry in that column.

Point to this seam and double-click to adjust the left column automatically

The current measurement for this column appears here

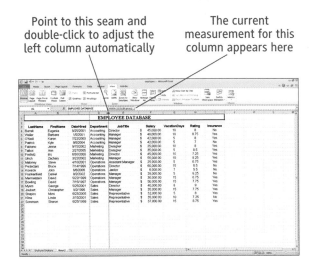

Figure 5-2
Use your mouse to double-click or drag the columns to the desired width.

▶ **Click and drag.** Again pointing to the same seam shown in Figure 5-2, when your mouse pointer turns to a two-headed arrow, drag. Drag to the right to widen the column or to the left to narrow it.

Tip

The AutoFit Column Width command in the Home tab's Format button menu does the same thing as double-clicking the column letter seam. Just select the columns first and then make the button menu selection.

▶ **Use the Ribbon.** If you prefer a more methodical approach, select the columns you want to adjust, use the Cells group of the Home tab, and click the Format button. In the menu displayed in Figure 5-3, choose Column Width and then use the dialog box shown in Figure 5-4 to adjust the column's width to a specific measurement. The number displayed when you open the dialog box is the current number of characters at the default point size that the cells in that column will house. The higher the number you enter, the wider the column will be.

Figure 5-3
Use the Format button menu to choose how to adjust your column width.

Figure 5-4
Enter a value to widen or narrow the selected column.

Tip

Don't remember how to select a column or series of columns? Click the column letter to select an individual column, or drag through the column letters of a series to select several contiguous columns all at once. If you want to select multiple but non-contiguous columns, press and hold the Ctrl key as you click each desired column's letter.

Changing Row Height

While the need to adjust column widths is more common than the need to adjust row heights, it's equally simple to make your rows the right height for their content. Here are your options:

▶ **Double-click.** Take your mouse and point to the dividing seam, as indicated in Figure 5-5, between the row numbers on the row you want to adjust and the one beneath it. When your mouse pointer turns to a two-headed (up and down-pointing) arrow, double-click. The row is automatically adjusted to the height of the tallest entry in that row.

Point to this seam and double-click to adjust the upper row automatically

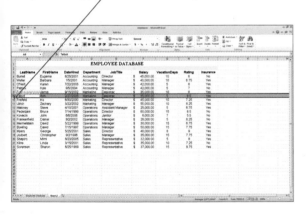

Figure 5-5
Use your mouse to double-click or drag the rows to the desired height.

▶ **Click and drag.** Again pointing to the same seam shown in Figure 5-5, when your mouse pointer turns to a two-headed arrow, drag. Drag down to make the row taller, or up to make it shorter.

Tip

The AutoFit Row Height command in the Home tab's Format button menu does the same thing as double-clicking the row number seam. Just select the rows first and then make the button menu selection.

▶ **Use the Ribbon.** For those who prefer a more step-by-step approach, adjusting rows can be done from a menu, too. Select the rows you want to make taller or shorter, and using the Cells group of the Home tab, click the Format button. In the menu shown in Figure 5-6, choose Row Height and then use the dialog box shown in Figure 5-7 to adjust the row's height to a specific measurement. The number displayed when you open the dialog box is the current setting, based on the default font size (which is measured in points), and a small allowance for space above and below the text/numbers in the cells in the row. When choosing a new setting, the higher the number you enter, the taller the column will be.

Tip

When you change the font size in any cell in a row, the row adjusts automatically, to accommodate that new height. If you manually adjust the row afterward, the new height you set will remain in place until you use one of the aforementioned methods to manually adjust its height.

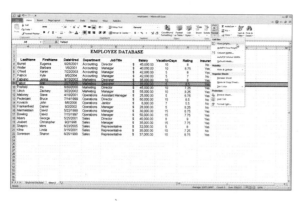

Figure 5-6
Use the Format button menu to choose
how to adjust your row height.

Figure 5-7
Enter a value to make the row taller or shorter.

Inserting and Deleting Columns and Rows

The most common things people forget when
planning and setting up a worksheet is a column
or row for some of the data they'll need to enter.
When setting up a list database, for example, it's
quite common to forget one of the fields, and
therefore need to add a column. Same thing
with rows—if you imagine setting up a budget
worksheet, it's easy to also imagine forgetting
one of the expenses and needing to go back and
insert a row where that item would appear in
the list, so the data can be entered.

Inserting One or More Columns

Luckily, as easy as it is to forget a row or column
when you're building your worksheet, it's that
easy to remedy the situation by adding one
or more rows and/or columns whenever and
wherever you want.

To add a column, choose one of these methods:

▶ **Right-click.** Right-click the letter of the
column to the right of where you need
an additional column. Choose Insert from
the pop-up menu, as shown in Figure 5-8,
and voila! A new column appears. If you
need more than one column, select as
many as you need, using columns to the
right of the spot where the new ones
should appear, and use this right-click
method. However many columns are
selected when you issue the command,
that's how many new ones you get.

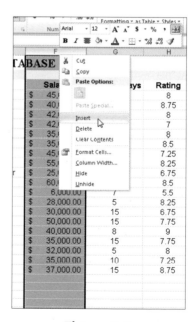

Figure 5-8
Right-click a column letter and choose
Insert to add a new column.

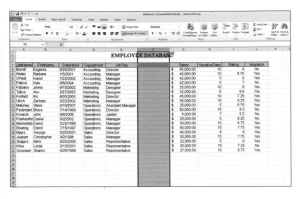

Figure 5-9
The inserted column appears to the right
of the column originally selected.

▶ **Use the Insert button.** Select the columns
to the right of where you want your new
ones to appear, and use the Insert button
on the Home tab. You don't need to click
the arrow to display the menu—just
click the Insert button itself, and your
new columns appear (see Figure 5-9).
If you do click the arrow, just choose
Insert Sheet Columns from the menu.

Tip

If you've used the Merge & Center button
to merge, say, a series of cells across the
top of a series of columns (to house a title
for the data), adding columns within that
range of columns will expand the merged
cell. If this will create an undesirable
change for your merged cell, unmerge it
(click in the cell and then use the Unmerge
Cells command in the Merge & Center
drop-down menu) before inserting the
columns, and then click Merge & Center to
merge and center the desired range of cells.

Inserting One or More Rows

Adding rows is similarly easy. It's all a matter of
selecting the row below the spot where you need
a new one—or, if you need two or more new rows,
selecting as many existing rows as you need
below the point where the new ones should
appear. Once the selection is made, pick your
procedure:

▶ **Right-click.** Right-click the row number
of the row below where you need the
new row. Choose Insert from the pop-up
menu, as shown in Figure 5-10, and in a
nanosecond, you have a new row. If you
need more than one row, select as many
rows as you need, using rows beneath the
point where the new ones should appear,
and use the right-click method. However
many rows are selected when you issue
the command, that's how many new rows
you get.

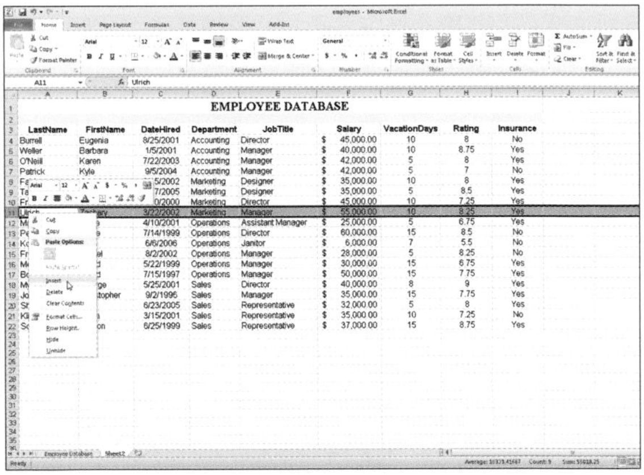

Figure 5-10
Select as many rows as you want to add, and
right-click them to access the Insert command.

▶ **Use the Insert button.** Select the rows below where you want your new ones to appear, and use the Insert button on the Home tab. There's no need to click the arrow to display the menu—just click the Insert button itself, and your new rows appear. If you do click the arrow, just choose Insert Sheet Rows from the menu. Figure 5-11 shows the new resulting row in place, awaiting content.

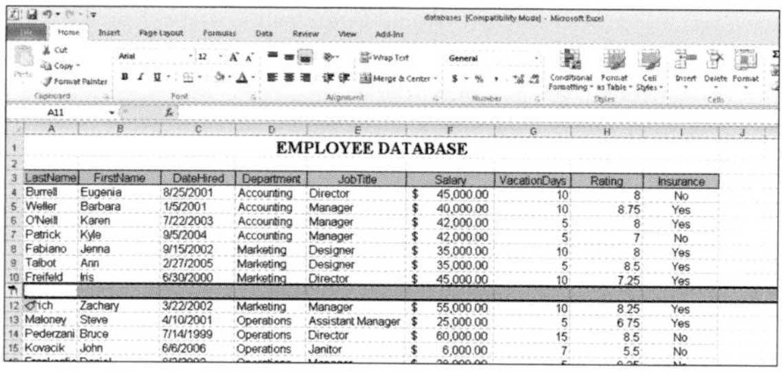

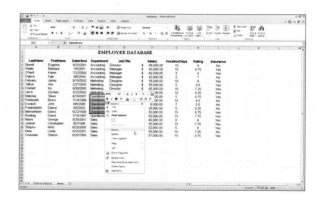

Figure 5-11
The inserted row appears below the
originally selected row.

Don't Forget to Adjust Your Formulas

When inserting columns or rows, keep your existing formulas in mind. If you add a row within a series of rows that contain cells that are included in a SUM formula that sums a range, the range will update to include the new row's cell. If you add a row at the bottom of an existing series, you'll have to update the formula manually to include the cell in the new row. The same goes for columns—if you add a column within a series, any formulas referencing the range that now includes that column will be updated. Not so if you add a column at the end of a series. Not sure how to edit a formula or check on the impact that a new row or column has had? Check out Chapters 2 and 3, on formulas and functions, respectively.

Inserting Cells

If you want to insert a single cell into a row or column, or add a quick range of cells—usually a block of cells within a column or row—you can do so by following these steps:

1. Select a range of cells equal to the number (and configuration) of the cells you want to insert. For example, as shown in Figure 5-12, if you want to insert five cells in a column, select five existing cells within the column, either to the right of or below where you want the new cells to appear.

Figure 5-12
Select the same number of cells that
you want to insert.

2. Right-click the selection and choose Insert from the pop-up menu. The dialog box shown in Figure 5-13 appears, offering you four choices as to how Excel can accommodate your request.

Figure 5-13
Tell Excel how to insert the desired cells within the worksheet at hand.

3. Make your choice between shifting the surrounding (and selected) cells to the right or down or inserting an entire row or column.

4. Click OK. If you're not happy with the results, remember that you can undo your actions (choose Edit > Undo or Ctrl+Z) and try again.

Deleting Columns and Rows

Do you have a row or column (or more than one) that you wish weren't there? Maybe you added too many, or you left too many blank rows or columns between sections of your worksheet. It's easy to get rid of them, whether they have content or not. Perhaps too easy, if there is content in them, so be careful before applying any of the following methods for column or row deletion—there could be content somewhere beyond the range of cells you can see, and you might not want to lose whatever that content is.

That warning out of the way, here are some simple ways to remove unwanted columns or rows:

▶ **Right-click.** Select the unwanted columns or rows, and right-click. From the resulting menu, shown in Figure 5-14, choose Delete.

▶ **Delete button.** Select the unwanted columns or rows, and click the Delete button (don't bother with the drop-down menu, just click the button itself) on the Home tab's Cells group.

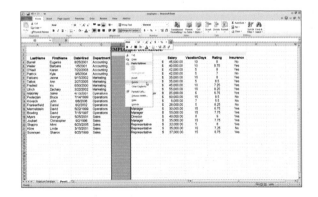

Figure 5-14
The Delete command applies to whatever's selected—a column or a row—and deletes its content as well as the cells themselves.

Tip

As tempting as it would be to delete a column and a row at the same time, Excel won't let you do that. If you attempt it, a prompt appears, indicating that you cannot delete the content of overlapping cells. Another thing that doesn't work? The Delete key, which only deletes the content of selected cells, not the cells (columns or rows) themselves.

Deleting Cells

Wait a minute, aren't columns and rows cells? Sure they are. But they're finite groups of cells, with fixed arrangements. You select an entire row by clicking its row number, or an entire column by clicking its column letter. Each of those clicks selects hundreds (or thousands, in the case of a column) of cells and when deleted, Excel needs only move everything next to the selected row or column over (or up) to fill the gap.

But what if you want to delete a block of cells, say the block shown in Figure 5-15? Because it's not an entire row or column, Excel can't just make a quick "fold" in the worksheet to bring the remaining parts back together. The presence of content in surrounding cells makes it even more complex—if not for Excel, for you, because you need to know what you'd like Excel to do with the content that remains after the deletion.

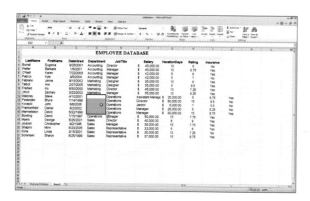

Figure 5-15
An unwanted range of cells can be removed with relative ease—you just need to know how you'd like Excel to go about it.

Fortunately, the Delete dialog box forces you to decide how the remaining cells should fill in the gap created by your deletion, by offering four logical choices. Here are the steps:

1. Select the cell or range of cells you want to delete.

2. Right-click the selection and choose Delete... from the pop-up menu. Note that this is different than the plain "Delete" command from the previous section on deleting rows and columns. Because a single cell or a manually-selected range of cells is selected, a variation on the Delete command is offered, including the ellipsis, indicating a dialog box will follow. As shown in Figure 5-16, the Delete dialog box appears.

Figure 5-16
Four choices await you when you choose Delete (with the ellipsis) from the pop-up menu.

3. Choose how you'd like Excel to make the deletion. You can:

   Shift cells left

   Shift cells up

   Delete the entire row

   Delete the entire column

4. Click OK to perform the deletion. Excel will move the adjacent cells' content into the remaining cells, per your instructions in the dialog box.

Formatting Cell Content

AS YOU TYPE ALONG, adding content to cells, Excel's default settings take effect. Normally, this is fine, left-aligning your text, right-aligning your numeric content, applying the standard 11 point Calibri font to the content, and formatting dates, times, and other content automatically. When your needs go beyond these defaults, or if you want to tweak them a bit, it's handy to know the most effective ways to change the formatting of one or more cells so that your content looks and works the way you want it to—everything you need is at your fingertips, literally.

Applying Fonts, Sizes, Styles, and Text Color

Using the Home tab, shown in Figure 5-17, you can change the appearance of any cell or range of cells with just a few clicks. Beginning with the Font group, after selecting the cells to which the formatting should apply, you can apply the following changes:

▶ **Font.** The default is Calibri, and if you click the drop-down arrow, you can choose from any of the fonts installed on your computer, making your selection from the graphic samples that appear in the menu, as shown in Figure 5-18.

▶ **Size.** This defaults to 11 points (based on 72 points per inch). Pick a larger or smaller number to make your content larger or smaller.

▶ **Increase or Decrease Font Size.** These two A icons (the bigger one is the Increase Font Size button, as you'd imagine) allow you to make content bigger or smaller, in two-point increments for each click of the button. These are handy to use when you don't know, for example, that you need 24-point text, but will recognize the right size when you see it applied.

▶ **Bold, Italic, and Underline.** These three styles (represented by the B, I, and U buttons) add emphasis.

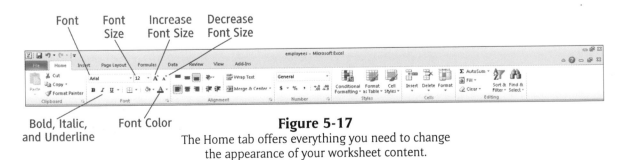

Figure 5-17
The Home tab offers everything you need to change the appearance of your worksheet content.

Figure 5-18
Pick a font based on the graphic
samples in the Font menu.

▶ **Font Color.** The A on top of a color block
(red by default) opens a palette of colors
drawn from various Office Themes
(showing a series of compatible shades)
or Standard colors (see Figure 5-19). The
More Colors link opens a larger palette in
the Colors dialog box, as shown in Figure
5-20, through two tabs—Standard and
Custom—and literally millions of color
choices.

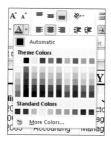

Figure 5-19
Utilizing a feature called Live Preview, you can mouse
over the palette to see the selected cells displayed in
any color available through the palette.

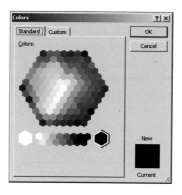

Figure 5-20
The Colors dialog box offers over a million
shades, through the Standard and Custom tabs.
Pick a color and click OK.

Adding Borders and Shading

Continuing with the options available in the
Font group of the Home tab, you can apply the
following to selected cells—bear in mind these
changes apply to the cells, rather than to the text
or numbers within them. As shown in row 3 of
Figure 5-21, the Fill Color and Borders tools fill
the cells with color and apply a custom border.

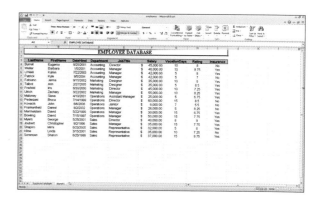

Figure 5-21
Use the Borders and Fill Color tools
to dress up your cells.

To apply these effects, select the cells, and click the drop-down arrows next to each of the buttons:

▶ **Fill Color.** This button presents a palette, much like the Font Color button. You can pick from Office Themes colors, or Standard colors, or click More Colors to open the dialog box shown in Figure 5-22.

▶ **Borders.** Click the arrow next to this button (the button shows the last border applied, or if not used yet, the bottom border) to display the menu shown in Figure 5-22.

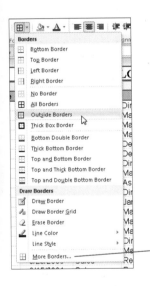

Figure 5-22
Apply borders to one or more sides of a single cell or range of cells.

— More Borders Command

Applying Borders with a Drawing Tool

The Draw Borders section of the Borders menu offers tools for using a drawing tool to apply borders. You can choose the drawn border colors and styles, using the palettes displayed by choosing the Line Color and Line Style commands.

▶ **More Borders.** This command, found at the foot of the Borders menu, opens a dialog box through which you can completely customize the sides of the cells to be given a border, including the thickness, style, and color of the borders. Figure 5-23 shows the Format Cells dialog box, open to the Border tab. You'll be seeing more of this dialog box and its other tabs as we move through the rest of this chapter.

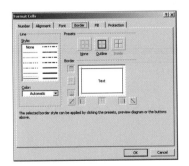

Figure 5-23
The Border tab in the Format Cells dialog box offers true border customization.

Working with Alignment and Spacing

Moving across the Home tab, the next group is called Alignment—and that's what its commands control for your worksheet cells and their content. You can choose how content is aligned horizontally and vertically, whether or not the content is indented, and even put content on a variety of angles. To use these tools (shown and identified in Figure 5-24), select the cells to which the changes should apply, and make your choice from the following buttons:

▶ **Vertical Alignment.** Use the Top, Middle, or Bottom Align buttons to control how the content of selected cells lines up vertically. Bottom alignment is the default.

▶ **Orientation.** Need to put your column headings at an angle? Long headings can take up less horizontal space if they're at an angle, as shown in Figure 5-25.

Alignment Options in the Format Cells Dialog Box

The Format Cell Alignment command opens the Format Cells dialog box, open to the Alignment tab (shown in Figure 5-26). Pick an exact angle for your content, using the half-clock on the right, and use alignment, control, and text direction options on the left side of the dialog box. These are mostly repetitions of what's available on the Home tab's Alignment group.

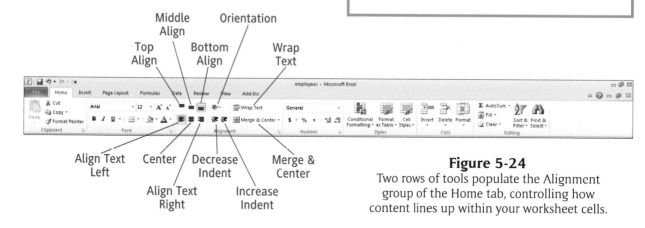

Figure 5-24
Two rows of tools populate the Alignment group of the Home tab, controlling how content lines up within your worksheet cells.

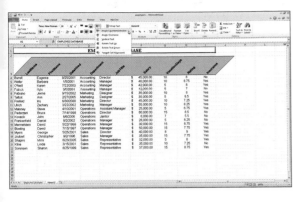

Figure 5-25
Angle your cells' content using the five choices
on the Orientation palette.

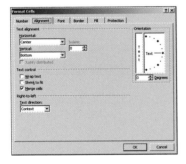

Figure 5-26
The Alignment tab of the Format Cells
dialog box offers more tools to do the same
things you can do from the Home tab.

▶ **Wrap Text.** Click this button to tell Excel
to allow wrapping within the selected
cells. This can come in handy for cells that
will contain long strings of text—sentences,
product descriptions, survey comments,
anything longer than a couple of words,
where you don't want the column to have
to be very wide to accommodate the full
display of the text.

▶ **Horizontal Alignment.** Choose from
Align Text Left, Center, and Align Text
Right buttons, to align cell content to
the sides or center of the selected cells.

▶ **Indent.** You can indent cell content,
moving it to the right within the cell with
each click of the Increase Indent button.
The Decrease Indent button moves the
text back to the left.

▶ **Merge & Center.** This button works to
toggle merging of selected cells on and
off, and also displays a menu, as shown
in Figure 5-27. The most common use of
this button is to merge a series of cells to
make a single title cell above a series of
columns. The list offers commands to
Merge Across (to merge a horizontal
series of cells), Merge Cells (to merge a
block of cells, including vertical ranges),
and Unmerge Cells, which removes the
merge and returns the cells to their individual states.

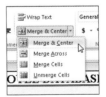

Figure 5-27
Merge & Center a title, using the button
or this handy list of options.

Applying Numeric Formatting

THE NUMBER GROUP OF THE HOME tab offers tools for controlling how Excel displays—you guessed it—numbers. From currency to percentages, all the basic tools are here, as shown in Figure 5-28.

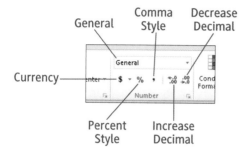

Figure 5-28
Got money? A date or time? Use the Number group of the Home tab to make your numbers look like what they really are.

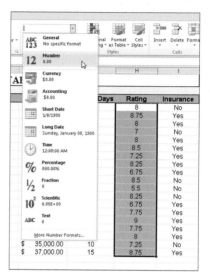

Figure 5-29
Pick a format for the cells in question.

To apply these formats to your numeric content, select the cells to which the formatting should apply, and then choose from the following buttons:

▶ **Number Format.** This button displays the default or current formatting in place for the selected cells. If you click the button arrow, a menu displays, as shown in Figure 5-29, offering eleven formatting options, plus a More Number Formats command, which opens the Format Cells dialog box to the Number tab, as shown in Figure 5-30.

Figure 5-30
The Format Cells dialog box offers Number formatting from 12 categories, each with its own set of customization options.

Sampling the Number Format Results

You'll notice that each of the options in the Number Format menu contains a sample of what that particular format will do to the selected cells. For the cell selected when Figure 5-29 was created, the number 8 is shown as a plain number, as currency, in accounting format, in two different date formats, as a time, a percentage, a fraction, in scientific notation, and as text. If you have more than one cell selected, it's assumed that they all need the same formatting, so the first cell in the selection is shown in each menu sample.

▶ **Currency.** Click this button to apply the currency for the country you indicated was the default when you installed Office 2010, or click the arrow to see a list of common currencies for countries including the US, UK, the European Union, China, and France, as shown in Figure 5-31.

Figure 5-31
Pick the currency style for the country whose money your selected cells contain.

▶ **Percent Style.** This command converts the numeric content of your cells to a percentage. If your cell contains .50, that becomes 50%. If it contains .555, that becomes 56%, because this format rounds up by default.

▶ **Comma Style.** Do you want a comma after thousands, as in 1,000 instead of 1000? Click this button and the comma is inserted, as well as two decimal places—so 1000 becomes 1,000.00. You can use the Decrease Decimal button (coming up next) to get rid of the decimals if you only want to see 1,000.

▶ **Increase Decimal and Decrease Decimal.** These two buttons add or remove decimal places. Each click of the respective buttons adds or removes one decimal place. Use them to customize Currency, Comma Style, and Percent Style formatting, as well as formatting applied through the Number Format command's choices, such as Accounting, which automatically applies two decimal places to numbers.

Figure 5-32
Right-click your way to a host of formatting options in the Format Cells dialog box, and a quick set of tools on the floating formatting toolbar.

Formatting Tabs Galore

Right-click any cell or selected range of cells and the pop-up menu shown in Figure 5-32 appears. Through this menu, you can choose the Format Cells command to access six tabs' worth of formatting commands, most of which are also represented on the Home tab. You can also use the floating formatting toolbar, shown in Figure 5-32, to apply basic font, size, color, and numeric formatting to the selected cells' content.

Applying Conditional Formatting

CONDITIONAL FORMATTING isn't really as complicated as some people think. It's simply formatting that's applied when certain conditions are met. Excel 2010 has expanded its powers, however, allowing all sorts of graphical enhancements to be added to your worksheets, but at its core, it's a simple feature—define what the conditions are (such as "Sales greater than $5,000,000") and tell Excel how to format the numbers that meet that criteria (make them bold and turn them green, for example).

Creating Cell Rules

The "rules" for conditional formatting are really just a set of criteria, or conditions, that all the cells in a selection are compared to. The cells that meet the conditions are then formatted according to the rules. Figure 5-33 shows a database of employee data, and the employees earning more than $50,000 are highlighted.

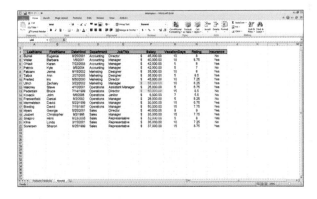

Figure 5-33
The condition—Salary greater than $50,000—is met by those records that are in green text, with their cells highlighted with a color fill.

There are two ways to set up the kind of rules that result in such formatting, and you'll try each of them here.

Highlighting Rules

The first method for applying conditional formatting you're going to look at is the Highlight Cells Rules command, following these steps:

1. With your worksheet (or a desired portion thereof) selected, click the Conditional Formatting button on the Home tab's Styles group.

2. Choose Highlight Cells Rules, and view the submenu, shown in Figure 5-34.

3. Select the conditions Excel should look for within the selected cells, from Greater Than to Duplicate Values, for a total of seven conditions to choose from. Each of the options results in a dialog box, and Figure 5-35 shows the Greater Than dialog box, which you'll use for this example.

The Salary column is selected prior to setting conditional formatting

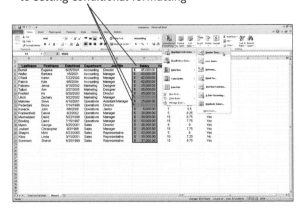

Figure 5-34
Select the section of your worksheet where the conditions can be found and then begin setting up conditional formatting.

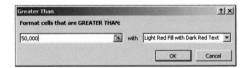

Figure 5-35
Two questions must be answered—greater than what, and when that value is found, how should it be formatted?

4. Enter a value in the field on the left side of the dialog box, and then choose the type of highlighting to apply from the drop-down menu on the right.

5. Click OK, and view your worksheet to see which cells were found to meet the conditions, and see that the selected formatting has been applied to them, as shown in Figure 5-36.

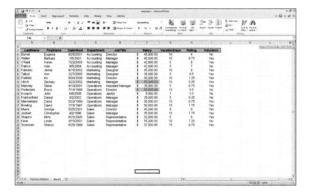

Figure 5-36
Two employees' salaries meet the conditions, and are formatted to stand out among the rest of the list.

Providing Formatting Conditions

Each of the commands in the Highlight Cells Rules submenu presents a similar dialog box, and all you have to do is provide the conditions and tell Excel what sort of formatting to apply, using the list of preset formatting combinations.

Tip

The Top/Bottom Rules command works just like the Highlight Cells Rules command, except that you're choosing from six rules for top and bottom values. The top 10, the bottom 10, the cells containing above or below average values—these can all be identified and formatted per your instructions in the resulting Rules dialog box.

Creating a New Rule

If you'd rather take a more methodical approach, with more ways to customize the conditions and the resulting formatting, you can use the New Formatting Rule dialog box, shown in Figure 5-37. This dialog box is opened by selecting a portion of your worksheet (where the conditions are to be found) and choosing New Rule from the Conditional Formatting button's menu.

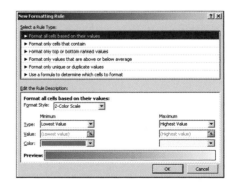

Figure 5-37
Work with various rule presets and create your own custom formatting for those cells that meet your conditions.

Once it's open, follow these steps:

1. Select a Rule Type, choosing from the six options offered.

2. Edit the rule. You can set the following options:

   - **Format Style.** Choose 2-Color Scale, 3-Color Scale, Data Bar, or Icon Sets. You'll learn more about these in the subsequent section of this chapter.

   - **Value Type Minimum and Maximum.** Choose what kind of value Excel should look for—numbers, percents, formulas, or set a Lowest and Highest Value. You choose Number here so you can set a range in the next field, to highlight everyone whose salary is between 50,000 and 100,000.

   - **Value.** Here's where you enter the values that Excel should seek—you'll enter 50,000 on the Minimum side, and 100,000 on the Maximum side.

   - **Color.** Choose from Themes colors, Standard Colors, or click More Colors to choose from any of millions of possible shades. You can apply different colors for the low and high values.

3. When you like the Preview colors (which varies, depending on your choice under Format Style), click OK. The formatting is applied, per the rules you created in the Edit the Rule Description section of the dialog box. Figure 5-38 shows the result, where the lowest to highest values were shaded from dark orange to light orange (lowest values having a darker cell fill color).

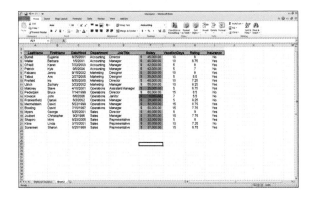

Figure 5-38
Colors were applied to the cells meeting the conditions.

Tip

Want to get rid of the conditional formatting, however it was applied? Click the Clear Rules command, found in the Conditional Formatting button's menu. The resulting submenu lets you choose which rules to clear—from the selected cells, or the entire worksheet. If you made a selection before issuing this command, simply choose the Clear Rules From Selected Cells command, and all formatting applied by your conditional formatting rules is removed.

Using Data Bars, Color Scales, and Icon Sets

These graphical, interactive tools are found in the Conditional Formatting button's menu. Your three options, Data Bars, Color Scales, and Icon Sets, allow you to select a range of cells and then choose how they'll be graphically quantified. As shown in Figure 5-39, if a Gradient Fill Data Bar is applied to the Salary column, the lowest salary ($6,000) gets a really short gradient bar, and the highest salary, $60,000, gets a long gradient bar. It essentially turns the selected column into a horizontal bar graph. The Color Scales and Icon Sets create a similar effect, applying colors and shapes (arrows, dots, flags, and so on) to indicate values within the selected cells.

To apply the effects—not just preview them as I suggested by having you mouse over them to see how they look applied to your data—simply click on one of the icons in the Data Bars, Color Scales, or Icon Sets palettes. If you edit your data, the effects change to reflect that, so that an increase, for example, in the $6,000 salary would result in a longer gradient bar.

Tip

If you ever want to get rid of the bars, scales, or icons, simply select the range and use the Clear Rules command from the Conditional Formatting button's menu. You can choose to clear the rules from the selected cells or the entire worksheet.

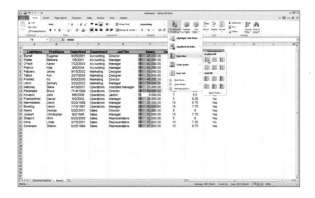

Figure 5-39
Mouse over the various Data Bars, Color Scales, and Icon Sets options, and see them applied to your selected data.

Applying Office Themes and Layouts

THE PAGE LAYOUT TAB, shown in Figure 5-40, contains tools for adjusting the overall look of your worksheet—not individual cells, but the entire worksheet itself. Your choices on this tab include:

▶ **Themes.** This tab group contains Themes, which are collections of formats that combine compatible colors, fonts, and border styles, and three separate buttons for Colors, Fonts, and Effects, if you want to customize things a bit more. Click any of the buttons to view a palette of options, each represented by color swatches and/or graphical examples of the impact the selection would have on your worksheet. Figure 5-41 shows the Effects palette and all the special effects that each offers.

▶ **Page Setup.** Working with any of the seven buttons in this group allows you to change how your worksheet will print—where page breaks will occur, what will print on each page (a pre-set print area, titles, and so on), and whether or not your page will have a background image—a photo or other image that appears behind the gridlines and your worksheet content.

Tip

Unless your photo or other image is very light, don't apply a background image. It can really interfere with legibility, as shown in Figure 5-42, where the photo makes it impossible to read the worksheet's content.

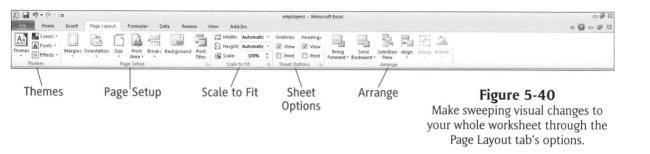

Themes   Page Setup   Scale to Fit   Sheet Options   Arrange

Figure 5-40
Make sweeping visual changes to your whole worksheet through the Page Layout tab's options.

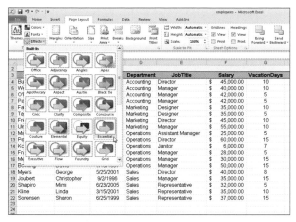

Figure 5-41
Choose from a series of special Effects for your worksheet elements—text, graphics, borders, and so on.

Figure 5-42
Background images, applied through the
Page Setup group of the Page Layout tab, are usually
a distraction from your worksheet content.

▶ **Scale to Fit.** Use these commands to force
a certain number of columns and/or rows
onto the printed pages of your worksheet.
You can specify the number of pages wide
or tall, or set a scale, which shrinks or
expands the worksheet to fit on the page.

▶ **Sheet Options.** These commands allow
you to choose what will be included on
your printed worksheet (using the Print
checkboxes) or only visible onscreen
(using the View checkboxes).

▶ **Arrange.** The six commands in this last
group of the Page Layout tab allow you to
change the stacking order of graphics on
the page—charts, pictures, drawn shapes
and lines, text boxes—just about anything
you add to the worksheet via the Insert
tab. You don't need to tinker with the
stacking order unless things overlap, but
if they do, these commands can be quite
handy to make sure the overlap doesn't
obscure something important. By default,
things stack in the order you added
them—last items on top.

Part II
Handling Larger Workbooks

Managing Large Amounts
of Excel Data

BECAUSE EXCEL IS SO ADEPT at managing data, people are not the least bit hesitant to enter large amounts of data into a worksheet. However, large worksheets bring with them their own rules for using them successfully. If you have a worksheet with lots of data, you probably already know what I mean, but let me explain.

Large worksheets are by their very nature, large. This often means you will not always see the entire worksheet at one time. In addition, large worksheets seem to gather together in large workbooks full of several sheets, each with its own purpose. Both of these tendencies make working within such structures a bit difficult, as you often need to switch between worksheets and scroll within them to locate the data you are looking for. You'll discover several techniques in this chapter that will help you not only move back and forth within large worksheets and workbooks with ease, but to quickly find the data you want.

Large workbooks may have several similar worksheets, such as January, February, and March sales figures. These similarities make it easy to build such workbooks, and to make sweeping changes, as you'll soon learn.

Working with Multiple Worksheets

AN EXCEL WORKBOOK STARTS out with three worksheets, although quite often, you may only use one. Each of these worksheets has a generic name, such as Sheet1, Sheet2, and so on, although you can rename them as needed. You can remove sheets from a workbook that you aren't using, and make the file slightly smaller and easier to use. You can also add sheets to a workbook, if you need to gather related information together (such as each month's sales figures) and yet keep them separate and unique. If you are building such a workbook, you can create the first month's sales worksheet, complete with formulas and formatting, and copy it over and over within the workbook, saving tons of time. In this section, you learn how to perform all of these tasks, and many more related to working within a workbook that contains multiple worksheets.

Tip

You can change the default number of worksheets if you like—just click the File tab to display Backstage view, and then select Options from the list on the left. The Excel Options dialog box appears. Select General from the list on the left to display the General options. In the When Creating New Workbooks section, type the number of worksheets you want Excel to include in all new workbooks in the Include This Many Sheets box. Click OK to save your changes.

Moving Between Worksheets

Even if you're not a terribly curious person by nature, if a workbook contains more than one worksheet, at some point or another, your curiosity will simply overwhelm you. What lies beyond this current worksheet? What treasures (or additional work) lay behind those other worksheet tabs? Well, thar may be dragons, as they used to say, or there may be treasures on those other worksheets. But the only way you will find out is to change from the current worksheet to another one.

You probably noticed by now that Excel lines its worksheets up along the bottom of the workbook window, each represented by a single tab, like a tab in a large notebook. The tab for the currently displayed worksheet appears in white, as shown in Figure 6-1.

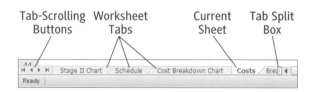

Figure 6-1
Each worksheet is represented by its own tab.

Here are some tips on how to move back and forth between worksheets:

▶ To change from one worksheet to another, simply click its tab.

▶ In workbooks with many worksheets, you may not see all the tabs at one time. Use the tab-scrolling buttons to adjust the tab listing until the tab of the worksheet you want to switch to is visible.

- To display the first few worksheet tabs, click the first tab-scrolling button. To display the last few worksheet tabs, click the last tab-scrolling button.

- To scroll the tab listing to the left or right one worksheet at a time, click one of the tab-scrolling buttons in the middle.

▶ Drag the tab split box to the right to increase the number of worksheet tabs displayed at any given time. (This will shorten the horizontal scroll bar a bit, but it will still be useable.) Drag the tab split box to the left to decrease the number of worksheet tabs displayed.

Inserting Additional Worksheets

Normally, a workbook contains three worksheets, although you can set up Excel so that new workbooks contain a different number of starting sheets. In any case, it's a simple matter to add worksheets to a workbook. You might want to use worksheets to separate similar, but different data in a workbook. For example, you might use separate worksheets, one for each month, to enter budget, sales, or inventory data.

There are several ways to insert a worksheet into a workbook. Use whichever of these methods suits you best at the time:

▶ Click the arrow on the Insert button on the Home tab, and select Insert Sheet from the menu that appears. A sheet is inserted in front of the current sheet. The newly inserted sheet becomes the currently displayed sheet. See Figure 6-2.

New Sheet

Figure 6-2
A new sheet is inserted in front of the current sheet.

► Right-click a sheet tab and select Insert from the menu that appears. The Insert dialog box appears, as shown in Figure 6-3. On the General tab, select Worksheet, and then click OK. A sheet is inserted in front of the sheet you right-clicked.

Figure 6-3
Select what you want to insert into the workbook.

► Click the Insert Worksheet button, located at the right end of the sheet tabs, as shown in Figure 6-4.

Insert Worksheet
Button

Figure 6-4
Insert a worksheet quickly using
the Insert Worksheet button.

New sheets are given names unique to the workbook such as Sheet4, Sheet5, and so on. The names of sheets that were added to the workbook at some other time are not reused even if they were renamed or removed. You can rename these newly inserted sheets if you want, in order to make their purpose more obvious to the users of the workbook. See "Renaming Worksheets."

Deleting Worksheets

If a workbook contains sheets you do not plan on using, you can remove the unwanted sheets and make the workbook file a bit smaller. If a sheet contains data, it can removed as well, although you should check to be sure you do not want that data before removing it.

Confirming a Sheet Deletion

Excel does stop to confirm whether you want to delete a sheet that has data on it before it actually does so, so have no fear when removing worksheets.

Follow these steps to remove a worksheet:

1. Click the tab of the sheet you want to remove.

2. Choose either of the following methods to remove the selected sheet:

   - Click the arrow on the Delete button on the Home tab, and select Delete Sheet from the menu that appears.

   - Right-click the sheet tab and select Delete from the menu that appears.

3. If the sheet contains data, a warning dialog box appears, as shown in Figure 6-5. Click Delete to delete the sheet. If you have reconsidered and no longer want to remove the sheet, click Cancel instead.

Getting Your Lost Data Back

If you delete a worksheet that contains data, you will not be able to undo your action, so be sure that removing the worksheet is what you want to do before you confirm. If you do accidentally delete a worksheet with data that you wanted to keep, immediately close the workbook and do not save your changes. (Of course, you will lose any changes you may have made and not saved just prior to accidentally deleting the worksheet, so consider that before you close the workbook without saving.)

Figure 6-5
If a worksheet contains data, you must confirm that you want it deleted before Excel will remove it from the workbook.

Tip

All of the previous methods described here remove only a single sheet from the workbook. However, you can remove multiple sheets in a single step if you want. Start by selecting the sheets you want to remove by pressing Ctrl and clicking each tab. Then follow any of the methods here (such as clicking the arrow on the Delete button on the Home tab and selecting Delete Sheet) to remove the sheets. If any of the worksheets contain data, click Delete to confirm.

Renaming Worksheets

Unlike people, worksheets are not immediately given meaningful names. Instead, worksheets typically bear generic-sounding names like Sheet1, Sheet2, and so on. If a workbook contains lots of data spread out over several worksheets, you can make it easier for users to locate the data they need by giving your worksheets names that correspond to the data they contain. For example, you might name worksheets April, May, June, and 2nd Qtr Totals.

Follow these steps to rename a worksheet:

1. Click the tab of the sheet you want to rename.

2. Choose any of the following methods to rename the selected sheet:

   - Click the Format button on the Home tab, and select Rename Sheet from the menu that appears.

   - Right-click the sheet tab and select Rename from the menu that appears.

   - Double-click the tab of the sheet you want to rename.

3. The current tab name is highlighted, as shown in Figure 6-6. Type a new name for the sheet, up to 31 characters. You can use numbers, letters, spaces, and special characters (such as $ and %) if you like.

Figure 6-6
Identify the contents of each sheet by renaming it.

4. Press Enter. The new name appears on the worksheet tab.

Tip

Press Esc (before you press Enter) if you change your mind and you no longer want to rename the worksheet.

Copying Worksheets

An easy way to build up a complex workbook full of worksheets is to create a single sheet, and to copy that sheet over and over as needed. When you copy a worksheet, all of its data, including row and column headings, formulas, and worksheet titles, are duplicated in the copy. In addition, formatting and column widths are also copied.

Using these copies, you can then make simple adjustments (changing the title from May Revenues to June Revenues, for example), and quickly create a new worksheet. The idea behind copying worksheets is that you are not stuck with the tedious process of recreating similar worksheets over and over again in a large workbook.

You can copy a worksheet to a place within the current workbook, or to any other workbook.

Follow these steps to copy a worksheet:

1. Click the tab of the sheet you want to copy. You can copy multiple sheets if you want by pressing Ctrl and clicking the tabs of the sheets you want to copy.

2. Choose either of the following methods to copy the selected sheet(s):

   - Click the Format button on the Home tab, and select Move or Copy Sheet from the menu that appears.

   - Right-click one of the selected sheet tab(s) and select Move or Copy from the menu that appears.

3. The Move or Copy dialog box appears, as shown in Figure 6-7. Select the open workbook to which you want to copy the worksheet(s) from thc To Book list.

Figure 6-7
Select where you want the worksheet copied.

4. Select a sheet in front of which you want the copied worksheet(s) placed within the selected workbook by selecting a sheet from the Before Sheet list.

5. Select the Create a Copy checkbox.

Adding New Data to the End of the Worksheet

If you want to place the copied worksheet(s) at the end of the worksheet tabs and in front of the Insert Worksheet button, choose (Move to End) from the Before Sheet list.

6. Click OK. The selected worksheet(s) are copied and placed where you indicated. The copies are given a name similar to the original worksheets, with the addition of a number, such as Qtr 2 Sales (2).

Tip

You can quickly copy a worksheet within the current workbook by pressing and holding Ctrl, dragging its tab along the row of tabs, and dropping the tab where you want the copy to go.

Moving Worksheets

Complex workbooks with lots of worksheets often benefit from good organization—and one way in which that happens is by moving worksheets around until they appear in a logical order. Now, of course, there is no right or wrong order, but sometimes the right order will present itself—for example, the Qtr 1 Budget should probably appear before (to the left of) the Qtr 2 Budget sheet in the tab list along the bottom of the Excel window.

You can move a worksheet to a place within the current workbook, or to any other workbook.

Follow these steps to move a worksheet:

1. Click the tab of the sheet you want to move. You can move multiple sheets by pressing Ctrl and clicking the tabs of the sheets you want to move.

2. Choose either of the following methods to move the selected sheet(s):

   - Click the Format button on the Home tab, and select Move or Copy Sheet from the menu that appears.

   - Right-click one of the selected sheet tab(s) and select Move or Copy from the menu that appears.

3. The Move or Copy dialog box appears (see Figure 6-7). Select the open workbook to which you want to move the worksheet(s) from the To Book list.

4. Select a sheet in front of which you want the worksheet(s) moved within the selected workbook by selecting a sheet from the Before Sheet list.

5. Click OK. The selected worksheet(s) are moved where you indicated.

Placing Data at the End

If you want to move the worksheet(s) to the end of the worksheet tabs and in front of the Insert Worksheet button, choose (Move to End) from the Before Sheet list.

Tip

You can quickly move a worksheet within the current workbook by simply dragging its tab along the row of tabs, and dropping the tab where you want to move it.

Changing Worksheet Tab Colors

Normally, a worksheet's tab is gray until you click it to make it active, in which case it then changes to white. When you're dealing with workbooks that contain only a few worksheets at most, this works out just fine. When working with complex workbooks that contain lots of data and worksheets, organizing the sheet tabs by color can be truly helpful. For example, in a workbook that chronicles the schedule, budget, and actual costs related to a long-term project, you might color the schedule and schedule time-line chart the same color, such as blue. Other related tabs, such as the actual costs sheets, might also bear the same color, such as red, as shown in Figure 6-8.

Figure 6-8
Use tab colors to visually organize worksheets in a workbook.

Use Color Sparingly

You do not need to add color to every sheet tab in a workbook. If a particular sheet is important, and you want to call attention to it so it's easy to find in a forest of sheets, you can color just that tab if you like.

Now, when you color a worksheet tab, that color appears on the tab when it is not selected, as shown in Figure 6-8. When the tab is selected, like the Actual Costs tab shown in Figure 6-8, only a hint of its tab color appears as a stripe across the bottom of the tab. In this case, if you look closely, you might see a hint of red in that stripe that runs along the bottom of the Actual Costs tab.

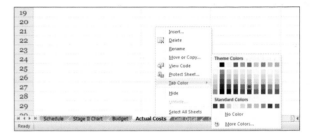

Figure 6-9
Select a color for the tab.

To change a tab's color, follow these steps:

1. Click the tab you want to color. You can select multiple tabs and color them all in one step—just press and hold Ctrl as you click each tab.

2. Choose either of the following methods to color the selected tab(s):

   • Click the Format button on the Home tab, and point to Tab Color from the menu that appears.

   • Right-click one of the selected sheet tabs and point to Tab Color from the menu that appears.

3. A palette of colors appears (see Figure 6-9). Click the color you want for the selected tab(s). The tab(s) are immediately changed to the color you selected, although the current tab appears in white with only a stripe of that color running along the bottom.

If you don't see a color you like, select More Colors from the palette. The Colors dialog box appears, as shown in Figure 6-10, displaying the Custom tab.

Start by clicking the Colors palette to choose a basic color. If you don't get the exact color you want to start with, you can click again or drag the pointer over the Colors palette.

Click to Select a Basic Color   Drag to Adjust Lightness/Darkness

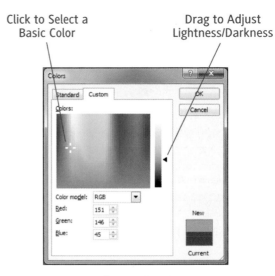

Figure 6-10
Mix a custom color for the tab if you want.

After selecting a good basic color, drag the Saturation slider to adjust the color's lightness/darkness.

If the Custom tab is too intimidating, you can quickly select a basic color without a lot of fuss. Click the Standard tab to display the standard colors, as shown in Figure 6-11. Just click any of the colored hexagons. After choosing a color, click OK to apply it to the selected tab(s).

Select a Standard
Color

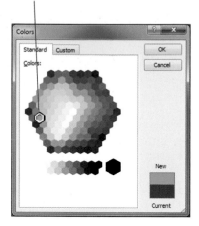

Figure 6-11
Select one of the standard colors
for the tab if desired.

Theme Colors Affect Tab Colors

If you select a theme color (a color that
appears in the top portion of the color
palette) and you later change themes, the
tab colors change to coordinate with the
new theme.

Tip

To remove the color from a tab, follow
the steps in this section, but select No
Color from the color palette.

Displaying Data Stored Elsewhere in the Workbook

Sometimes, especially in situations in which a worksheet contains a lot of data, you might want to be able to redisplay the contents of a cell in more than one location—either on that same worksheet, or on another worksheet in the same workbook. For example, suppose you set up a workbook with a worksheet that lists each of your company's products, and its selling price, based on whether it was sold through your catalog, online, or at a tradeshow. On other worksheets, you want to list the number of units sold for each item that month, through each of your various vertical markets. You want to display the current price on each of the monthly worksheets by simply redisplaying the prices you've already entered on the price sheet, as shown in Figure 6-12.

Displaying Data from Another Workbook

You can also display data stored in a different workbook. See the section "Displaying Data Stored in Another Workbook" for help.

Here's how to display data stored elsewhere in the workbook:

1. Click the cell where you want the data to appear.

2. Type the equals (=) sign.

Corresponding Data   Reference to Elsewhere
in the Workbook

Cell Reference

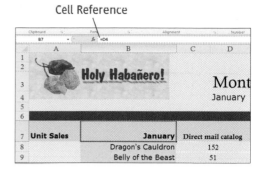

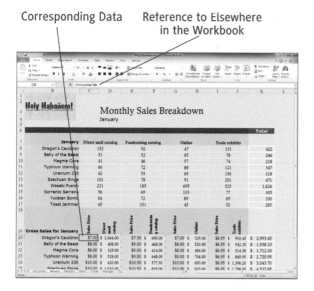

Figure 6-12
Don't retype data—simply redisplay it when needed.

Figure 6-13
Reference a cell in the same worksheet
with a simple address.

Cell Reference

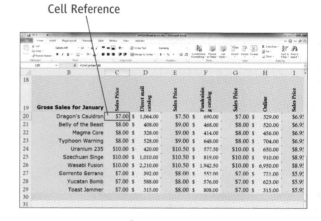

Figure 6-14
Reference a cell in another worksheet by
including a reference to that sheet.

3. Perform one of the following actions:

   • If the cell whose contents you want to
   display is located in the current worksheet, scroll if necessary so you can see
   the cell, and then click it. You can also
   simply type the cell's address, such as
   =D4. (See Figure 6-13.)

   • If the cell whose contents you want to
   display is located on another worksheet,
   click that worksheet's tab. Then scroll if
   necessary so you can see the cell, and
   click it. If you want to type the cell's
   address yourself, you need to follow the
   rules: type the name of the worksheet in
   single quotations (as in 'Unit Prices'),
   followed by an exclamation point (!), followed by the cell address—for example,
   type ='Unit Prices'!B8. (See Figure 6-14.)

4. Press Enter. The contents of the referenced
cell appear in the result cell you selected in
Step 1.

Referencing a Cell in a Formula

You can reference a cell and use its contents
in a formula. For example, you might want
to reference the price of an item stored on
another worksheet, and multiply it by the
number of items sold this month—without
actually displaying the price on the sales
worksheet. For example, you might type
='Unit Prices'!B8*C20.

Displaying Data Stored in Another Workbook

You can reference data stored in another workbook when needed, and display that data in the current workbook. Typically, this is done for convenience, so you do not need to open that other workbook in order to look up related information. For example, you might want to reference the product codes in an inventory workbook, for use in your marketing analysis workbook.

You can also reference the data in that other workbook for use in a formula. For example, perhaps you want to reference the current inventory total for a product, for use in a sales projection-planning-budget worksheet. Follow these steps:

1. Open both workbooks—the workbook in which you want the referenced data to appear, and the workbook that contains that data.

2. Click the cell where you want the data to appear.

3. Type the equals (=) sign.

4. Change to the workbook that contains the data you want to reference. Change to the worksheet that contains the data by clicking that worksheet's tab. Then scroll if necessary so you can see the cell containing the data, and click it.

   If you want to type the cell's address yourself, you need to follow the rules: first type the name of the workbook in square brackets (as in [HHQtr1Breakdown.xlsx]), followed by the name of the worksheet, followed by an exclamation point (!), followed by the cell address —for example, type =[HHQtr1Breakdown.xlsx]January!K8. (See Figure 6-15.)

Cell Reference   Source Data

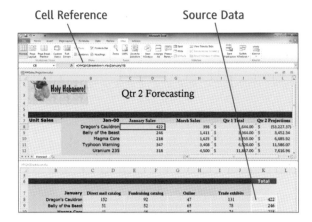

Figure 6-15
Reference a cell in another workbook when needed.

5. Press Enter. The contents of the referenced cell appear in the result cell you selected in Step 1.

After you create a reference to data in another workbook, whenever you reopen the workbook in which you created the reference, you will see a warning just above the Formula bar, as shown in Figure 6-16. The warning is telling you that this workbook depends on data saved in another workbook but nothing in this workbook has been updated automatically. Because the data in the other workbook might have changed, Excel recommends that you click the Enable Content button to update it. If you don't want to update the worksheet with data from the other workbook (because it's wrong, or you're in a hurry, or whatever), just ignore the warning and simply continue working. You can close the warning bar by clicking its Close button (the X) over there on the right if you want.

Figure 6-16
Update the data referenced in another workbook when needed.

Linking to Elsewhere in the Same or Different Workbook

A hyperlink (or simply, a link) is a bit of text or a graphic that, when clicked, displays related information elsewhere in the same worksheet, in another worksheet, or within another workbook. You can also link to other files such as Word documents, audio or video files, or new workbooks. In addition, you can link to a Web page or an e-mail address.

Theme Colors Affect Hyperlink Colors

If a hyperlink is text, it typically appears in a blue, underlined font. When a text link is used, it is often changed to purple, underlined text so users can easy determine if a link has been visited in the current working session. However, if your worksheet uses a different theme than the default (which is Office), the text color for your hyperlink may be different, as the hyperlink color is determined by the theme you select. For example, in Figure 6-17, the worksheet shown uses the Slipstream theme, so the hyperlink appears in aqua, and changes to blue when clicked. However, regardless of the theme you apply to a worksheet, if you apply a non-theme color to the hyperlink text, it will not change color when clicked.

When you move the mouse pointer over a hyperlink, whether the link is a bit of text or a graphic, the mouse pointer changes to a hand to indicate that if you click, the linked file, Web page, or e-mail address will be opened. (See Figure 6-17.) This behavior makes it easier to distinguish links from regular text and graphics.

In addition, when the mouse pointer moves over a hyperlink, a ScreenTip appears, displaying the location of the linked file, URL of the linked Web page, or address of the e-mail link—as shown in Figure 6-17. You can tell Excel to display different information in the ScreenTip if you want, by entering that information when you create the link.

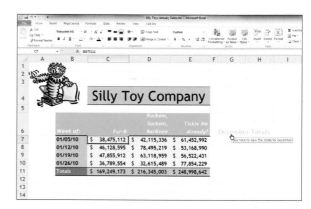

Figure 6-17
The mouse pointer changes when placed over a hyperlink, and a ScreenTip appears.

Linking to the Same Workbook

To create a hyperlink to a place within the current workbook, follow these steps:

1. Click the cell containing the text you want to use as the link, or click a graphic.

2. Click the Hyperlink button on the Insert tab. The Insert Hyperlink dialog box appears, as shown in Figure 6-18.

3. Click the Place In This Document button from the Link To list.

Type the Cell
To Link to

Select the Worksheet
To Link to

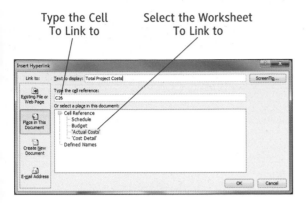

Figure 6-18
Create a link to another location
in this same workbook.

4. Enter the address of the cell you want to link to in the Type The Cell Reference text box. If you want to link to a cell on a different worksheet, select that worksheet from the Cell Reference section of the Or Select A Place In This Document box, and then type the cell address.

Tip

To save time, you can give the cell(s) within the worksheet that you want to link to range names, and then select one of those range names from the Defined Names section of the Or Select A Place In This Document box to link to that particular cell.

5. To enter a ScreenTip for the link, click the ScreenTip button, type the description to display in the ScreenTip, and click OK to return to the dialog box.

6. Click OK. The link is inserted into the worksheet. When you click the link, the cursor is moved to the cell you linked to.

Linking to a Different Workbook or Other File

To create a hyperlink to a place within a different workbook or to some other file such as a Word document, follow these steps:

1. Click the cell containing the text you want to use as the link, or click a graphic.

2. Click the Hyperlink button on the Insert tab. The Insert Hyperlink dialog box appears, as shown in Figure 6-19.

Select the Workbook
To Link to

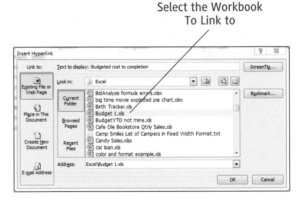

Figure 6-19
Create a link to another workbook or other file.

3. Click the Existing File or Web Page button from the Link To list.

4. Enter the path to the file you want to link to in the Address text box, or select the drive and folder containing the file from the Look In list and then select the file.

Figure 6-20
Create a link to a Web page.

5. To link to a specific place within a file such as
another Excel workbook or a Word document,
click the Bookmark button. To link to a cell
on a specific worksheet, select that worksheet from the Cell Reference section of the
Or Select A Place In This Document box. If
you've created a range name or a bookmark
in a Word file, select it from the Defined
Names section in the Or Select A Place In
This Document box. Click OK to return to
the dialog box.

6. To enter a ScreenTip for the link, click the
ScreenTip button, type the description to display in the ScreenTip, and click OK to return
to the dialog box.

7. Click OK. The link is inserted into the worksheet. When you click the link, the file you
linked to is opened and displayed.

Linking to a Web Page

To create a hyperlink to a Web page out on the
Internet, or on your company's network, follow
these steps:

1. Click the cell containing the text you want to
use as the link, or click a graphic.

2. Click the Hyperlink button on the Insert tab.
The Insert Hyperlink dialog box appears, as
shown in Figure 6-20.

3. Click the Existing File or Web Page button
from the Link To list.

4. Enter the path to the page you want to link
to in the Address text box, or click the
Browse the Web button, and use your Web
browser to display the page you want to link
to. After displaying the page, do not close
your browser, but simply switch back to Excel
and the dialog box—the Web page address
automatically appears in the Address box.

5. Some Web pages are designed with bookmarks that link to places on that page. To
link to a specific place within the page, click
the Bookmark button, and select a place
from those listed. Click OK to return to the
dialog box.

6. To enter a ScreenTip for the link, click the ScreenTip button, type the description to display in the ScreenTip, and click OK to return to the dialog box.

7. Click OK. The link is inserted into the worksheet. When you click the link, the Web page you linked to is displayed in a Web browser.

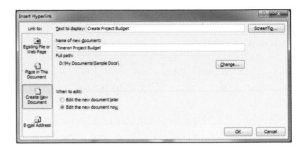

Figure 6-21
Create a new workbook to link to.

Linking to a New Workbook

To create a hyperlink to a new workbook, follow these steps:

1. Click the cell containing the text you want to use as the link, or click a graphic.

2. Click the Hyperlink button on the Insert tab. The Insert Hyperlink dialog box appears, as shown in Figure 6-21.

3. Click the Create New Document button from the Link To list.

4. Type a name for the new workbook in the Name of New Document text box.

5. If you want to edit this new workbook now, select Edit the New Document Now. Otherwise, select Edit the New Document Later.

6. To enter a ScreenTip for the link, click the ScreenTip button, type the description to display in the ScreenTip, and click OK to return to the dialog box.

7. Click OK. If you indicated that you wanted to edit the workbook now, it is opened in Excel so you can enter data. Regardless, the link is inserted into the worksheet. When you click the link, this new workbook is displayed.

Linking to an E-Mail Address

To create a hyperlink that generates an e-mail message pre-addressed to a particular address, follow these steps:

1. Click the cell containing the text you want to use as the link, or click a graphic.

2. Click the Hyperlink button on the Insert tab. The Insert Hyperlink dialog box appears, as shown in Figure 6-22.

Figure 6-22
Create a link that generates an e-mail message.

3. Click the E-mail Address button from the Link To list.

4. Enter the e-mail address you want to link to in the E-Mail Address text box. Excel automatically adds the text, mailto: in front of the address you type.

Tip

If you've e-mailed this address recently, select the address to use from the Recently Used E-Mail Addresses list.

5. Type a description for the e-mail message in the Subject box.

6. To enter a ScreenTip for the link, click the ScreenTip button, type the description to display in the ScreenTip, and click OK to return to the dialog box.

7. Click OK. The link is inserted into the worksheet. When you click the link, an e-mail message appears, automatically addressed to the e-mail address link.

Using and Managing Links

After creating a link, simply move the mouse pointer over it and click when the pointer changes to a hand to activate the link. Here are some tips for managing links:

▶ To edit the text in a cell that contains a hyperlink, you can't just click and edit because as soon as you click, the link is activated. Instead, click a cell nearby and use the arrow keys to navigate to the cell. Then type new text for the link or edit the existing text using the Formula bar. Press Enter to save your changes.

▶ To edit the place to which the link points, move the cursor to the link cell. Click the Hyperlink button on the Insert tab, and the original information you used to create the link appears. Make any changes you want, and click OK to save them.

▶ To remove a hyperlink, move the cursor to the link cell. Click the Hyperlink button on the Insert tab and click the Remove Link button. The link is immediately removed, along with the text used to create the link.

Using Find and Replace

WHEN YOU WORK WITH large workbooks, you may often find yourself wishing you could locate a specific piece of data quickly. Using Find, you can. Find allows you to search through data, formulas, and comments in a worksheet to locate the exact piece of information you are searching for. Once something is found, you can optionally replace that something with something else. In a large workbook, this feature is quite useful, as you can make massive changes throughout the workbook to the name of a product, the reported value of an investment, or any other data.

Searching for Data

As mentioned earlier, Excel can search a worksheet's data, formulas, or comments. When searching though formulas, Excel searches not only the formulas themselves, but also the data in the cells to which they refer. If you search through data or comments, Excel searches only through the actual data entered in cells, or the comments attached to cells. You might search a large worksheet for a particular employee, office, or product, and then make some changes to that item's data.

Tip

You can search the current worksheet only, or all the worksheets in a workbook.

1. If you want to search within a limited range, select that range of cells. Otherwise, click any cell in the worksheet/workbook you want to search.

2. Click the Find & Select button on the Home tab.

3. Select Find from the pop-up menu. The Find and Replace dialog box appears, as seen in Figure 6-23.

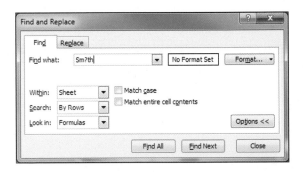

Figure 6-23
Search a worksheet or a workbook for specific data.

4. Type the data to find in the Find What box.

5. To set options, click the Options button and make your selections:

- To search for data that uses a particular format, click the Format button, select the format to search for (such as Currency format), and click OK to return to the dialog box. You can select a cell that contains the formats to find by clicking the Choose Format From Cell button in the Find Format dialog box and clicking a cell.

- Normally, Excel searches only within the current worksheet. To search within the entire workbook, select Workbook from the Within list.

- In order to decrease the time in which it takes Excel to locate the data you're searching for, you might want to indicate the direction in which you want Excel to search the sheet. Just open the Search list and select either By Rows or By Columns.

- Normally, Excel searches formulas and the cells to which they refer. To search data or comments only, open the Look In list and select Values or Comments.

- To match text by exact upper- and lowercase, select the Match Case checkbox.

- To find cells that contain only the contents you are searching for, select the Match Entire Cell Contents checkbox.

Using Wildcards for Single Characters

You can use wildcards when searching, such as * or ?. Use ? to represent a single unknown character, as in Sm?th to find Smith and Smyth, for example. Use * to represent any number of unknown characters, such as some*, which matches something, someday, and somebody. If you are looking for data that contains a ? or * you must type a tilde ~ in front of the character so Excel doesn't treat it as a wildcard, as in ~? or ~*.

6. Click either Find Next (to highlight the first cell that matches your criteria) or Find All (to display a list of all matching cells).

- If you clicked Find Next, the cursor moves to the first matching cell. If you want, you can continue searching to the next matching cell by clicking Find Next again. Continue clicking Find Next to search for matching cells one at a time.

- If you clicked Find All, a list of matching cells appears at the bottom of the Find and Replace dialog box, as seen in Figure 6-24. You can drag a corner of the dialog box to make it wider and longer in order to make the list easier to use. Select a cell in the list to move the cursor to that cell.

7. When you're through searching, click Close.

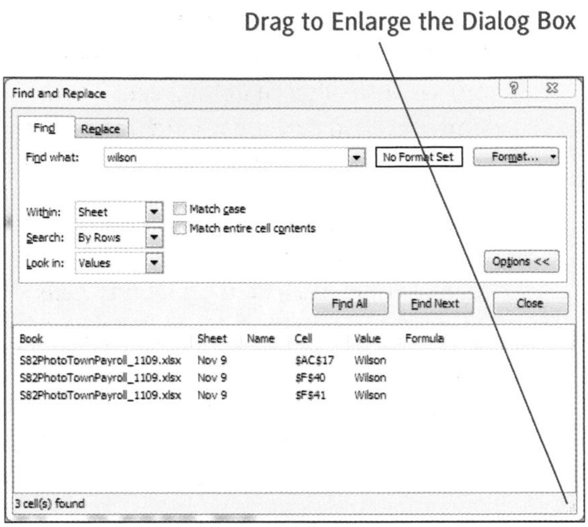

Drag to Enlarge the Dialog Box

Figure 6-24
When you click Find All, a list of matching cells is produced.

Replacing Cell Data

Excel can find data in a worksheet, and can replace it with other data as well. When performing a search and replace, you can choose to replace individual instances of the matching data, or all matches. Again, you can search and replace data in the current worksheet or the entire workbook. Follow these steps:

1. If you want to search within a limited range, select that range of cells. Otherwise, click any cell in the worksheet/workbook you want to search.

2. Click the Find & Select button on the Home tab.

3. Select Replace from the pop-up menu. The Find and Replace dialog box appears, as shown in Figure 6-25.

Figure 6-25
Search for specific data and replace it.

4. Type the data to find in the Find What box.

5. Type the data to use as the replacement in the Replace With box.

Searching for Special Characters

Wildcards such as * (to replace multiple characters) or ? (to replace a single character) can be used in searching. If you are looking for data that contains a ? or * you must type a tilde ~ in front of the character so Excel doesn't treat it as a wildcard, as in ~? or ~*.

6. To set options, click the Options button and make your selections:

   • To search for data that uses a particular format, click the Format button next to the Find What list, select the format to search for (such as Currency format), and click OK to return to the dialog box. You can select a cell that contains the formats to find by clicking the Choose Format From Cell button in the Find Format dialog box and clicking a cell.

   • To replace data and apply a particular format, click the Format button next to the Replace With list, and follow the process described previously for selecting formats.

   • Normally, Excel searches only within the current worksheet. To search within the entire workbook, select Workbook from the Within list.

   • In order to decrease the time in which it takes Excel to locate the data you're searching for, you might want to indicate the direction in which you want Excel to search the sheet. Just open the Search list and select either By Rows or By Columns.

   • Normally, Excel searches formulas and the cells to which they refer. To search data or comments only, open the Look In list and select Values or Comments.

   • To match text by exact upper- and lower-case, select the Match Case checkbox.

   • To find cells that contain only the contents you are searching for, select the Match Entire Cell Contents checkbox.

7. Perform one of the following:

   • Click Find Next to highlight the first cell that matches your criteria. The cursor moves to the first matching cell. If you want, you can continue searching to the next matching cell by clicking Find Next again.

   • Click Find All (to display a list of all matching cells). A list of matching cells appears at the bottom of the Find and Replace dialog box. Drag a corner of the dialog box to make it wider and longer in order to make the list easier to use. Select a cell in the list to move the cursor to that cell.

   • Once a cell is highlighted, click Replace to replace the matching data with the replacement data you entered in Step 5.

   • To replace all matching cells without highlighting each one first, click Replace All.

8. When you're through searching and replacing, click Close.

Managing Worksheet Views

WHEN ENTERING DATA, especially in a large worksheet, you may often want to change the view. For example, you might want to zoom in to see a smaller area of the worksheet, or zoom out in order to reduce the size of the worksheet onscreen so you can see more of it. Excel has many special views you can use for particular purposes, such as adding headers and footers or adjusting where page breaks occur. In this section, you learn how to control the view of the worksheet so you can work efficiently.

Zooming In and Out

Zooming in increases the size of data onscreen so you can view it more clearly. It also reduces the number of cells shown onscreen, so zoom in when you want to review a specific, smaller area of a worksheet. Zooming out is the exact opposite of zooming in—the size of data is reduced as more cells are displayed onscreen. Zooming is measured by percentages. At 100% zoom, data is shown onscreen in the approximate size it will appear when printed. At 200%, data is shown at approximately twice its size. At 50%, data is shown at approximately half its normal size.

Zooming Has No Effect on Printouts

Zooming in and out affects the size of text as it appears onscreen, but it does not affect the size of text when printed.

There are various ways in which you can zoom:

▶ To zoom to 100%, click the 100% button on the View tab.

▶ To zoom in on the currently selected cells, click the Zoom to Selection button on the View tab.

▶ To enter a custom zoom percentage, click the Zoom button on the View tab. The Zoom dialog box appears, as shown in Figure 6-26. Select the zoom percentage you want. The Fit Selection option zooms in on the currently selected cells. The Custom option allows you to type in the exact zoom percentage you want, from 10% to 400%. After making a selection, click OK to zoom to that percentage.

Figure 6-26
Zoom in to an exact percentage.

▶ Zoom using the mouse by pressing and holding Ctrl and rolling the wheel on the mouse up (to zoom in) or down (to zoom out).

▶ Zoom using the Zoom slider, located at the bottom-right corner of the Excel window as shown in Figure 6-27. Drag the slider to the left to zoom out, drag to the right to zoom in. Zoom out by 10% increments by clicking the minus button to the left of the zoom slider; zoom in by 10% increments by clicking the plus button instead.

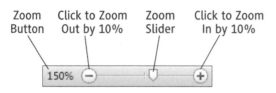

Figure 6-27
Zoom using the Zoom slider.

▶ Click the Zoom button shown in Figure 6-27 to display the Zoom dialog box and enter a zoom percentage.

Changing Worksheet Views

Excel has many preset views that are helpful when working with any worksheet, but especially large ones that contain lots of data. There are four preset views: Normal, Page Layout, Page Break Preview, and Full Screen. Each view serves its own special purpose.

Normal view is just that—normal. Data is displayed in rows and columns clearly marked so you can enter data easily. This is the view in which you'll do most of your work within Excel. To change back to Normal view at any time, click the Normal button on the View tab, or click the Normal view button located just to the left of the Zoom slider (refer to Figure 6-28).

Using Page Layout

In Page Layout view, data is displayed as it might look when printed, page by page. To switch to Page Layout view, click the Page Layout button on the View tab, or click the Page Layout view button. In Page Layout view, the zoom is automatically switched to 100%, and only the first page appears, surrounded by the empty page margins, as shown in Figure 6-28. To view the next page of the printout, click either the horizontal or vertical scroll bar (depending on the layout of the worksheet).

Page headers and footers also appear. A header is data that appears at the top of every page in the printout, whereas a footer is data that prints at the bottom of every page. Rulers appear so you can adjust the size of the margins and header/footer space as you like. Simply drag the margin edge on the Ruler to adjust the margin size. To create a header, click in any one of the three boxes that make up the header (left, center, or right) and type the data you want to appear there. The Header & Footer Tools tab appears with buttons for inserting special data such as page number, the current date or time, or the file name.

Using Page Break Preview

Page Break Preview is a special view designed to show you where page breaks occur in a printout, while allowing you the opportunity to adjust them. To change to Page Break Preview, click the Page Break Preview button on the View tab, or click the Page Break Preview view button. If you see a Welcome to Page Break Preview dialog box reminding you that you can adjust page breaks using this view, simply click OK to dismiss it.

Drag to Adjust Margin   **Type In One of the Header Boxes to Add Header Information**

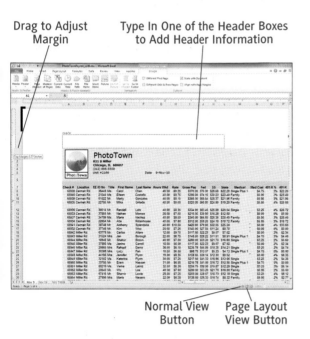

Normal View Button   **Page Layout View Button**

Figure 6-28
Page Layout view displays your data
as it will look when printed.

Page breaks are displayed as blue dashed lines on the worksheet; each page is marked with the text *Page*, followed by some number so you know which page you are viewing. (See Figure 6-29.) If you drag a page break and drop it elsewhere in the sheet, you are telling Excel to place the break there. The page break becomes solid, so you can tell your manual page breaks from Excel's automatic ones. In addition, page numbers and the size of data are automatically adjusted so everything fits on the pages you have designated. To remove a page break, drag it off the printout. To remove all manual page breaks and return to automatic page breaks, click the Breaks button on the Page Layout tab and select Reset All Page Breaks from the pop-up menu.

Checking the Page Layout for Printouts

If you move a page break to include more rows or columns on a single page, you won't really see much of a change to data size onscreen. You will notice a difference, however, when you print the worksheet. If you want to see in advance how much the text will be reduced in order to cram in those extra rows or columns on a page in which you've moved the page break, check the Scale percentage, located on the Page Layout tab, in the Scale to Fit group.

Manual Page Break   **Automatic Page Break**   **Page Break Preview View Button**

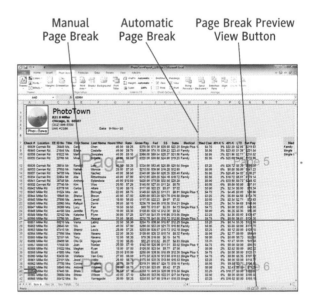

Figure 6-29
Page Break Preview allows you to view
and change page breaks.

Using Full Screen

When you change to Full Screen view (by clicking the Full Screen button on the View tab), the current view settings are retained, but the Ribbon, Quick Access Toolbar, Zoom slider, and view buttons are removed to maximize viewing space, as seen in Figure 6-30. The worksheet tabs are still displayed along the bottom of the window so you can switch from one sheet to another. To exit Full Screen view, press Esc.

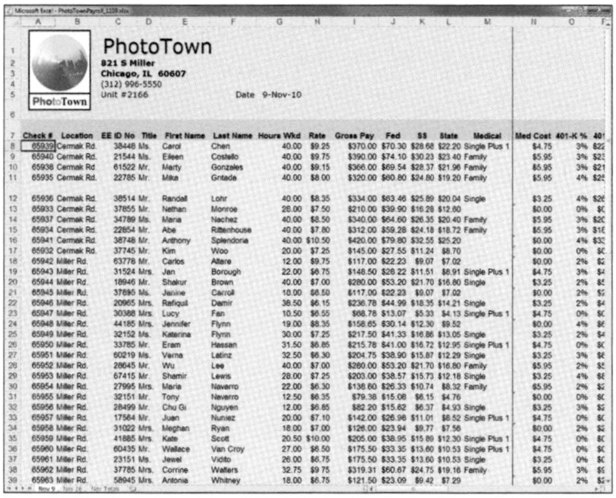

Figure 6-30
Full Screen view maximizes the viewing area of the worksheet.

Tip

Because the zoom slider is removed when you change to Full Screen view, you may want to adjust the zoom before entering this view.

Freezing Row and Column Headings

One of the most annoying things about working with a large worksheet, such as a worksheet with lots of rows, is that you can easily scroll down and out of view of the column headings. At that point, you will find yourself staring at lots of unlabeled data, trying to decipher what it all means. Without the column headings to guide you, this can be quite difficult at times. The same thing holds true if your worksheet uses row labels, and you scroll to the right and out of sight of them. One way to solve this problem is to freeze the row and/or column headings in place, so you can scroll down or to the right as far as you like, and still identify what it is you're looking at.

To freeze row and column headings, click a cell below the column headings and to the right of any row headings you want to freeze. Then click the Freeze Panes button on the View tab and select Freeze Panes. A dark line appears just above and to the left of the cell you clicked—these lines mark the "frozen" area of the sheet as shown in Figure 6-31. After freezing row and column headings, scroll down or to the right to view the data you want; the headings always stay in view. Here I split the screen to freeze the column headings and to keep the customer names in view, and then I scrolled to the right in the lower-right pane to view the amount of that customer's last purchase. To unfreeze row and column headings, click the Freeze Panes button on the View tab and select Unfreeze Panes.

Frozen Row
Heading

Scroll to the Data
You Want to View

Frozen Column
Headings

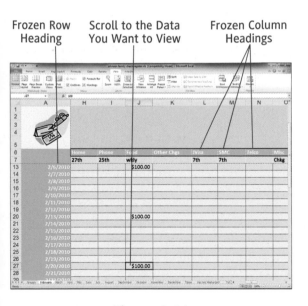

Figure 6-31
Freeze row and column headings so you can
scroll anywhere within a large worksheet.

Tip

If your row headings are located in column A, click the Freeze Panes button on
the View tab and select Freeze First
Column to freeze them without clicking
any particular cell first. Select Freeze Top
Row from the pop-up menu to freeze column headings (assuming they are located
in row 1 of the worksheet).

Splitting the Excel Screen

Splitting the Excel window is similar to freezing
row and column headings, because it enables
you to see non-contiguous parts of the worksheet at the same time. The way splitting differs
is that its focus is not on row and column labels.
Instead, splitting can be used to literally split the
window into up to four viewing panes, divided
horizontally and vertically), so you can see four
different areas of the worksheet at once.

When you split the screen, up to two split bars
appear as shown in Figure 6-32. If you click a
cell in the first row for example, and then split
the screen, a split bar appears to the left of this
cell, vertically splitting the screen in two. These
two vertical panes scroll together when you scroll
up or down in either pane, but independently if
you scroll left or right within a pane. If you click
a cell in the first column instead, a split bar
appears above the cell, splitting the screen horizontally in two. The two horizontal panes scroll
together when you scroll left or right in either
pane, but independently when you scroll up or
down. If you click any other cell, the screen is
split both horizontally and vertically (above and
to the left of the cell you click). Two of the four
panes scroll together when you scroll left or
right/up or down.

Horizontal
Split Bar

Vertical Split
Bar

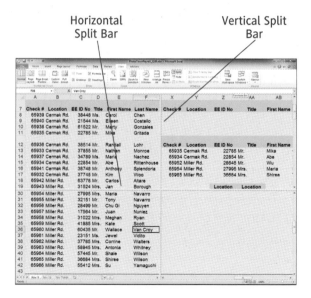

Figure 6-32
Split the screen to create views of
non-contiguous areas of the worksheet.

To split a screen, click any cell and then click
the Split button on the View tab. The split bars
appear above and/or to the left of this cell. Click
within any pane and scroll to get the view you
want. In Figure 6-32, I split the screen into four
parts, scrolled down in the bottom left pane to
view one of the last employees—Shiree Wilson.
In the upper-right pane, I scrolled to the right
to view the paycheck breakdown for that same
employee. To remove the split bars, click the
Split button on the View tab again.

Tip

You can also split a worksheet using the
horizontal or vertical split bars. For
example, drag the horizontal split bar
from its place just below the Formula bar
down onto the worksheet, and drop it
where you want to split the screen horizontally. To split the screen vertically,
drag the vertical split bar from its place
at the right end of the horizontal scroll
bar to the left and drop it where you
want to split a worksheet vertically. By
the way, no matter whether you drag
split bars onto a worksheet to split it or
use the Split button, you can still drag
the split bars once they are in place to
adjust the size of the panes.

Hiding Rows and Columns

One way that you can easily simplify a large
worksheet and make it easier to work with is to
temporarily hide the rows or columns you aren't
currently working on. Doing so instantly shrinks
a large worksheet and makes it workable. In addition, hidden rows or columns are not included
when you print a worksheet, so hiding rows or
columns enables you to quickly print exactly
what you want (such as non-contiguous rows or
columns), while hiding data you don't want to
share.

To hide rows or columns, select the rows or columns to hide by dragging over their row or column labels. For example, to hide rows 11–13, drag over the row labels 11, 12, and 13 to select those rows. Then click the Format button on the Home tab and point to Hide & Unhide from the pop-up menu. Another pop-up menu appears; select Hide Rows or Hide Columns, depending on what you are trying to hide. As an alternative, you can right-click the selected rows/columns and choose Hide from the pop-up menu.

Hiding rows or columns does not delete the data in them, so don't worry about that. When a row or column is hidden, it's pretty obvious because the row number or column letter is missing from the top or left of the Excel window. For example, if you hide row 23, you'll see the row numbers 21, 22, and 24 on the left side, but not 23.

The same is true of columns—if you hide columns C-E, you'll see the letters A, B, F, and G across the top, as shown in Figure 6-33.

Tip

You can also hide the contents of an individual cell if you feel like it. If a cell's contents are hidden, it simply appears empty. However, if someone clicks the cell, its contents are displayed in the Formula bar. The idea is that someone would need to know to click the cell, and for the most part, if a cell appears empty, they probably won't. To hide the contents of a cell, click it, and click the Dialog Box Launcher in the Number group on the Home tab. The Format Cells dialog box appears with the Number tab displayed because you are going to apply a custom number format that makes the cell contents disappear. Select Custom from the Category list. In the Type box on the right, type three semicolons (;;;). The Sample will show nothing, because the effect of this format is hiding the data. Click OK, and the cell's contents are hidden. Repeat this process to hide the data in other cells.

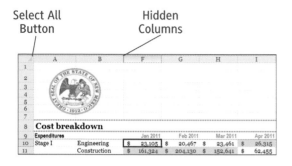

Figure 6-33
The column labels for hidden columns may call attention to the fact that they are hidden.

To unhide rows or columns, select the rows or columns to unhide by dragging over the row or column labels next to the hidden rows/columns. For example, to unhide rows 11–13, drag over the row labels 10 and 14 to select those adjacent rows. Then click the Format button on the Home tab, point to Hide & Unhide, and finally select Unhide Rows or Unhide Columns from the pop-up menu. Again, to quickly unhide the selected rows or columns, right-click the selected rows/columns and choose Unhide from the pop-up menu. To quickly unhide all hidden rows or columns in a worksheet, click the Select All button, and then click the Format button on the Home tab, point to Hide & Unhide, and select Unhide Rows (or Unhide Columns).

Hiding by Dragging

You can hide rows or columns by dragging if you want. For example, to hide column D, drag its right edge to the left until the column width is zero. To unhide the column later on, drag its hidden edge to the right. Now, you have to position the pointer exactly right to be able to pull this off, and not widen a visible column. Move the pointer in place, between the two visible columns that flank the hidden column. Move slightly to the left. When the pointer is in the right position, it appears with arrows pointing left and right, with two lines between the arrows. Once the pointer changes to this kind of double-headed arrow, drag to the right to widen the hidden column.

Sorting Data

PICTURE YOURSELF MAKING YOUR LONG list of names and addresses or products—or anything for that matter—and putting it in order. Putting a list in order accomplishes several goals, including making your list easier to read and use, making it appear more orderly, and giving the content a perceived priority. Of course that priority can change, as the same list can be put in order—or *sorted*—by any field within the list. Using a list of locations, for example, you can sort by the city or by the state. Or by any of the other fields containing information about each location, such as population or an economic rating. The order is up to you, and Excel 2010 gives you several options for achieving the order you seek.

Sorting from the Ribbon

THIS SORTING METHOD IS incredibly easy. Simply click on any cell in the column (field) you want to sort by, and click the A-Z or Z-A sorting buttons on the Data tab. The buttons are shown in Figure 7-1, where you also see a list of cities sorted by their State field.

Figure 7-1
Sort your list by any field, simply by being in any cell in that column and using the two Sort buttons on the Data tab.

The A-Z button, which sorts in ascending order, is also known as a "Smallest to Largest" sort in Excel. Its companion, the Z-A button, sorts in descending order, and is known as "Largest to Smallest." When sorting a field containing text, the sorts are easy to forecast—an A-Z sort will sort from A to Z. If you're sorting a numeric field, a Smallest to Largest sort (A-Z) will place the lowest numbers at the top of the list, followed by numbers increasing in value. Figure 7-2 shows the same list of cities, sorted this time by Local Population, in Largest to Smallest (Z-A) order, which places the city with the highest population at the top of the list.

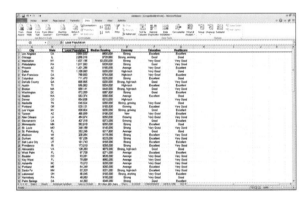

Figure 7-2
Sort numeric fields just as easily—from largest to smallest (as shown here) or smallest to largest.

Working with the Sort Command

WHEN YOU NEED TO GO beyond a single field sort, the Sort command (also found on the Data tab) is your ticket to multiple-field sorting. It's also a great way to lay the groundwork for a Subtotal report, which you'll read about in the last section of this chapter.

So why would you want to sort by more than one field? Well, sticking with the list of cities, imagine that you wanted to sort them by state *and* by city, so that all the cities are in state order, and within each group of states that that sort creates, the cities would be in alphabetical order. Figure 7-3 shows that sort in place.

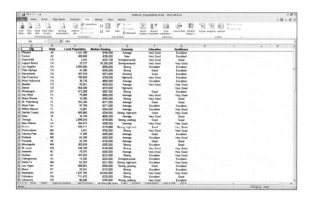

Figure 7-3
You can sort by more than one field to put your list in a more usable order.

Using Sort to Create Groups

What do I mean about the Sort command creating groups? Well, if you sort the cities list by state, because there are multiple cities in individual states, each state becomes a group—Arizona, then California, then Colorado, and so on. Each state's cities can then be placed in order within the state-based groups—to provide an even more useful, easily-understood list.

To use the Sort dialog box, shown in Figure 7-4, simply click the Sort button and begin choosing the fields by which you want to sort, in the order you want to sort by them. The dialog box gives you the opportunity to choose the fields to sort by, as well as to set each one to its own sort order.

Figure 7-4
Use the Sort dialog box to set multiple-field sorts.

To use the Sort dialog box, follow these steps:

1. Click in any cell in the database/list. Unlike using the A-Z or Z-A sort buttons, it doesn't matter which column you're in—you just have to be in a cell that contains data.

2. Click the Sort button. The dialog box shown in Figure 7-4 appears.

3. Choose your first field to sort on by clicking the Sort by drop-down menu, as shown in Figure 7-5. All of the fields in your database should appear in this list.

Figure 7-5
Choose from your list of field names and pick the field you'll sort by first.

Formatting Headers

What, no field names? If you see Column A, Column B, and so on instead of your field names in the Column Sort by section of the dialog box, you need to either tell Excel you have a header row (click the My Data Has Headers checkbox) or perhaps make a change to your list's layout. Having a title row directly above the headers row can confuse Excel and make it see the row with your field names as data and not as a header row. Delete any row above the headers, or put at least one blank row between them so that Excel can see where your headers are and where your data begins and ends.

Tip

The best field to sort by first is the one with the most duplicate entries. This creates groups (as explained in the note, "Using Sort to Create Groups"), and makes it easier to choose second- and third-level fields to sort by within those groups. Using the Cities list, a good choice for first field is State, then perhaps by economy or healthcare rating, and then by city. The State groups are then broken down by their ratings, and then for each group of ratings within a state, the cities will be in alphabetical order. The last field in your multiple-field sort should be one with few or no duplicates.

4. Click the Sort On drop-down menu to choose from alternatives to Values (the default), as shown in Figure 7-6. You can choose to sort on the color of the cell (if you've applied fills to certain cells), by font color, or by cell icon. As most of the time you'll only want to deal with the value in the cells, you don't have to change from the default here.

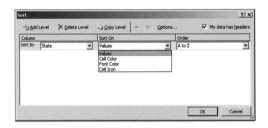

Figure 7-6
Sort by the values in the selected field, or perhaps by the color of the cells or their content.

5. Choose the order to sort by. You can choose from A to Z, Z to A (as shown in Figure 7-7), or Custom List. The last choice opens the Custom Lists dialog box, which contains the built-in and user-created custom lists that are typically used to speed up data entry of frequently used lists of names, numbers, and values like days of the week or months of the year. Your most useful choice? A to Z or Z to A, depending on which values (largest or smallest) you want to see first.

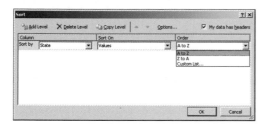

Figure 7-7
Choose the order for the sort on the selected field.

6. Add another level by clicking the Add Level button. The Then By drop-down menu appears, as shown in Figure 7-8, from which you can choose the second level of your sort.

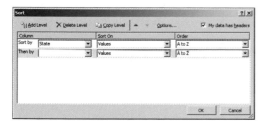

Figure 7-8
Select the second level for your sort.

7. Repeat Steps 4 and 5 for the new field, deciding what to sort on and what order the sorted records should appear in.

8. Continue adding sort levels until you have all the fields you want to sort by listed, in the order they should be sorted, in the dialog box.

9. Click OK to apply the sort to your list. Figure 7-9 shows a completed sort instruction, which sorts by state, then by healthcare rating, then by city.

Figure 7-9
Sort by as many fields as you want—although sorting by too many fields can reduce the usability and ease of use of the resulting sorted list.

Tip

Use the Copy Level button to duplicate a selected level in the Sort dialog box. When to use it? Because you wouldn't sort on the same field twice, use it when you want to sort by the same Sort On and Order values, and then just change the Column designation. This shortcut saves you two of the three steps involved in establishing a new level for your sort.

To get rid of a sort level you created by mistake or no longer want, simply click the Delete Level button while your mouse is in any of the options for the unwanted level. The level is gone, and you can continue creating levels or click OK to perform the sort as you've set it up.

Reordering and Adjusting Your Sort

What are those triangles and the Options button about? Click the triangles to reorder your sort levels—using the up-pointing triangle to move a selected level up in the sort, and the down-pointing arrow to move a selected level down in the sort. This can be handy if you re-think the order of your sort levels and don't want to have to delete one or more of them and start over. The Options button allows you to fine-tune your sort even further, turning on Case sensitivity and changing the orientation of your sort—converting from a top-to-bottom sort to a left-to-right sort. The default, of course, is top-to-bottom.

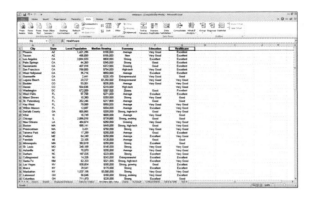

Figure 7-10
The list of cities, sorted by their healthcare rating, within each state. The cities are alphabetized.

Tip

If you need to look at a list from more than one perspective—using fields which might not have a lot of duplicate entries by which to create sorted groups—consider creating a PivotTable report (check out Chapter 15, "Using PivotTables") to create a more flexible, powerful report than a simple sort can give you.

As you can see in Figure 7-10, the resulting sorted list makes it easy to see which cities in which states have the best healthcare rating. The groups created by sorting on fields with duplicate records—State and Healthcare—make it easy to interpret the data. Instead of Healthcare, the Economy or Education fields could have been used (one or the other), depending on what's of interest to you or those who'll be viewing the list. Sorting by two of the ratings would make it harder to use the list in an "at a glance" way, however, as it would break up the groups created by duplicate entries in just one of the rating fields.

Creating a Subtotal Report

ASIDE FROM PUTTING YOUR LIST in some logical, useful order, what good does sorting do you? Well, it sets your list up to become a *Subtotal Report,* a handy, informative tool that turns those sorted groups into calculated sections of a report like the one shown in Figure 7-11, based on the sort completed in Figure 7-10, grouping the cities by state and their healthcare rating.

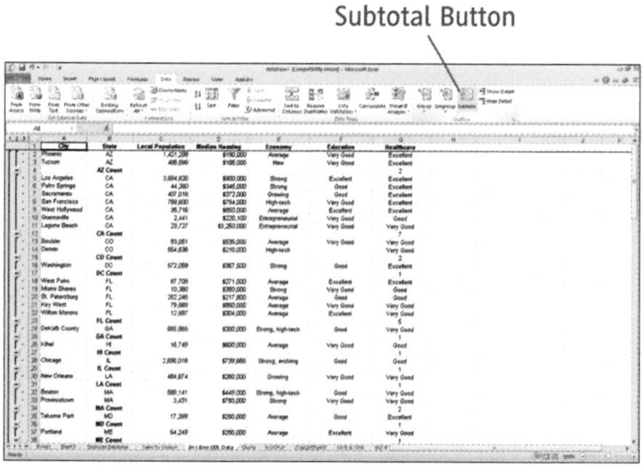

Subtotal Button

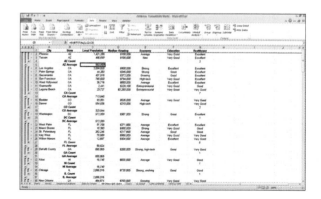

Figure 7-11
Your sorted groups become useful sections of an informative Subtotal Report.

To make this report, you need to have gone through the multiple-field sort steps in the previous section of this chapter, using the Sort command and dialog box. A subtotal report can be made by a single-field sort, but only if the sort creates groups—sorting the cities list by state, for example, or by one of the ratings. Sorting by city, local population, or median housing will not create groups to be subtotaled.

Tip

Creating multiple-field sort with the Sort dialog box is the more effective way to prepare for a Subtotal Report, but it's not the only way. You can also make your own groups, as discussed in the last sections of this chapter, beginning with "Creating Manual Groups from Sorted Rows."

The term "Subtotal" is key to understanding what a Subtotal Report is. As shown in Figure 7-11, there are calculations performed on the sort-generated groups, such as counting (for non-numeric fields), or creating a sum or average for numeric fields. The numeric field need not be one you sorted on, however, as shown in Figure 7-12, where the Local Population is averaged by state.

Figure 7-12
Perform a calculation on the fields in your Subtotal Report.

Once you've sorted your list—let's go with the sorting shown in Figure 7-10, at the end of the multiple-field sort process—follow these steps to create your Subtotal Report:

1. On the Data tab, click the Subtotal button, shown in the callout in Figure 7-11.

2. In the resulting Subtotal dialog box (shown in Figure 7-13), you will begin choosing which fields to subtotal.

Figure 7-13
Pick your subtotal fields—typically those you sorted by before starting the report—and decide which calculation to perform.

3. Click the At Each Change In drop-down menu, and see a list of all your fields, as shown in Figure 7-14.

Figure 7-14
Pick the field that represents the first-level grouping within your sorted list. State is the best choice here.

4. Click the Use Function drop-down menu to choose what calculation you want performed on the field you'll choose in the Add Subtotals To list (see next step). A wide variety of accounting, statistical, and analytical functions are offered, as shown in Figure 7-15.

Figure 7-15
Using the Local Population field, choose Average, to see the average home values in each state.

Expanding and Collapsing Your Subtotal Report

The first thing you'll notice about your Subtotal report is the appearance of numbers and columns on the left side of your worksheet, to the left of Column A (which might not be a field in your list). These columns allow you to expand and collapse your report, showing more or less detail for some or all of the groups within the report. As shown in Figure 7-17, you can collapse everything down to show just the grand total (click the 1 button), or as shown in Figure 7-18, you can expand only the major subtotals (click the 2 button). Figure 7-18 shows the average housing value for each state, without showing you individual cities within each state. Click the 3 button to bring back all the detail.

5. Pick the field to apply the calculation to. For example, if you're going to average the housing values in the cities in each state, choose Average from the function list, and click to place a checkmark next to Local Population from the Add Subtotal to list.

6. As this is the first subtotal you're creating, there's no need to adjust the remaining options in the dialog box (these are discussed in the next section, where you add levels to the initial report). Click OK to create the report, shown in Figure 7-16.

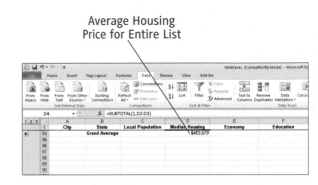

Average Housing Price for Entire List

Figure 7-17
Only care about the bottom line? Collapse your report to show just—and only—that.

Figure 7-16
Subtotal reports are best built one level at a time. Here's the first subtotal for the Cities list, averaging housing values by state.

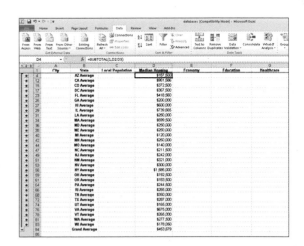

Figure 7-18
Remove the detail, but show more than just the grand total by clicking the 2 button, to show all the groups' subtotals.

Now, this needn't be the end of your subtotaling fun. As stated, this is just the first level, and you can add more subtotaled levels to the report. Follow these steps to count the number of cities per state.

1. With any cell in the list/report active, call up the Subtotal dialog box again by clicking the Subtotal button on the Data tab (Outline group).

2. Pick, as needed, a new field that represents a group created by your sort. If, for example, you sorted by both state and healthcare, you could choose healthcare for this second level of sorting.

3. Choose the function to apply. Let's pick Count this time.

Tip

Be sure to remove any checks next to other fields chosen in the Add Subtotals To list when you add your second level of subtotals. In this example, be sure only Healthcare is checked, so that only that field is counted.

4. Pick the field to count. Let's pick city this time, to count the cities in within each state.

5. Remove the checkmark next to Replace Current Subtotals. This will allow your first level subtotaling to remain in the report.

6. Click OK. The second level of the report is added to the first, as shown in Figure 7-19.

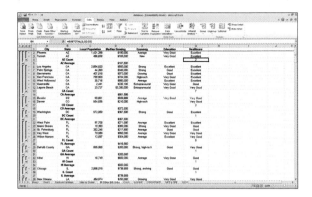

Figure 7-19
Now you have subtotals on two fields—an average of housing prices, and a count of cities with particular healthcare ratings.

Depending on the complexity and depth of your list—the number of fields by which you can group your data, basically—you may want to create Subtotal reports with more than two levels of subtotaling going on. You can continue to add levels, choosing fields and selecting functions, until you achieve the level of detail you're looking for.

Tip

To remove your subtotal report—taking your list back to its sorted, pre-report state, simply open the Subtotal dialog box and click the Remove All button. The numbered columns on the left are gone, as are the calculations.

Creating Manual Groups from Sorted Rows

WHAT IF YOU DON'T WANT to create subtotals, but you do want to group your data by sorted sections? For example, what if you want to create groups for each state in your Cities list, but don't want to apply any kind of calculation to the list—you just want to be able to expand and collapse your view of the list to show only certain states and their cities?

Excel 2010 makes this easy, with the Group button, shown in Figure 7-20. The button is found in the Outline group of the Data tab, and is paired with an Ungroup button, which allows your groups to be—that's right—ungrouped.

Group Button

Figure 7-20
Create your own groups from a sorted list—with the Group button.

To use the Group button, follow these steps:

1. With your list sorted, to create groups from one or more of the fields, select the rows that make up a group. Figure 7-21 shows the cities in California turned into a group.

2. Click the Group button. 1 and 2 buttons appear on the left side of the worksheet, allowing you to collapse this group (use the 1 button) or expand it to show all the cities in that group (click the 2 button).

3. Continue selecting series of rows, clicking the Group button for each one. Figure 7-22 shows several grouped states.

1 Button   2 Button

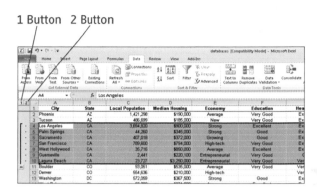

Figure 7-21
Select the series of rows that make the group you'd like to be able to set apart within the list.

Figure 7-22
Group the states you want to be able to expand or collapse. Those not grouped will always appear in detail, but the ones you group can be collapsed and removed from view in the list.

To get rid of a group, select it (drag through the rows that make up the group) and click the Ungroup button. Pretty simple! If you've made several individual groups, you will have to Ungroup them individually.

Filtering Data

PICTURE YOURSELF AT A RESTAURANT. You've just sat down and are looking at a menu filled with dozens of food choices. How do you decide what to eat? First, you know that your allergies mean you will avoid all seafood. Next, knowing you had pasta last night, you don't feel like eating pasta tonight, so you can rule out those options. You had a big lunch and don't want something heavy for dinner as well, so you avoid the red meat choices. Now, you are looking at chicken and a couple of vegetarian options. Making your decision from this more limited selection is much easier. This decision-making process is an example of filtering.

Excel's AutoFiltering feature works in the same way; it provides you with a method of filtering out, or temporarily hiding, the data that you don't need to see. None of your data is deleted, but you are able to see only those records that are important to you at any given time. A bookstore manager can filter her sales data to see only the nonfiction sales for the month. The accounts receivable manager at your doctor's office could filter out all patients who paid in full during their visit and see only those patients who still owe money.

This chapter shows you how you can use the Filter command in Excel to easily manage the data in your worksheets.

Creating an AutoFilter

THE EASIEST WAY TO FILTER your data is to use the AutoFilter feature in Excel. To create an AutoFilter, click anywhere in your worksheet table and choose Data > Sort & Filter > Filter. Excel recognizes that all of the adjacent cells are part of your table and applies a filter arrow to the top cell in each column, as seen in Figure 8-1.

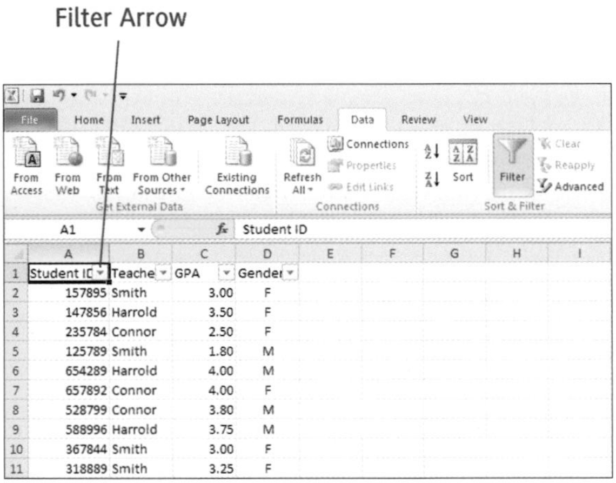

Caution

The AutoFilter feature does not work on protected worksheets. Learn more about protecting worksheets in Chapter 13, "Setting Security Options."

Figure 8-1
The AutoFilter feature applies a filter arrow to each column in your worksheet's table.

Applying the Filters

Clicking the filter arrow in each column header displays a drop-down menu of the unique entries in that column. In Figure 8-2, you can see that the unique values in the Gender column are F and M.

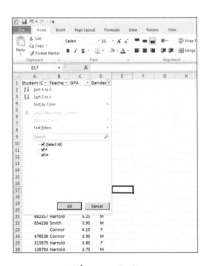

Figure 8-2
The filter arrow displays the column's unique values.

To apply a filter to your data, follow these steps.

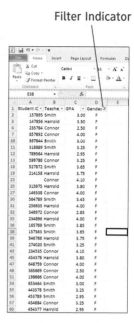

Filter Indicator

Figure 8-4
The arrow on the column header becomes
a funnel once a filter has been applied.

Tip

The AutoFilter's drop-down menu will show up to 10,000 unique data points, such as product numbers. You may need to use additional criteria to filter some of your tables.

1. Remove the check mark from the Select All option. The check marks are automatically removed from the rest of the unique entries.

2. Click the filtering option you want to see on your worksheet and click OK to apply the filter. In Figure 8-3, selecting the F option from the Gender column will filter out any records with an M in that column.

   The correct filtered data is displayed in the worksheet and the filter arrow has changed (see Figure 8-4). Once a filter is applied, the image next to the column title changes to look like a funnel to indicate that a filter is in use.

To remove the filters from the worksheet and return to the full unfiltered list of data, choose one of the following options:

▶ Click the filter button next to the column header and choose Clear Filter (see Figure 8-5).

▶ Click the Select All option and then click OK.

▶ Choose Data > Filter from the Ribbon.

Figure 8-3
Select only those values you want to see in your filtered worksheet data.

Number of Records Displayed

Whenever a filter is applied to your data, the number of records displayed appears in Excel's status bar. In Figure 8-6, Excel found that 28 of the 59 records in the worksheet database fit the filter.

Figure 8-5
Clearing a filter.

44	464376 Ms. Connor	3.90	M
46	554376 Mrs. Harrold	3.75	M
49	654899 Mr. Smith	2.25	M
50	696563 Mrs. Harrold	4.00	M
52	890084 Ms. Connor	3.80	M
53	338090 Mrs. Harrold	3.75	M
58	653533 Ms. Connor	3.30	M
59	Mrs. Harrold	4.00	M
61		3.64	28
62			
63			
64			
65			

School Grades / Sheet2 / Sheet3
Ready   28 of 59 records found

Figure 8-6
The status bar displays the number of
records matching your filter.

Copying Filtered Data

After you have filtered your data to display only
the files relevant to your needs, you can copy
that data to the Microsoft Clipboard. From the
Clipboard, you can paste the filtered data into
another area of your worksheet, or into any
other Microsoft application.

Use your mouse to select the filtered data and
choose Home > Copy to copy the data to the
Clipboard. Look closely at the highlighted cells in
Figure 8-7. Excel automatically performs a non-
adjacent cell selection to copy only the filtered
data. Notice that the marquee, or the marching
ants, appears between filtered data cells.

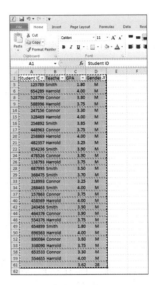

Figure 8-7
Excel copies only filtered data to the Clipboard.

Choose one of the following options to paste
your data.

▶ **To paste your data into a new Excel
worksheet, or into another area of the
existing worksheet, select the first cell
in the destination worksheet and
choose Home > Paste.** Once pasted into
the new area of the worksheet, the new
data is formatted as an unfiltered table.
Take a closer look at the row numbers
displayed in Figure 8-8; the data hidden
in the original area of the filtered worksheet table has now been permanently
removed.

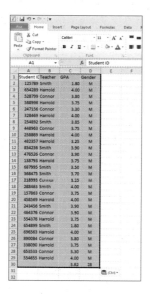

Figure 8-8
Excel deletes everything but the filtered
data when you paste filtered data.

▶ **To paste your data into another
Microsoft application, open the new
application and position your cursor
where desired, then press Ctrl+V to
paste your data into the application.**
Figure 8-9 illustrates how your data will
appear when pasted into PowerPoint 2010.

Student ID	Birth Date	Teacher	GPA	Gender
147856	9-Dec-00	Mrs. Harrold	3.50	F
654289	23-May-00	Mrs. Harrold	4.00	M
588996	4-Nov-00	Mrs. Harrold	3.75	M
789564	25-Oct-00	Mrs. Harrold	2.95	M
328469	17-Mar-00	Mrs. Harrold	4.00	M
214158	1-Jan-00	Mrs. Harrold	3.75	F
258869	5-Aug-00	Mrs. Harrold	4.00	M
482357	6-Jul-00	Mrs. Harrold	3.25	M
315975	21-May-00	Mrs. Harrold	3.80	F
138793	20-Mar-00	Mrs. Harrold	3.75	M
256635	14-Mar-00	Mrs. Harrold	4.00	F
234896	21-Mar-00	Mrs. Harrold	4.00	F
546786	3-Apr-00	Mrs. Harrold	3.75	F
458569	19-Jan-00	Mrs. Harrold	4.00	M
454378	25-May-00	Mrs. Harrold	3.80	F
554376	15-May-00	Mrs. Harrold	3.75	M
696563	3-Mar-00	Mrs. Harrold	4.00	M
338090	9-Aug-00	Mrs. Harrold	3.75	M
487665	27-May-00	Mrs. Harrold	4.00	M
454377	6-Mar-00	Mrs. Harrold	2.95	F

Figure 8-9
Filtered data can be copied into any
Microsoft application.

Tip

**Once the data has been pasted into the
new application, it can be formatted
using the application's standard formatting tools, as shown in Figure 8-10.**

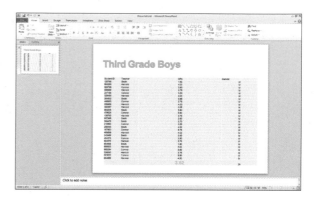

Figure 8-10
Excel data can be formatted with
standard editing tools.

Filter Arrows Aren't Copied

The filter arrows are overlaid onto your
worksheet; they are not part of your worksheet. As such, they will not be copied with
your data.

Performing a Secondary Filter Selection

SOMETIMES FILTERING data for one criterion is not enough. The sample worksheet you've seen earlier in this chapter reflects the grade point averages (GPA) of the third grade students in three classes. If you wanted to calculate the GPA of girls, you could apply a filter on the Gender column. But what if you wanted to see the GPA of only the girls in Mr. Smith's class? In this instance, you would need to apply a secondary filter.

The secondary filter starts with the data you already filtered and further reduces the number of records to review. You are not limited to applying two filters; you can apply as many filters to your data as you feel are necessary. Apply secondary filters by following these steps.

1. Choose Data > Sort & Filter > Filter to turn on the AutoFilter feature.

2. Click the filter arrow for the column you will filter first.

3. Click the Select All option to remove the check marks from all of your data points and then apply the first filter. In Figure 8-11, the first filter was applied to the Teacher column to select all of Mr. Smith's students.

4. Click the filter arrow for the next column you will filter and choose your filter criteria. In this example, you filter the Gender column to show only females (see Figure 8-12). Notice that both the Teacher and the Gender columns now show a filter indicator instead of the filter arrow.

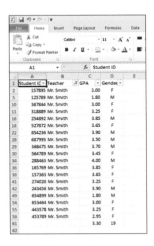

Figure 8-11
The first filter selects all of Mr. Smith's students.

Tip

If you have applied multiple filters to your worksheet, you can clear all of them at once by choosing Data > Sort & Filter > Clear.

Figure 8-12
Two filters were applied to this worksheet.

Exploring Special Filters

YOU'VE LEARNED HOW TO PERFORM a simple filter on your data, but Excel provides even more ways to filter your data. Use the AutoFilter feature to find missing data in your worksheet, to display a list of the 10 best sales districts, and even to see which invoices are due to be paid next month.

Searching for Blank Cells

Suppose you are the school administrator in this example and you are responsible for accurately maintaining this database of grades. The three teachers submitted their data to you on Friday, but some of the data was missing. You decide to enter the data you have and leave blanks where the data was missing and plan to fill in the missing data on Monday.

You can scroll through the database searching for the blank cells manually, but using Excel's AutoFilter would be so much easier. Excel can easily find the missing data in your worksheet, regardless of how big your spreadsheet becomes.

1. Choose Data > Sort & Filter > Filter to turn on the AutoFilter feature.

2. Click the filter arrow in the column header where you want to find blank cells.

3. Click the Select All option to remove the check marks from all of your data points.

4. Scroll to the bottom of the entry list and click the (Blanks) option and click OK. As shown in Figure 8-13, the (Blanks) option will always appear at the end of the entry list. If there are no blanks in the column, there will be no (Blanks) option to click.

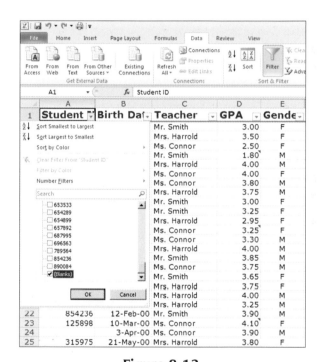

Figure 8-13
The (Blanks) option appears at the bottom of the entry list.

Excel will display only those records with blank cells in the column you selected (see Figure 8-14).

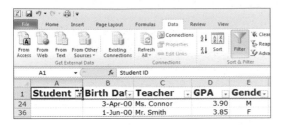

Figure 8-14
Excel found two records with blank entries
in the Student ID column.

Tip

**To view only the non-blank data, turn on
the AutoFilter, make sure that the Select
All option is checked and then scroll to
the bottom of the entry list and remove
the check mark from the (Blanks) option
(see Figure 8-15). Finally, click OK.**

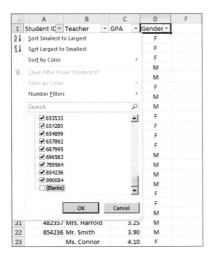

Figure 8-15
Add a check mark to all filter options except
(Blanks) to find non-blank data.

Filtering by Values

Excel's AutoFilter recognizes your data as either
numbers (values) or as text. If the data in your
cells is numerical, the AutoFilter will include
special filter options called Number Filters
(see Figure 8-16).

Figure 8-16
Number filters in Excel 2010.

1. To create a number filter, click the filter
   arrow in the column header containing the
   data you want to filter and click Number
   Filters.

2. Select the filter that best meets your needs.
   Table 8-1 describes the results of these filters
   on the GPA worksheet.

Table 8-1 Custom AutoFilter Options for Values

Filter	Sample Criteria	Records Displayed
Equals	3.25	Students with a GPA equal to 3.25
Does Not Equal	4.00	Students with a GPA not equal to 4.00, including any students above or below 4.00
Greater Than	4.00	Students with a GPA higher than 4.00
Greater Than or Equal To	3.50	Students with a GPA of 3.50 or higher
Less Than	3.50	Students with a GPA lower than 3.50
Less Than or Equal To	3.50	Students with a GPA of 3.50 or lower
Between	3.00 and 4.00	Students with a GPA of 3.00, 4.00, and those in between
Top 10		Students with the highest (Top) or lowest (Bottom) GPA
Above Average		Students with a GPA higher than the average GPA for the database as a whole
Below Average		Students with a GPA lower than the average GPA for the database as a whole

3. Enter your specific criteria in the resulting dialog box (see Figure 8-17) and click OK to apply the filter.

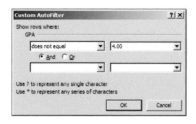

Figure 8-17
Each numbered filter can be further customized in a dialog box.

Filtering by Date

Excel provides two types of date filters: common and dynamic. Common filters use the same sort of comparison filters as the number filters do (for example, Equal To, Greater Than). Regardless of the date on which you perform the filter, your filtered results will look the same. For instance, if there are three records that are equal to January 10 today, there will be three records equal to January 10 tomorrow (provided no one changes your data).

Dynamic filters factor in today's date when performing the filter. For example, performing a filter to find all invoices coming due Next Week will produce a different result today than it will if you perform the same filter sometime next month. Dynamic filters include Today, Last Year, Next Month, and even Quarter 1. Figure 8-18 illustrates the full range of date filters available in Excel.

Figure 8-18
Date filters in Excel 2010.

1. To create a date filter, click the filter arrow in the column header containing the data you want to filter and click Date Filters.

2. Select the filter that best meets your needs.

3. Enter your specific criteria in the resulting dialog box and click OK to apply the filter.

Filtering by Time

Use the date AutoFilters in Excel to filter by time as well. For example, to filter by an earlier time than 8:00 in the morning, choose the Before filter, enter 8:00 AM, and then click OK.

Filtering by Color

If you are the type of person who likes to color-code your data, Excel has a filter just for you. If your database includes colored cells or colored fonts, the AutoFilter will include an option to filter by color (see Figure 8-19).

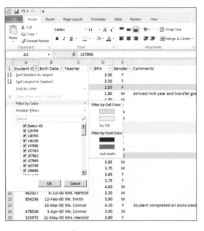

Figure 8-19
Filtering by color.

Tip

In determining the order of dates, Excel prioritizes year, then months, then days. January is always the first month of a year and the first month of a quarter.

Creating Custom Filters

EXCEL'S AUTOFILTER FEATURE is fast and accurate, but it's not always enough. Custom filters make it possible to compare parts of your data in order to display exactly the information you are looking for.

Filtering Text

To filter your text data, click the appropriate filter arrow and choose Text Filters. Make a selection from the list of available filters, enter your specific criteria in the resulting dialog box and click OK to apply the filter (see Figure 8-20).

Table 8-2 describes each of these filters and the results that would be produced by filtering an address book database.

Figure 8-20
Results of a text filter containing "student" in the Comments column.

Table 8-2   Custom AutoFilter Options for Text

Filter	Sample Filter	Records Displayed
Equals	Illinois	Anyone with an address in Illinois
Does Not Equal	Massachusetts	Anyone with an address anywhere other than Massachusetts
Begins With	New	Anyone with "New" at the beginning of the address. For example, New York, New Jersey, New Hampshire, and New Mexico
Ends With	ota	Anyone with "ota" at the end of the address. For example, South Dakota, North Dakota, and Minnesota
Contains	iss	Anyone with "iss" anywhere in the address. For example, Mississippi and Missouri
Does Not Contain	nn	Anyone without "nn" in the address. For example, Wisconsin, but not Pennsylvania

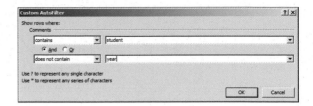

Figure 8-21
The Custom AutoFilter dialog box.

The Custom AutoFilter dialog box provides yet another more specific filter opportunity. Suppose you want to search for a word that begins with M, but is only eight characters long. Use the question mark symbol as a wildcard. For example, if you enter M???????, Excel will return Missouri, Maryland, and Michigan. The ? takes the place of a single character. Use an asterisk (*) as a wildcard if you don't know the exact number of characters.

Adding Multiple Comparison Criteria

You can use the Custom AutoFilter dialog box (see Figure 8-21) to compare more than one criterion. Excel uses the comparison operators AND and OR to combine comparison filters. For instance, creating a custom filter that begins with M *and* ends with I would find both Mississippi and Missouri. A custom filter that begins with F *or* begins with G would find both Florida and Georgia.

To create a Custom AutoFilter, select your initial filter using one of the methods described in this chapter. Then, in the Custom AutoFilter dialog box, choose the AND or OR option. From the second drop-down menu, select another filter option and type your filter term in the box. Click OK to apply the filter.

Using PivotTables on Columns

All of Excel's filters temporarily hide rows that contain the data you want to filter out of the worksheet. The filters cannot be applied to columns. If you need to filter data from a column, you can create a PivotTable to reposition your data. Learn how to do this in Chapter 15 "Using PivotTables."

Caution

The AutoFilter feature hides rows that don't meet your criteria, including rows holding your summary data. Be sure to check the summary row in your filter criteria if you want to display a calculation of the entire database, not just your filtered data, as shown in Figure 8-22.

Using Formulas with Filtered Data

AS YOU LEARNED IN CHAPTER 2, "Working with Formulas," Excel has a number of built-in formulas for calculating data in your worksheet. SUM, COUNT, and AVERAGE are three of the most frequently used and most useful formulas available.

Filtering your data means temporarily hiding the part of the data in your worksheet that does not fit the filter criteria and these formulas base their calculations on the total number of records in your database, not the filtered records. Figure 8-22 illustrates how formulas like SUM will return the same number when you have one or 100 records showing in your filtered results.

Luckily, you can use the SUBTOTAL function to perform calculations on filtered cells. The SUBTOTAL function calculates only the visible cells and ignores all hidden data (see Figure 8-23).

The syntax is =SUBTOTAL(*function number described in Table 8-3, range of cells to calculate*). For example, =SUBTOTAL(1,A1:A100) will calculate the average of the data in cells A1 to A100. To calculate the sum of the data in the same cells, type =**SUBTOTAL(9,A1:A100)**.

Figure 8-23
The SUBTOTAL formula is used for calculations on filtered data.

SUBTOTAL Formula

Table 8-3   SUBTOTAL Functions

Function Number	Formula
1	AVERAGE
2	COUNT
3	COUNTA
4	MAX
5	MIN
6	PRODUCT
7	STDEV
8	STDEVP
9	SUM
10	VAR
11	VARP

SUM Formula

Figure 8-22
The SUM formula will not recognize filtered data. Clearly 5+10 does not equal 2,175.

Preparing to

Print

ICTURE YOURSELF SHOPPING at your favorite clothing store. You are trying to find the perfect outfit for an important occasion. You've made it to the fitting room with your treasures and begin to try them on. You try on each outfit in turn and check the fit. One is too big in the waist, one is too long in the sleeve, and one is too tight in the neck, but you keep trying because you know that somewhere there is with the perfect fit.

Use the Print Preview features in Excel to help you find the right fit for your printed documents before you send them to the printer. This chapter describes all of the options available to you before you print.

Setting the Print Area

IT SOUNDS SIMPLE, but the first step in any printing project is deciding what to print. Unless you specify otherwise, Excel assumes you want to print the entire active worksheet. However, that might not be true. You may need to print only one of several data tables from a worksheet, or you may choose to print only a portion of a table. The range of cells that you want to print is called the *print area*.

To specify the print area:

1. Highlight the range of cells that you want to print.

2. Choose Page Layout > Page Setup > Print Area (arrow) and select Set Print Area (see Figure 9-1).

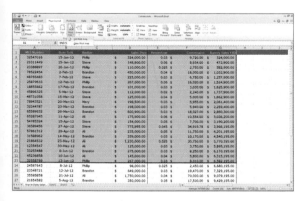

Figure 9-1
Setting the print area.

3. Excel surrounds the highlighted range with dotted lines as shown in Figure 9-2. Only the data within the lines will be printed.

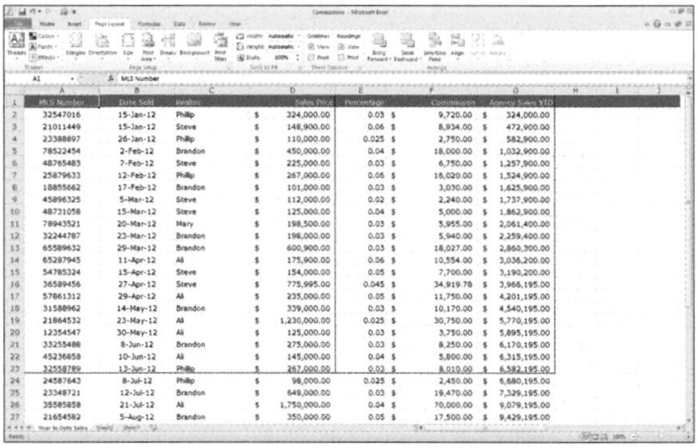

Figure 9-2
Dotted lines surround the print area.

The print area you defined is saved with the worksheet and becomes the new default print setting for that file. You can clear the existing print area and set a new one at any time. To clear the print area, choose Page Layout > Page Setup > Print Area (arrow) and select Clear Print Area. Clearing the print area returns to the default print settings (that is, printing the entire worksheet).

Previewing Your Worksheet

EXCEL WORKSHEETS CAN incorporate large amounts of data, not to mention charts and other images. Once you've established the print area and before you send all of that information to the printer, it's a good idea to get into the habit of previewing your work, to make sure that there are no surprises when your file reaches the printer.

Choose File > Print to open Excel's preview window (see Figure 9-3). The preview displays your worksheet exactly as it would appear if you printed the file on paper. For instance, if the selected printer prints only in black and white, the preview window will also display in black and white, even if your worksheet includes color objects.

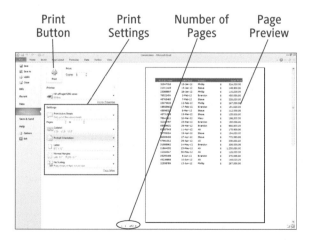

Print Button   Print Settings   Number of Pages   Page Preview

Figure 9-3
Excel's preview window.

Printing Multiple Copies

Click the up or down arrows next to the Copies option at the top of the Print Preview window to print multiple copies of the file in a single print job.

Changing Orientation

A piece of paper can be turned vertically or horizontally. That directionality is called the paper's *orientation*. Take a closer look at the Print Preview window. The preview shows the file in a vertical (portrait) format. Excel's default orientation is Portrait. With this orientation set, Excel will need two pages to print the selected print area.

You can change the orientation to try to reduce the number of pages required to print the worksheet. Click the arrow on the orientation option and select Landscape Orientation (see Figure 9-4). Excel changes the preview to reflect the new paper orientation. Figure 9-5 demonstrates that while more columns fit on this wider paper orientation, the print selection still requires two pages to fit.

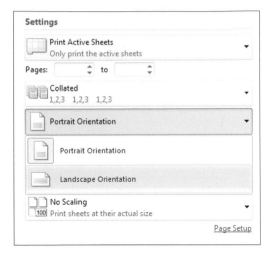

Figure 9-4
Specify Portrait or Landscape Orientation
from the Print Preview window.

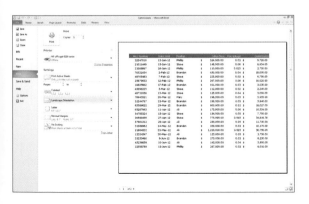

Figure 9-5
Changing to Landscape Orientation still
did not reduce the page count.

Choosing a Paper Size

Your printer is capable of printing on several sizes of paper. In North America, the most common paper sizes are Letter (8.5×11 inches) and Legal (8.5×14 inches). The default paper size in Excel is Letter.

To change the paper size, click the arrow on the paper size option and select the desired paper size from the drop-down menu (see Figure 9-6). The printer you have selected will determine which paper sizes you see in the list.

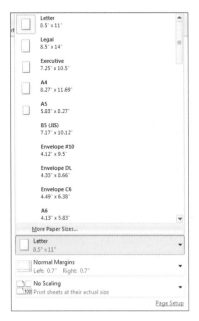

Figure 9-6
Choosing a paper size.

If the paper size you are looking for is not on the drop-down menu, you can add your own paper size. Click the More Paper Sizes button at the bottom of the list to open the Page Setup dialog box.

Click the Options button to open the Document Properties dialog box for your selected printer. Then, click the Custom button on the Paper/Quality tab (see Figure 9-7) and enter the measurements for your custom paper size.

Older Printers Beware...

Not all printers are created the same. Older printers may not allow custom settings. If yours doesn't, simply choose one of the predefined paper sizes.

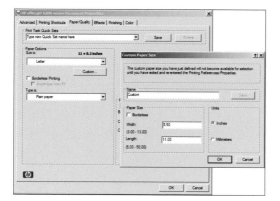

Figure 9-7
Adding a custom paper size.

Making It Fit

Scaling is a special tool used by Excel to force a print area to fit within a required number of pages. Scaling works similarly to the zoom feature on your camera. Excel does not change the formatting on the worksheet itself, but instead it adjusts the content to fit the available space. Table 9-1 describes the scaling options available in Excel 2010.

To change the scaling option, click the arrow and select the desired scaling option from the drop-down menu (see Figure 9-8).

Figure 9-9 illustrates how applying the Fit Sheet on One Page scaling option to the current worksheet affects the Commissions file. The preview window now confirms that the print area fits on a single page.

Table 9-1   Scaling Options

Scale	Description
Fit Sheet on One Page	Entire print area is scaled to fit on a single page
Fit All Columns on One Page	Entire print area is scaled to be one page wide, but may still require several pages in length
Fit All Rows on One Page	Entire print area is scaled to be one page long, but may still require several pages in width

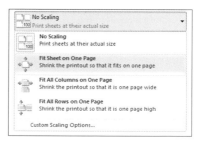

Figure 9-8
Select a paper size.

Figure 9-9
Worksheet scaled to fit on one page.

Switching Worksheet Views

EXCEL PROVIDES SEVERAL ways to view your data. Most of the time when you work in Excel you will be working in the Normal view, but your data is fully editable in any of these views.

▶ **Normal view:** The default view you see when you open Excel. Page breaks are indicated with dotted lines.

▶ **Page Layout view:** This view is a more powerful version of the Print Preview window.

▶ **Page Break preview:** This view condenses the print area of the worksheet and enables you to manually adjust page breaks.

To switch to another view, choose View > Workbook Views from the Excel Ribbon. Alternatively, you could use the View icons in the status bar (see Figure 9-10).

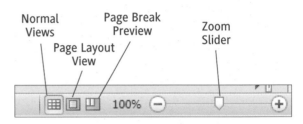

Figure 9-10
Excel's status bar contains the View icons and Zoom slider.

Tip

Use the Zoom slider to change the magnification level within each view.

Adjusting Page Layout

FIGURE 9-11 DEMONSTRATES that unlike the Normal view, the Page Layout view displays portions of the worksheet that are usually hidden until you view them on the Print Preview window. Instead of using dotted lines to indicate a page break, the Page Layout view shows an actual break in the worksheet as if you were looking at a piece of paper. Using this view allows you to make changes to elements of your document that are not normally visible, such as margins, titles, and headers and footers.

Figure 9-12
Excel's Page Layout tab.

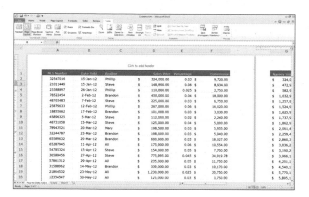

Figure 9-11
Excel's Page Layout view.

Returning to Normal

When you finish working in any view, you can return to Normal view by choosing View > Workbook Views > Normal.

The Ribbon's Page Layout tab (see Figure 9-12) includes five groups of elements that can be changed:

► **Themes:** As you discovered in Chapter 5, "Making the Worksheet Look Good," the Themes group contains a number of built-in tools to control the colors and fonts used in your worksheet.

► **Page Setup:** Control the margins, print area, page orientation, and printed appearance of your worksheet from the Page Setup group, as described in Table 9-2. Many of these controls are also available in the Print Preview window.

► **Scale to Fit:** As in the Print Preview window, the Scale to Fit group contains controls to help you fit your data onto a specified number of pages.

► **Sheet Options:** This group contains controls to make gridlines or cell headings appear on the screen and printed page.

► **Arrange:** The Arrange group controls the alignment of the graphical elements of your worksheet. You learn more about those elements in Chapter 12, "Inserting Illustrations."

Table 9-2   Page Setup Tools

Button	Description
Margins	Adjusts the whitespace at the top, bottom, and sides of your data.
Orientation	Changes the paper layout from portrait to landscape.
Size	Changes the size of the paper to which you will be printing.
Print Area	Highlights the area of the worksheet that you want to print.
Breaks	Sets or removes manual page breaks.
Background	Adds a picture behind your worksheet data.
Print Titles	Adds repeating rows and columns to the printed page.

Working with Margins

Margins are the whitespace found at the top, bottom, and sides of printed pages. There is no correct margin size. The right size is a personal choice for aesthetic or functional purposes. Use one of the three built-in margin settings by choosing Page Layout > Page Setup > Margins and selecting one of the options in the drop-down menu (see Figure 9-13).

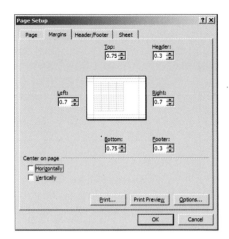

Figure 9-14
Manually adjust margins from the Margins tab.

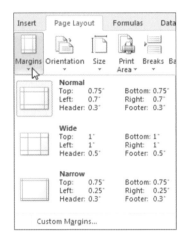

Figure 9-13
Built-in margin options.

Tip

Center the worksheet data horizontally and vertically on the printed page by checking those options on the Margins tab of the Page Setup dialog box.

Choosing Custom Margins from the drop-down menu will open the Page Setup dialog box. The Margins tab displays a miniature worksheet and small up and down arrows, called *spinners*, for each of the modifiable margins as shown in Figure 9-14. To change a margin, click the appropriate spinner arrow or type the value manually.

Margins can also be changed from the Print Preview window once the print area has been established. Just follow these steps:

1. Choose File > Print to open the Print Preview window.

2. Click the Margins icon in the lower-right corner. Excel displays the margins over the worksheet (see Figure 9-15).

3. Drag the square margin handles to manually adjust the margin settings.

Figure 9-15
Drag sizing handles to adjust margins
in the print preview.

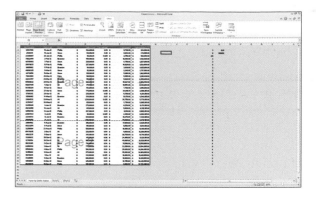

Figure 9-16
Viewing page breaks.

Tip

The Margins icon also displays column
handles. Drag these handles to resize the
column widths so that all of your data is
visible.

Tip

Each time you open the Page Break preview, you will see a Page Break Preview
message. Check the Do Not Show This
Dialog again box to prevent the message
from reappearing.

Manually Changing Page Breaks

If you want to see where Excel breaks your data
to a new printed page, you can select View >
Workbook Views > Page Break Preview. Not only
can you see blue dotted lines and page-number
labels (see Figure 9-16) to indicate the breaks,
you can change where the breaks occur.

To move a page break, position the mouse over
the blue lines until the mouse pointer turns into
a double-headed arrow. Click and drag the page
break lines into the desired position. Excel will
adjust the page scaling so that the information
fits on the requested number of pages.

Besides moving existing page breaks, you will
also be able to insert page breaks at any point
in the worksheet from the Page Break preview.
Page breaks can be placed vertically (between
columns) or horizontally (between rows). Select
the first cell in the row or column you want to
be placed on a new page and then choose Page
Layout > Page Setup > Breaks from the Ribbon.
Select Insert Page Break from the drop-down
menu. Excel adds a solid blue line to indicate a
manual page break as shown in Figure 9-17.

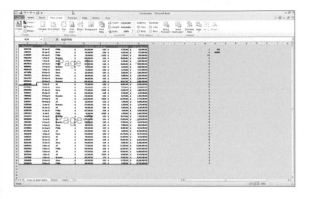

Figure 9-17
Manual page breaks appear as solid blue lines.

Creating Backgrounds

Pictures can add life and context to your worksheet data and the Page Layout tab offers an interesting option: add an image as a background on your worksheet. What makes this so interesting is that the image cannot be printed; it is only visible within Excel. This limitation can work well within a corporate environment where including an image, for example a corporate logo, might be a requirement.

Caution

Background images cannot be edited once they are inserted. Smaller images will be tiled to fill the sheet.

To add a sheet background, first open the worksheet upon which you want to add the background image, and then follow these steps:

1. Choose Page Layout > Page Setup > Background. Excel opens the Sheet Background dialog box.

2. Select a picture for the sheet background, and then click Insert. The image is placed behind the gridlines and cell contents, as shown in Figure 9-18.

Delete Background Button

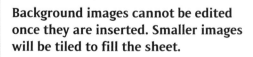

Figure 9-18
Background images cannot be printed.

Delete Your Background

The Backgrounds button changes to a Delete Background button once a background image has been inserted. Click this button to remove a background image from your worksheet.

Printing Gridlines and Headings

As a rule, worksheet elements are visible on the worksheet views, but are not printed. However, two of these sheet options can be printed.

▶ **Gridlines:** Lines between cells in the worksheet

▶ **Headings:** Row numbers and column letters

To force Excel to print these elements, click the Print check box under the appropriate option on the Page Layout tab as in Figure 9-19.

Figure 9-19
Sheet options can be printed.

Including Titles

In most instances data tables will include a label, or title, describing the data that will be included in that row or column. Because that information is only included once on the worksheet, it will print only once. If your worksheet is more than one page long, the second page will not include the descriptive title (see Figure 9-20).

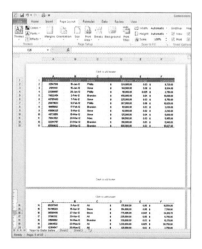

Figure 9-20
Multiple pages without titles.

You can use Page Layout tools to force Excel to repeat those titles on every page of your printed document. Choose Page Layout > Page Setup > Titles. Excel opens the Page Setup dialog box with the Sheet tab selected (see Figure 9-21).

Collapse Button

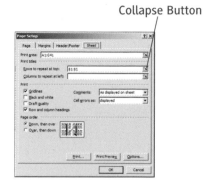

Figure 9-21
Specifying which titles to include on every page.

Then, follow these steps to repeat rows or columns on your printed document:

1. Click the Collapse button at the end of the Rows to Repeat at Top option. The dialog box is collapsed to show only that option box.

2. Use your mouse to select the row, or rows, that you want to repeat at the top of every page and click the Collapse button again to return to the full dialog box.

3. If necessary, repeat the process with the Columns to Repeat at Left option.

4. Click OK to close the dialog box.

Figure 9-22 illustrates the effect of repeating the row titles on this document. The second page now includes descriptive labels at the top of the page.

Figure 9-22
Row 1 is repeated on each page.

Adding Headers and Footers

HEADERS AND FOOTERS are text and images that appear at the top (header) and bottom (footer) of a printed page. They are repeated on all pages of a single print job and may include information such as the file name, page number, date and time, and a logo.

Excel includes a number of predefined headers and footers. All you have to do is tell Excel where to put the information. With the Page Layout view selected, follow these steps:

1. Click in the header or footer area. This area is divided into three sections: left, centered, or right based on where the text will be aligned on the page. Excel adds a new Header & Footer Tools Design tab.

2. Choose Header & Footer Tools Design > Header & Footer > Header (or Footer). The drop-down menu reveals several predefined text options (see Figure 9-23).

3. Select the option you want to add. Predefined text will be inserted into the center area of the header or footer.

Adding a Header/Footer in Normal View

You can also add a header or footer from the Normal view by choosing Insert > Text > Header & Footer from the Ribbon.

You are not limited to these predefined headers and footers. Table 9-3 indicates the elements that may be included in a custom header or footer.

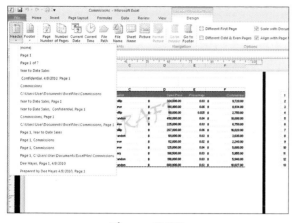

Figure 9-23
Predefined header and footer options.

To add a custom header or footer, select the Page Layout view and follow these steps:

1. Click in the area of the header or footer where you would like the custom text to be aligned on the page. Excel adds a new Header & Footer Tools Design tab.

2. Choose Header & Footer Tools Design > Header & Footer Elements and select any combination of the elements you want to see on your printed document. Excel inserts the code associated with the element, as shown in Figure 9-24. Alternatively, you can type directly into the header or footer area.

Table 9-3   Header and Footer Tools

Button	Code	Description
Page Number	&[Page]	Inserts the current page number
Number of Pages	&[Pages]	Inserts the total number of pages that will be printed
Current Date	&[Date]	Inserts the current date
Current Time	&[Time]	Inserts the current time
File Path	&[Path]&[File]	Inserts the complete path, including file name, for this workbook
File Name	&[File]	Inserts the file name for this workbook
Sheet Name	&[Tab]	Inserts the name of the worksheet as displayed on the sheet tab
Picture	&[Picture]	Enables you to insert a picture; also used for watermarks, as described in the next section
Format Picture		Displays the Format Picture dialog box to adjust the size and scale of the picture

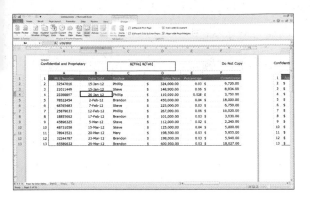

Figure 9-24
Customizing the header and footer.

3. Switch between the header and footer area of the page by choosing Header & Footer Tools Design > Navigation > Go to Header (or Go to Footer).

4. If you want to create a separate header or footer for the first page, or for odd and even pages, click the appropriate check boxes in the Options group of the Header & Footer Tools Design tab.

Figure 9-25 illustrates how these custom headers and footers can add useful information to your printed pages.

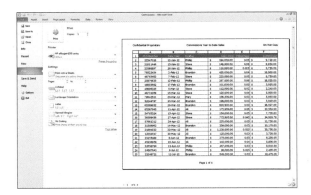

Figure 9-25
Previewing a custom header and footer.

Caution

Excel recognizes an ampersand (&) in the header or footer as part of its internal code and will ignore any ampersand you type unless you type it twice. For instance, to include the words "Cats & Dogs" in the header and footer, you need to type "Cats && Dogs."

Inserting a Watermark

YOU LEARNED EARLIER IN THIS CHAPTER that background images do not print, but there may be a very good reason for you to want to include an image on a printed document. You might want to include a company logo in the header or text across the body of the page to indicate that the material is confidential or is still a draft. A graphic that appears behind the text of a printed document, as illustrated in Figure 9-26, is called a *watermark*.

	A	B	C	D	E	F
1	MLS Number	Date Sold	Realtor	Sales Price	Percentage	Commission
2	32547016	15-Jan-12	Phillip	$ 324,000.00	0.03	$ 9,720.00
3	21011449	15-Jan-12	Steve	$ 148,900.00	0.06	$ 8,934.00
4	23388897	26-Jan-12	Phillip	$ 110,000.00	0.025	$ 2,750.00
5	78522454	2-Feb-12	Brandon	$ 450,000.00	0.04	$ 18,000.00
6	48765483	7-Feb-12	Steve	$ 225,000.00	0.03	$ 6,750.00
7	25879633	12-Feb-12	Phillip	$ 267,000.00	0.06	$ 16,020.00
8	18855662	17-Feb-12	Brandon	$ 101,000.00	0.03	$ 3,030.00
9	45896325	5-Mar-12	Steve	$ 112,000.00	0.02	$ 2,240.00
10	48731058	15-Mar-12	Steve	$ 125,000.00	0.04	$ 5,000.00
11	78943521	20-Mar-12	Mary	$ 198,500.00	0.03	$ 5,955.00
12	32244787	23-Mar-12	Brandon	$ 198,000.00	0.03	$ 5,940.00
13	65589632	29-Mar-12	Brandon	$ 600,900.00	0.03	$ 18,027.00

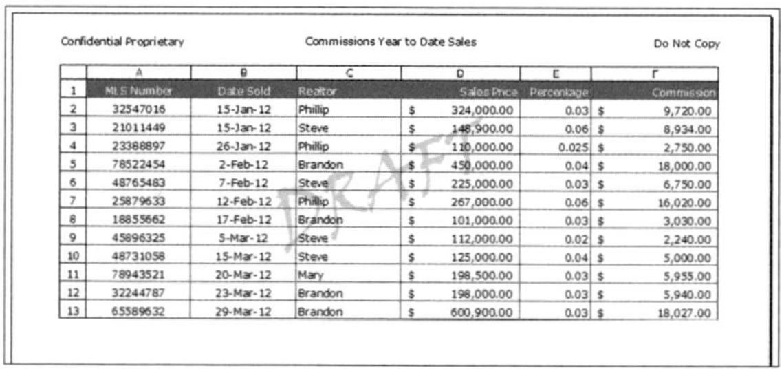

Figure 9-26
A watermark appears on every page of your printed document.

Tip

Keep watermark images simple and faintly colored so that they do not interfere with the readability of your data.

The same steps are required to add an image to your header or a watermark to the body of your document. The difference is the size of the graphic. Watermarks should include enough whitespace around the image to force it to fall in the center of your page. In either case, follow these steps.

1. Choose Insert > Text > Header & Footer from the Ribbon. Excel adds a new Design tab.
2. Click the Picture button on the Design tab of the Header & Footer Tools (see Figure 9-27). Excel opens the Insert Picture dialog box.
3. Select the desired picture from the file list and click Open to add the picture to your worksheet. Excel adds the picture code (&[Picture]) to the centered header selection box.

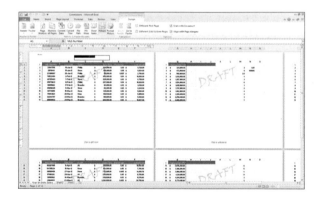

Figure 9-27
Adding a watermark to the header.

Modifying Watermarks

Watermark images, or any other image included in a header or footer, can be modified by choosing the Format Picture button in the Design tab.

Printing and Other

Output Formats

PICTURE YOURSELF BREAKING GROUND for your dream house. You have put in hours of planning and meetings with architects and designers so that you are prepared to lead your team of carpenters, electricians, and HVAC specialists in the construction. All you need is a copy of the plans to distribute to your crew. For many people, the ability to print out the product from their work is worth more than the time spent creating it in the first place.

Printing your Excel workbooks is easy. This chapter focuses on getting a complete printout of your work and showing you some simple tips and tricks along the way.

Printing Your Workbooks

CHAPTER 9, "PREPARING TO PRINT," focused on the steps necessary to ensure that the printed version of your worksheet displays exactly the way you envisioned. Now that all of your print settings are established, you are ready to see the fruits of your labor.

1. Make sure that your computer is connected to a printer.

2. Choose File > Print. Excel displays the Print Preview window.

3. Review your document in the preview window (see Figure 10-1) and adjust the print settings as necessary.

4. Click Print. Excel prints your file and closes the Print Preview window.

Tip

Use a keyboard shortcut, Ctrl+P, to access the Print Preview window.

Figure 10-1
Printing your worksheet from Excel 2010.

Handling Special Printing Needs

NOT ALL PRINT JOBS ARE the same and there are times when simply choosing File > Print is not enough. Instructions for handling some of those special cases can be found in this section.

Selecting Multiple Worksheets to Print

Suppose you had a workbook that kept track of your sales figures for the entire year. You might have chosen to create a separate worksheet for each month's sales and another worksheet that summarizes the year-to-date sales figures.

At the end of each month, you choose to print a hard copy of your month's sales and the summary information for your files. You could print the entire workbook and throw away the unwanted pages, or you could use this more eco-friendly alternative.

1. Select only the worksheet tabs that you want to print. Table 10-1 describes the key combinations required to select multiple worksheet tabs.

2. Choose File > Print and print the document as you normally would. Excel prints the tabs you selected and ignores all of the other tabs.

Table 10-1   Printing Multiple Worksheets

Print	Mouse and Keystroke Combination
A single worksheet	Click the sheet tab at the bottom of the Excel window.
Adjacent worksheets	Click the first sheet tab, then hold Shift and click the last sheet tab you want to print. Excel will highlight all of the sheet tabs in between.
Non-adjacent worksheets	Click the first sheet tab, then press Ctrl+additional sheet tabs you want to print. Figure 10-2 illustrates how Excel highlights only the selected tabs.

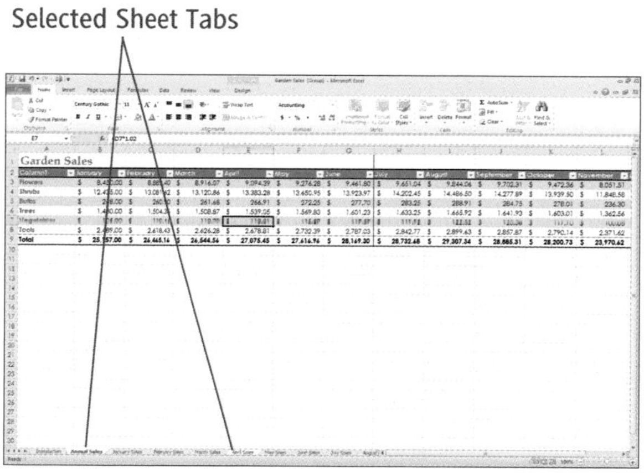

Selected Sheet Tabs

Figure 10-2
Selecting multiple sheets in a workbook.

Changing Orientation in the Same Print Job

As you discovered in Chapter 9, "Preparing to Print," orientation refers to the direction of the printed page. Excel will print your file in portrait (vertical) or landscape (horizontal) format. By default, Excel will print all of the pages in a workbook using the same page orientation. However, you can use the features provided in Excel to customize the orientation to fit your data.

You can specify the print orientation for each worksheet in a workbook file.

1. Select the first worksheet tab that you want to print.

2. Choose Page Layout > Page Setup > Orientation (arrow) and select the appropriate orientation for the data on the worksheet.

3. Select the worksheet tab corresponding to any other worksheets that you want to print and choose the appropriate orientation for each worksheet.

4. Select the worksheets that you want to print, following the steps in the previous section.

5. Choose File > Print and confirm the page orientation in the Print Preview window.

6. Click the Print button to print. Figure 10-3 demonstrates how pages in the same print job can have two different orientations.

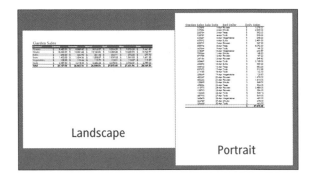

Landscape

Portrait

Figure 10-3
You can specify the print orientation for each worksheet in a print job.

Printing Multiple Pages on a Single Sheet

Excel worksheets are created to manage your data. They are generally formatted to serve that purpose, and not necessarily to accommodate printing. Have ever wished you could put the information from two worksheets together on a single printed page? Well, you can do that too. Just follow these steps:

1. Select a worksheet that will print on multiple pages. You could also select multiple worksheets.

2. Choose File > Print. Excel displays the Print Preview window.

Caution

Not all printer models will be able to perform this task.

3. Click the Printer Properties link under your selected printer. Excel displays a dialog box for your printer.

4. Click the Finishing tab and set the number of pages you want to print on a single page in the Pages Per Sheet drop-down menu, as shown in Figure 10-4.

5. Click OK to close the Properties dialog box.

6. Print the document as usual.

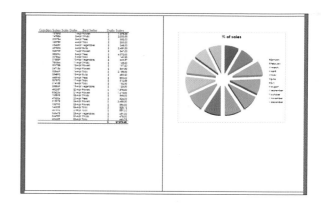

Figure 10-5
Both sheets must be formatted with
the same page orientation.

Figure 10-4
The Finishing tab.

Figure 10-5 illustrates an example with two worksheets printed on a single page. A chart and its associated data are presented together. Notice that both worksheets are printed in a portrait orientation. When printing multiple pages on a single sheet, you will need to keep the same page orientation for all worksheets.

Making Comments Visible

With Excel you can add comments to provide context to the data in your worksheet; think of them as an asterisk added to a data table you see in a newspaper. For instance, you might want to add a comment to your worksheet to explain that sales were low in a given month because the store had to be closed for a week during a flood.

Normally comments are visible on the worksheet only as a small red triangle in the upper-right corner of the cell. As you move the mouse pointer over a cell with a comment, a small pop-up window displays the comment (see Figure 10-6). You can learn more about adding comments to a cell in Chapter 14, "Collaborating with Others."

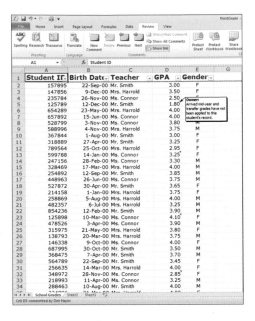

Figure 10-6
A small red triangle in the corner of the
cell indicates a comment.

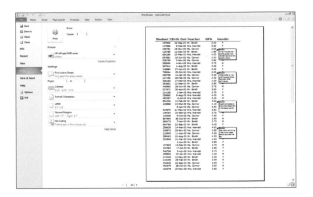

Figure 10-7
Comments can be printed as pop-ups
on the worksheet.

Figure 10-8
Comments can be printed at the end
of the document.

Excel does not print comments by default;
however, it does provide two methods by which
you can print your comments.

▶ **Print comments as displayed on the
worksheet.** In this case, Excel shows
the comments in their pop-up windows
(see Figure 10-7).

▶ **Print comments at the end of the document.** In this case, Excel prints comments
on the last page of the printed document
(see Figure 10-8).

Follow these steps to print comments with your
worksheets:

1. Choose Page Layout > Page Setup and click
   the Dialog Box Launcher to open the Page
   Setup dialog box.

2. Click the Sheet tab.

3. Click the Comments arrow and specify how you want your comment printed from the drop-down list (see Figure 10-9).

4. Click OK to close the dialog box.

5. Print your worksheet as usual.

Figure 10-9
The Comments option on the Sheet tab.

Showing Off Your Formulas

Formulas are equations that perform calculations on the contents of Excel's data cells. Formulas are extremely useful, as you discovered in Chapter 2, "Working with Formulas." So useful, in fact, that there is sure to come a time when you will want to see exactly what formulas you used in the worksheet.

To show the formulas you used in your worksheet, choose Formulas > Formula Auditing > Show Formulas. Excel displays the contents of each cell as they were entered in the Formula Bar. As illustrated in Figure 10-10, dates are converted to the internal code that Excel uses to perform calculations on them.

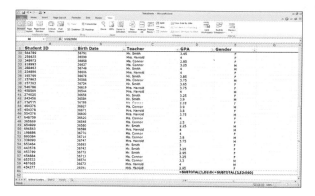

Figure 10-10
Showing formulas in Excel.

After Excel displays the formulas on the worksheet, you can print the worksheet as usual. Click the Show Formulas button again to hide the formulas and return the worksheet to normal.

Adjusting Cells for Large Formulas

In most cases, you will need to adjust the cell widths to accommodate the wider formulas.

Printing Named Ranges

As you learned in Chapter 1, "Creating a Basic Excel Worksheet," named ranges can be used to quickly find frequently used data. This data can be in adjacent cells or in non-adjacent cells. In both cases, set the print area using the named range as described in these steps.

1. Select the named range. Click the down arrow in the Name box of the worksheet and select your desired name from the list (see Figure 10-11). Excel highlights the cells selected by the named range.

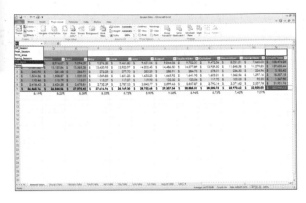

Figure 10-11
The named area is highlighted on the worksheet.

2. Choose Page Layout > Page Setup > Print Area (arrow) and select Set Print Area to make the print area the same as the named range, as shown in Figure 10-12.

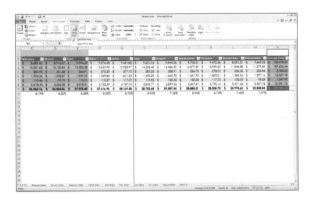

Figure 10-12
The print area is the same as the named range.

If the range is a set of adjacent cells, print the worksheet as usual. If the cells in the range are not adjacent, choose one of the following methods for printing:

▶ **Print the report as usual.** Excel will add a page break between each group of adjacent cells, forcing the range in this example to print on two pages (see Figure 10-13).

▶ **Print the report with multiple sheets on a single page as described earlier in this section.**

▶ **Use the named range to verify which rows or columns will be used and then hide the unused rows or columns as shown in Figure 10-14 before manually setting the print area.** Excel will not print hidden rows and columns and your named range will print as if the cells were adjacent.

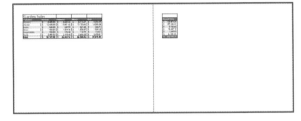

Figure 10-13
Excel adds a page break between non-adjacent ranges.

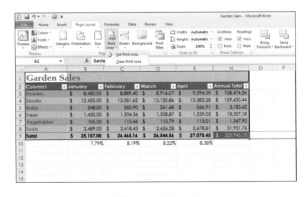

Figure 10-14
Unused columns F–M are hidden and will not print.

Printing Charts

CHARTS ARE A GRAPHIC VERSION of your data. Printing a worksheet that includes a chart will print both the chart and your associated data. You could also print the chart separate from the data on its own page. Just follow these steps:

1. Click to select the chart.

2. Choose File > Print. Excel displays the selected chart scaled to the full page in a Print Preview window (see Figure 10-15).

3. Print the chart as you would any other Excel document.

If necessary, you can easily use the print settings to force your color printer to print the chart in black and white. Click the Page Setup link at the bottom of the Print Preview window. Excel will display the Page Setup dialog box with a Chart tab instead of a Sheet tab, as shown in Figure 10-16. Click the Chart tab and select Print in Black and White.

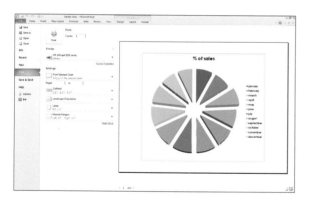

Figure 10-15
Print a chart.

Figure 10-16
You can print charts in black and white.

Creating a Chart Is Fun

Find out more about creating and formatting charts in Chapter 11, "Generating Excel Charts."

Printing a Draft

ALTHOUGH THE POWER OF EXCEL lies in its ability to manage data, it is also flexible enough to add images, charts, and colors to highlight your data. All of those "extras" take time to print and may not be necessary for all of your printing needs. You can reduce the amount of time a worksheet takes to print by stripping out all of the images, charts, and lines.

1. Choose Page Layout > Page Setup and click the Dialog Box Launcher to open the Page Setup dialog box.

2. Click the Sheet tab.

3. Click the Draft Quality option (see Figure 10-17).

4. Click OK to close the dialog box.

5. Print your worksheet as usual.

Printing a draft does not change the format of your worksheet; the text and colors remain, as illustrated in Figure 10-18. Read Chapter 12, "Inserting Illustrations," to learn more about adding images to your worksheets.

Figure 10-17
Setting the Draft Quality option.

Figure 10-18
Images, charts, and lines are not printed in draft format.

Changing Printers

IF YOU ARE LUCKY ENOUGH to have access to multiple printers, you will need to make sure that Excel sends your printed document to the correct printer. To specify another printer, follow these steps:

1. Choose File > Print to open the Print Preview window.

2. Click the Printer down-arrow and select your desired printer from the resulting list (see Figure 10-19).

3. Review your print preview and click Print when you are ready to send your document to the printer.

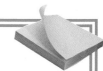

Caution

Anytime you change printers, remember to check the print preview by choosing File > Print to be sure that the new printer has retained your page break preferences and other printer settings.

Figure 10-19
Select the new printer from the drop-down menu.

Printing Without Opening Excel

ANOTHER QUICK PRINTING method is found in Windows Explorer, and you don't even have to open the file to do it. You won't be able to change any print settings, but Excel will print the active worksheet from the last time the file was opened.

Right-click on the file name and choose Print from the shortcut menu (see Figure 10-20). Windows will open the selected workbook in Excel (even if it is not already open) and print the file. Windows will then close the workbook and Excel (unless it was already open).

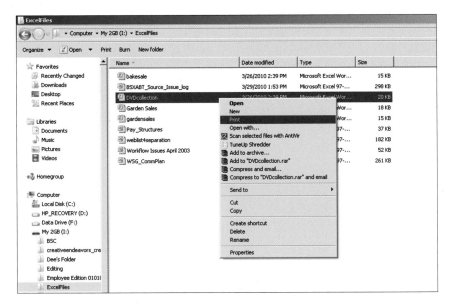

Figure 10-20
Print a worksheet from Windows Explorer.

Choosing an Alternative to Printing

IF YOU ARE SHARING your data with clients or co-workers in another location, it is not always practical to print a copy of your document. In cases like these, you should consider another alternative output.

Creating a PDF

PDF, or Portable Document Format, is a file format developed by Adobe Systems Incorporated that enables people to view and print documents even if they don't have access to the original application, in this instance, Excel.

1. Choose File > Save As to open the Save As dialog box.

2. Select PDF from the Save As Type drop-down menu, as illustrated in Figure 10-21.

3. Click the Save button in the Save As dialog box to save the files and return to your Excel file.

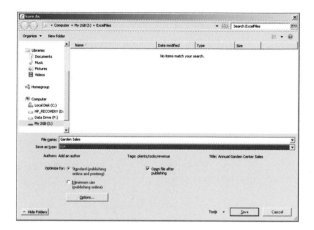

Figure 10-21
Save your file as a PDF document to be viewable by anyone.

Tip

PDF files can be opened in the free Adobe Reader available at http://www.adobe.com/downloads.

E-Mailing Your Worksheet

As an alternative to printing your worksheet and sending a hard copy to your audience, you could e-mail the file to your audience and have them print the file for themselves. Two important things to remember about this option:

▶ **If you are e-mailing your file, you run the risk of your viewers changing the file in such a way that they will not see the data as you intended.** Chapter 13, "Setting Security Options," will help you decide how much protection you want to add to your file, if any.

▶ **Whenever you open a worksheet, Excel restores the active worksheet and print settings from the point at which you last saved the file.** If you are e-mailing your file, make sure that you are aware of what your viewers will see when they open your file.

To e-mail a copy of your worksheet:

1. Choose File > Save & Send > Send Using Email.

2. Select your preferred Send As option:

   Send as Attachment: Opens an e-mail message with a copy of the file in the original file format (.xls or .xlsx) attached (see Figure 10-22).

   Send as PDF: Opens an e-mail message with a copy of the file in PDF format attached.

3. Complete the e-mail message as usual and click Send.

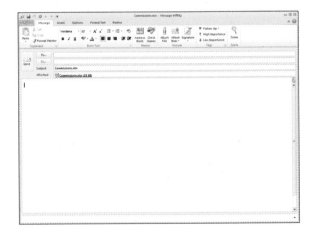

Figure 10-22
Use e-mail as an alternative to printing.

Printing from the Quick Access Toolbar

ONCE YOU HAVE ESTABLISHED all of the settings that will make your printed document the perfect reflection of your hard work, you use Excel's Quick Print feature to simplify your printing process.

First, add the Quick Print button to the Quick Access Toolbar, and then click the button to print.

1. Click the Customize Quick Access Toolbar button.

2. Click Quick Print on the drop-down menu (see Figure 10-23).

Caution

The Quick Print option will not print comments even if that option was selected in your print settings.

When you click the Quick Print button (see Figure 10-24), Excel sends your document to the Windows print queue—a sort of holding area before your document is sent to the printer. This is exactly what you need if your computer is not permanently connected to a printer. Excel displays a message (see Figure 10-25) during the Quick Print process informing you of its progress. You will not be able to edit your worksheet until after this message disappears.

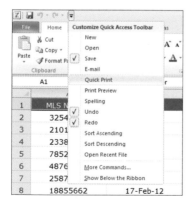

Figure 10-23
Quick Access Toolbar options.

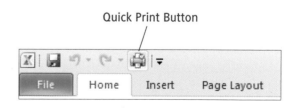

Figure 10-24
Click the Quick Print button to send your document to the print queue.

213

Figure 10-25
The Quick Print progress message.

Documents in the print queue will print as soon as your computer is connected to a printer. While documents are still in the print queue, you can cancel (delete) a print job or pause a job at the top of the queue in order to print another document sooner.

To affect documents in the print queue, follow these steps:

1. Double-click the printer icon in the far right of your Windows taskbar (see Figure 10-26).

Print Queue Icon

Figure 10-26
The Print Queue icon is found in the Windows taskbar.

2. Right-click on the Excel file name that you want to change.

3. Select Pause or Cancel from the shortcut menu (see Figure 10-27).

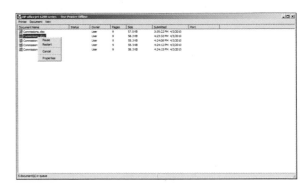

Figure 10-27
The Print Queue shortcut menu.

4. If necessary, select Restart from the shortcut menu to restart a paused document.

5. Choose Printer > Close to close the print queue window.

Print Preview a Different Way

The Print Preview command is also available from the Customize Quick Access Toolbar menu. Clicking Print Preview from the Quick Access Toolbar is a shortcut to choosing File > Print from the Ribbon.

Part III
Working with Graphics

Generating

Excel Charts

PICTURE YOURSELF TURNING YOUR text-and-number-filled worksheet into a chart, an easily understood graphical representation of your data. Charts turn tons of boring or potentially confusing data into a picture, a snapshot of the information that makes a statement. Sales are up? No need to wade through lots of other numbers to see that if the bar or column is taller than the one for last month or last quarter. Survey responses look good for your candidate? You can tell right away by looking at the Pie chart, and seeing that "Strongly Agree" was the most frequent answer, and shown by that slice being the biggest in the pie. Although charts aren't always appropriate—or even possible, depending on your data—they can make the difference between data that only those who entered it understand and data that anyone can grasp and make quick, effective use of.

Creating a Basic Chart

LUCKY FOR US ALL, given how important charts can be to the effective use and distribution of our data, they're really easy to create. They're even easier in Excel 2010, where simply selecting the data to be charted and clicking a button for the type of chart you want—Column, Bar, Pie, Line, and so on—gives you an instant chart.

Selected Data   Insert a Chart   The Value Axis Allows You to Quantify Each Plotted Data Point   Each Column Is a Data Point   The Category Axis Identifies Chart Data   Chart Legend

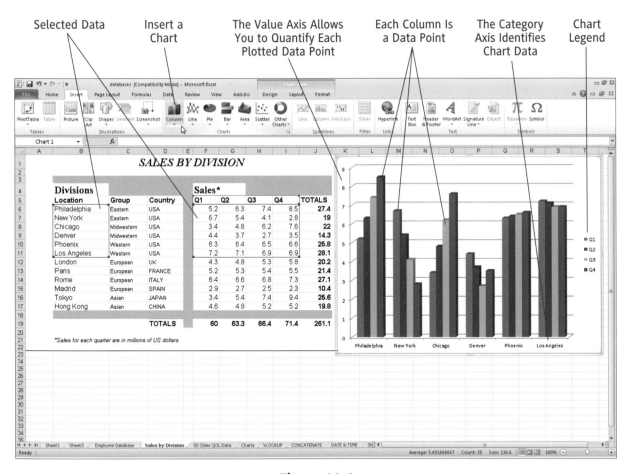

Figure 11-1
The selected data on the left winds up in a chart—with just a few clicks of the mouse.

218

Selecting the Right Source Data

The one tricky part of this very easy process is selecting the data to be charted. This is the point in the process with the largest margin for error, but you can eliminate that by understanding how charts work. Charts plot data points, which are grouped in logical data series, along a horizontal x or "category" axis, and a vertical y or "value" axis. Sales for a given city over the course of a year would be one series, with each of the month's data being the data points. If you're tracking multiple cities, as you will in the examples throughout this chapter, one quarter or month's worth of data for all the cities would be another collection of data points, making yet another data series. Figure 11-1 shows the source data and the resulting Column chart, where six cities' sales are plotted in the chart, on a quarterly basis. The quarters are in the chart's legend, to help you identify the colored bars and interpret the chart.

So inserting, or adding, a chart to your Excel worksheet is quite simple, but it does require a little preparation. First, you need to decide which data you want to plot in the chart, and at the same time—because it affects the amount of data you select—which kind of chart you want to create. You also want to decide if the chart will live on its own worksheet or be placed alongside the data from which it is created. You can always move a chart after you've created it (as I'll discuss later in this chapter), so that's not something you have to be completely sure of from the start.

Choosing the Right Kind of Chart

Although you'll actually select the chart type after you've selected your data, it's important to decide on the type of chart you'll be creating before you make the selection. Excel gives you six main choices for chart types (all listed on the Insert menu, as shown in Figure 11-1), plus an Other Charts button, which gives you five more types to choose from. Your six main choices, however, are:

▶ **Column:** As shown in Figure 11-2, you can create five different types of Column charts, ranging from 2D rectangular columns to 3D pyramid columns. Each of the five types has at least three subtypes, with individual columns for each data point or stacked columns, showing multiple data points per column. Your choice is both cosmetic—do you prefer the more modern 3D look, or do you want a simple, flat, 2D chart—and logical. The logical part of the decision rests on choosing between individual and stacked columns, and whether or not the columns are on one row or in multiple rows. If you strive for real simplicity, with little or no contemplation required of the person viewing the chart, go for individual columns in one row.

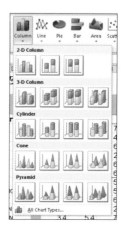

Figure 11-2
Choose the kind of Column chart you want to create.

▶ **Line:** The Line chart button offers 2D and 3D lines, and allows you to choose whether or not each of the data points plotted over the course of each line is represented by a dot. Using dots makes the value of each point more obvious, but not using them allows for a more obvious, uncluttered trend to be depicted. If you don't care exactly what the sales were in a particular month but you want it to be completely obvious that sales have been rising steadily, a 2D line with no dots will be your best choice.

Column, Line, and Bar Charts, Oh My!

Column, Line, and Bar charts are great for showing both trends and comparisons. If the columns in a chart, for example, show sales figures over the course of a year, the height of the columns not only shows what the sales were for each location, but because they appear in date order, they also show the sales trend over the 12 months. The columns, lines, and bars can also be compared, so that one can easily see that one location's sales are higher or lower than another location's sales. The other great feature of Column, Line, and Bar charts? They can show multiple data series in one chart (unlike Pies, as discussed shortly). So you can pack a lot of data into a still-easy-to-understand chart.

▶ **Pie:** As shown in Figure 11-3, your Pie chart options include 2D and 3D variations, plus pies with an optional bar. You can also choose a pie with an exploded slice, which means a slice that's pulled away from the pie for emphasis.

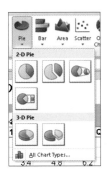

Figure 11-3
Compare your data in a simple or more complex Pie chart.

Don't Mix Your Pies

Pie charts can show only one data series at a time. If you want to show sales for several locations for one quarter or one month, that's one data series. If you want to look at a single location for the entire year, that's another data series, and would be in a separate pie, not combined in one pie. Why? Because for a Pie chart to be effective, each slice needs to be a different color. If you're charting the New York location's sales for a whole year, you'd have 12 different-colored slices, and all would be clear. If you tried to show both New York and Los Angeles' sales for a year, you'd have 24 slices, and need 24 different colors—and it would be impossible to simply compare, say, March sales for New York and Los Angeles, in such a complex pie.

▶ **Bar:** Bar charts are the same as Column charts, except that the bars run horizontally, rather than vertically. Your choices here are the same as in the Column button menu, in terms of dimensions and shapes.

▶ **Area:** An Area chart combines the trend and comparison features of Column, Bar, and Line charts with the simple comparison features of a pie. As shown in Figure 11-4, your choices are between 2D and 3D Area charts that stack or appear in rows.

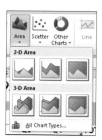

Figure 11-4
Area charts can be a useful variation on Column and Pie charts.

▶ **Scatter:** Scatter charts are used to show frequency—the number of people who gave a particular response to a survey question, medical test results, anything that shows how often something happens over time or under specific circumstances. They're a little more difficult for the viewer to interpret, so you'll want to use them only when the viewers are familiar with the data and the information that the chart is meant to impart. Figure 11-5 shows your Scatter chart options, including lines connecting the scattered dots.

Figure 11-5
Study and survey data can be plotted to show frequency in a Scatter chart.

Other Charts Too

What about the Other Charts button? It offers five additional chart types for you to choose from—Stock, Surface, Doughnut, Bubble, and Radar. These are less commonly used chart types, but some of them, such as Doughnut and Surface charts, can be used in the same way as Pie, Line, and Area charts, respectively. Figure 11-6 shows the Other Charts menu, and the variations on each of the five chart types.

Figure 11-6
Specialized needs find a home in the Other Charts category.

Selecting Chart Data and Creating the Chart

So now that you know what kind of chart you need—one that shows comparisons, trends, or both, most likely—you can begin choosing the data that will be plotted in the chart. To do so, follow these steps:

1. Open the worksheet containing the data you want to chart.

2. Using your mouse and/or keyboard, select the cells containing the data you want to plot in the chart. You should include column and row headings, as shown in Figure 11-7, because this information will become part of the chart, populating the category axis and the legend.

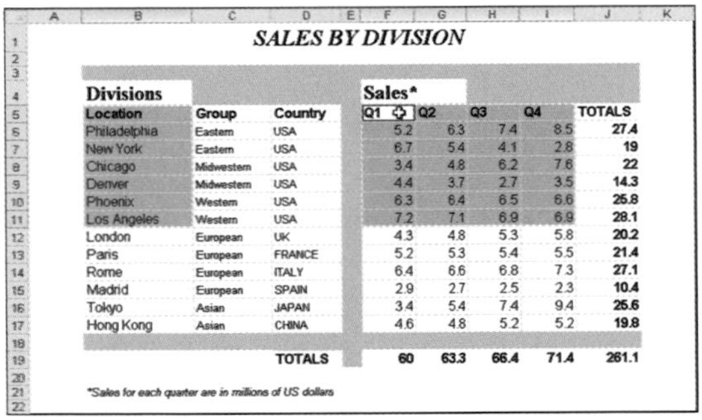

Figure 11-7
Select the headings and numeric data that you want to use in your chart.

3. Click the Insert tab to display that ribbon.

4. Click the button for the type of chart you want—Column, Line, Pie, Bar, Area, Scatter, or one of the Other Charts—and make a selection from the drop-down menu.

5. Observe the resulting chart, shown in Figure 11-8, overlapping your data.

Chart Tools Section of the Ribbon Is Now Active

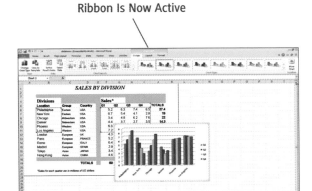

Figure 11-8
The default location for the chart is rarely where you want it—it covers the data used to make it.

6. As needed, drag the chart to an unpopulated section of the worksheet, so your data is not obscured. Figure 11-9 shows a chart in transit.

Tip

When moving your chart within the same worksheet, mouse over the border and keep an eye on your mouse pointer—when it turns to a four-headed arrow, you're ready to drag the chart to a new location.

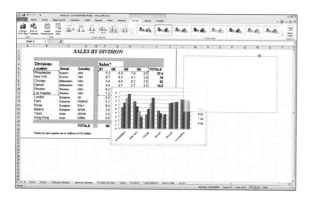

Figure 11-9
Drag and drop your chart to a spot where
it doesn't cover up any data.

Tip

The Move Chart button (on the Design
tab, within the Chart Tools section of the
ribbon) opens a dialog box asking where
you want to take your chart. Shown in
Figure 11-11, you can choose New Sheet
(which creates and names the new sheet
for you) or choose an existing sheet from
the Object In option. Make your choice
and click OK—the chart is moved automatically, ready for formatting and
enhancement, as needed.

If you want to move your chart to its own sheet,
it's easy to do—you can hover over one of the
chart's borders, and when your mouse pointer
turns to a four-headed arrow, right-click. From
the resulting pop-up menu (shown in Figure
11-10), choose Cut. Then go to the worksheet
where you want to place the chart, and right-
click again, choosing Paste from the pop-up
menu. Once the chart is in place, you can
enlarge it even more, for greater visibility.

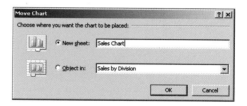

Figure 11-11
Use the Move Chart dialog box to send your
chart packing—to a new or existing sheet
elsewhere in the open workbook.

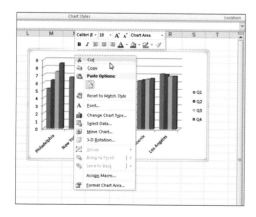

Figure 11-10
Cut and then paste your chart to a new
worksheet—or an existing sheet with more room
on it—to give your chart some real elbow room.

Resizing Your Chart

Once your chart is where you want it (assuming you've got it in a worksheet with other content, not on its own sheet, where resizing is not needed), you can resize it easily—just point to any corner, and when your mouse turns to a two-headed arrow (as shown in Figure 11-12), press and hold the Shift key and drag. Drag outward to enlarge the chart, or inward to reduce its size. Why press the Shift key? To maintain your chart's *aspect ratio*, or proportions. If you drag without pressing that key, you risk elongating or narrowing the chart. Although that's okay to do—and sometimes you want to do just that—sometimes it distorts the chart's content and size relative to other objects—the legend, titles, and so on.

Figure 11-12

Resize your chart by dragging from a corner handle.

Tip

If you elect to place your chart on a new sheet (in the Move Chart dialog box), it is automatically full size within that new sheet, and therefore cannot be resized. Although your mouse pointer will turn to a two-headed arrow when you point to a corner, you are not able to make the chart larger or smaller if it's on its own sheet.

Changing the Chart Options

ANY ASPECT OF YOUR CHART can be changed. Anything. You can change to a different type of chart entirely, you can change the color of your columns, bars, lines, or pie slices, you can add titles, you can move and resize the legend, and you can add labels to your chart to identify data and values. Figure 11-13 shows a Pie chart with a chart title and slice labels that indicate the percentage of the total that each slice represents.

Switching Your Chart's Focus

The focus of your chart is determined by which data is on the category (the X, or horizontal) axis. Why? Because this is the most obvious and first-noticed information in your chart if it's a Column or Line chart, two of the most commonly used chart types. Excel makes it easy to swap the data that's currently in your legend for what's currently in the category axis, thus changing the focus of your chart. Still not clear on this? Look at Figure 11-14, where the chart on the left has the cities in the category axis and the quarters in the legend, and the chart on the right that's set up in the opposite way—quarters along the category axis and cities in the legend. Neither chart is "better" than the other, but depending on your audience, one of the charts will be more effective than the other. Salespeople, for example, who are likely to be competing with other locations' sales numbers, will want to see the city data along the category axis, whereas accountants or auditors will be more interested in when the sales were made, and want to see quarterly data along the horizontal axis.

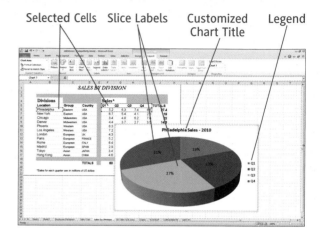

Selected Cells   Slice Labels   Customized Chart Title   Legend

Figure 11-13
Want a title on your chart? Need to add more information? It's all just a few clicks away in the Chart Tools section of the ribbon.

Figure 11-14
Switch your rows and columns to change the focus of your chart.

To switch your chart's focus, click once on the chart to activate it, and then go to the Design tab in the Chart Tools section of the ribbon. The first button in the Data group, also shown in Figure 11-14, is the Switch Row/Column button. One click and your legend and category axis data switch—a second click and they switch back. It couldn't be easier!

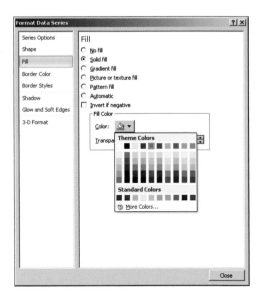

Figure 11-15
Use the Format Data Series dialog box to change any aspect of the series you double-clicked.

Tip

If your Pie chart ever appears as one big slice—no segments and all one color—click the Switch Row/Column button. Chances are, you've got your data in the wrong place (row vs. column), and clicking the button will give you the individually colored slices you seek.

Changing Chart Colors

When you click one of the Chart buttons—to insert any kind of chart, based on selected data—a default set of colors is applied to the bars, columns, pie slices, lines, or other shapes. If you don't like one or more of these colors, you can easily change them. Here are some of your options:

▶ **Double-click any column, bar, slice, or line.** As soon as you do, the Format Data Series dialog box opens, as shown in Figure 11-15, through which you can choose new Fill and Border Colors, or even customize the shadows and other 3D effects in your chart. Click the aspect of the series you want to change, using the list of Series Options on the left side of the dialog box, and use the resulting tools to make your changes.

▶ **Use the Format tab.** Found within the Chart Tools section of the ribbon, the Format tab offers Shape Fill, Shape Outline, and Shape Effects tools you can use to change the appearance of one or all of your bars, columns, slices, or lines. To select just one data point for a change, click once on it in the chart, and you'll see handles on the single slice or all the points in a single data series (all the Los Angeles bars or columns, for example). The changes you then make using the Format tools will apply only to the selected point/series. Figure 11-16 shows the Shape Fill drop-down menu, and all the options it offers for changing the fill of the selected data point or series.

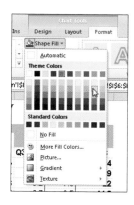

Figure 11-16
Choose from Theme Colors, Standard Colors, or apply pictures, gradients, or textures to the selected data point or series.

Tip

Color choices for the various parts of your chart aren't just cosmetic. Sure, you like blue, or maybe your company's logo is green, so you want everything to match. But another thing to consider is color blindness. Ten percent of men and 7% of women have a form of color blindness that makes it difficult or impossible to tell green from red. This means that you should avoid using green and red together, because to this portion of the population, both colors will just look gray. This is especially bad if the colors are adjacent, making, for example, two pie slices meld together into one big gray slice.

▶ **Use the Design tab.** This tab, also found within the Chart Tools section of the ribbon, offers some preset color combinations that will recolor your entire chart— all the bars, columns, lines, or slices. To use them, just click on the chart itself (to make sure it's the active element on your worksheet) and then just click the Chart Styles button for the color scheme you'd like to use. Note that there's a scroll bar at the end of this section of the ribbon —meaning there are lots of styles to choose from, in addition to the first eight that appear as shown in Figure 11-17.

lines that give quantitative context to your chart's bars, columns, or lines). Figure 11-18 shows a chart with customized formatting applied to each of these chart elements.

Figure 11-17
The Chart Styles buttons instantly recolor all the bars, columns, lines, or slices in the active chart.

Formatting Your Chart Wall, Area, and Gridlines

As is the case with your data points, you can also easily edit the appearance of your chart wall (the background, which is white, by default), the chart area (also white by default, it's the space within the wall that contains your plotted data), and gridlines (the horizontal and/or vertical

Chart Area Has | Gridlines | Chart Wall Has
Solid Color Fill | Are Thicker | Gradient Fill

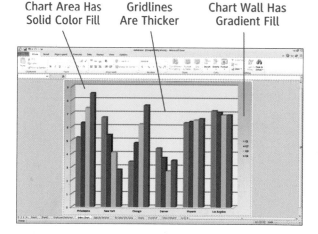

Figure 11-18
Every filled area of your chart—not just its bars, columns, and slices—can be re-colored or filled with a gradient, picture, texture, or pattern.

Here are your options for formatting these elements of your active chart:

▶ **Double click.** Whichever part of your chart you want to reformat, double-click it. An appropriate Format dialog box appears. Figure 11-19 shows the Format Chart Area dialog box, which allows you to customize the area's appearance, with options from Solid, Gradient, Picture, Texture, or Pattern fills. Whichever one you pick (by clicking the radio button next to it) results in a set of options appearing to allow you to customize that effect. Figure 11-19 shows the Texture fill options, and you can see the chart behind it, filled with a subtle textured effect.

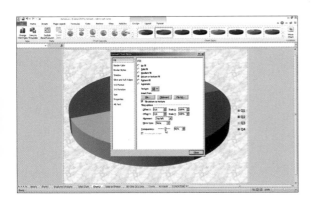

Figure 11-19
Pick the fill you want to apply to your chart area, and see it applied as you tweak the settings in the Format Chart Area dialog box.

▶ **Use the Format tab.** The same Shape Fill tool you used to color a single data point or series can be used to fill the chart area or floor. Whichever one is selected, using the Shape Fill drop-down menu and making a color selection will recolor it.

▶ **Click the Format Selection button.** Found on the Format tab, this first button on the ribbon opens the Format dialog box for whichever chart element is selected. Figure 11-20 shows the Format Major Gridlines dialog box, and your options for changing the color of the lines. There is also a Line Style option on the left, which allows you to make your lines thicker or thinner. To makes sure this is the dialog box you get, either click on one of the gridlines in your chart, or click the button above the Format Selection button, which gives you a list of the available chart elements you can reformat.

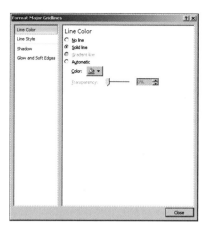

Figure 11-20
Want lighter, darker, brighter, or more subtle gridlines? Here's your solution: the Format Major Gridlines dialog box.

Tip

If you're using a 3D chart style, you can change its 3D rotation. Click the 3D Rotation button (see the Layout tab's Background group, within Chart Tools) and use the resulting dialog box (the Format Chart Area dialog box, which opens to facilitate formatting other aspects of the chart, too) and change the rotation using the X and Y fields to move it horizontally and vertically. The chart changes as you click the triangles on these two fields or after you enter new values manually. Once you like what you see, click the Close button.

Customizing Your Legend

Second only to the category axis in terms of the impact on a chart's usability, the legend is very important. The legend lets people know what the colors in your chart mean, so that they know, for example, that the blue columns are New York and the green ones are Philadelphia. Without the legend, your charts—regardless of the type—would be pretty, but useless.

Your legend can be customized in two ways. You can format the font used, picking a different font entirely, or simply making the text larger, for better legibility. Formatting options are found on the Format tab, where you can choose from Text Fill, Text Outline, and Text Effects options (see Figure 11-21) and on the Home tab, where your standby tools for Font, Size, Style, and Color are found in the Font section of the ribbon.

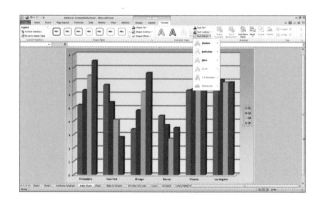

Figure 11-21
Format your legend text with the Format tab's Text tools.

You can also format the placement of the legend, placing it on the left, right, or along the bottom of the chart. To make these changes, double-click the legend, and use the resulting Format Legend dialog box, shown in Figure 11-22.

Figure 11-22
Pick the position for your legend from this list of five choices.

Tip

Don't forget the Layout tab, for anything that pertains to the placement and structure of your chart. Along with a Legend button, which provides the same options for the position of your legend that are found in the Format Legend dialog box, you can customize the placement of your axes, gridlines, chart wall, and chart floor.

Adding Titles

Just like your worksheet probably benefits from a title—typically housed in a row above the data—your chart can also benefit from something to tell viewers what the chart is about.

"2010 Sales" is an example, as shown in Figure 11-23. The chart also has a category axis title, "US Locations," to clarify that the cities listed are just those in the US, not including the other international locations the company has.

Chart Title   Axis Titles
Button   Button

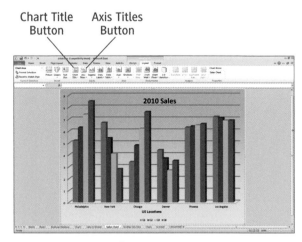

Figure 11-23
Give your chart a title to help clarify its subject.

To add a title like the one shown in Figure 11-23 —or to add titles to further explain your category or value axes—use these tools, found on the Layout tab, within the Chart Tools section of the ribbon:

▶ **Chart Title:** This button offers three options: None, Centered Overlay Title, and Above Chart. If you choose either of the last two options, a Chart Title text box is automatically added to your chart, as shown in Figure 11-24. To change the instructional text to your chart's desired title, just click on the text and begin typing. Your text appears on the Formula bar, and when you press Enter, it replaces the "Chart Title" text. You can then use the Home and Format tabs to format the text.

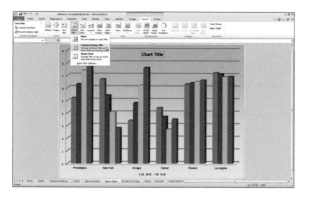

Figure 11-24
"Chart Title" is easily replaced with the chart title that makes sense for the active chart.

▶ **Axis Title:** This button works much like the Chart Title button, except it gives you two choices (Primary Horizontal Axis Title and Primary Vertical Axis Title), and each one has a submenu of choices, as shown in Figure 11-25. Pick an option that adds a title (such as Vertical Title, for a value axis title that runs up and down), and then type your text to replace the instructional text. After typing and inserting the title (by pressing Enter), you can use the Home and Format tabs to format the title's size and color.

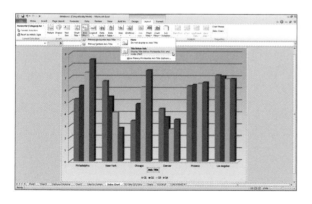

Figure 11-25
Clarify your category (horizontal) or value (vertical) axis with a title.

Add Text Boxes to a Chart

Axis and chart titles aren't the only text you can add to your chart. You can also add random text boxes, appearing anywhere you want them on the chart—overlapping the chart area, to point out or explain a particular data point, or anywhere overlapping the chart wall. To add such a text box, click the Text Box button on the Layout tab. Your mouse pointer turns into a crosshair, which you can use to draw a box the size you want the text box to be. Once you draw the box and release the mouse, you see a blinking cursor, awaiting your text. Type the text and then use the Home tab's formatting tools to dress up the text as desired. If you have more text than will fit in the box, use the white handles to resize the box.

Enhancing Your Chart with Data Labels and Tables

Sometimes between chart and axis titles, the category axis labels, and the legend, you still need to clarify or provide details pertaining to some or all of the data in your chart. Although it's not a good idea to clutter your chart with too much stuff, you can add data labels (such as the Line chart labels shown in Figure 11-26) and/or a data table (as shown in Figure 11-27) to show the actual data behind the chart's bars, columns, slices, and lines.

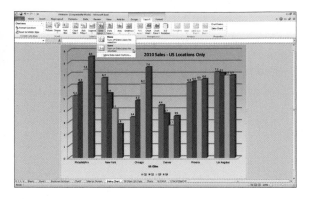

Figure 11-26
Each point along the line is now clearly
quantified with the actual data.

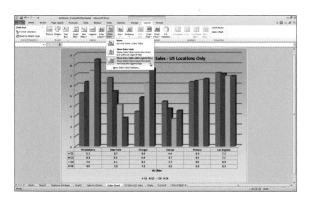

Figure 11-27
A table of the data that was included in your
chart provides more details for viewers
who want to know exact figures.

Adding Data Labels

To add data labels, click the Data Labels button
and pick Show. The values for each of your data
points appear automatically. Once the labels are
in place, you can move them by dragging them
with your mouse, and you can format them
using the Home tab's tools to increase font size,
change font color, and so on. Figure 11-28 shows
the labels enlarged, courtesy of the Home tab's
font size tool.

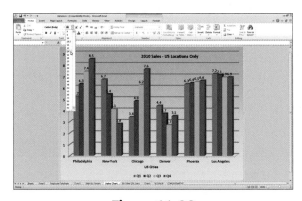

Figure 11-28
If you want data labels, you might as
well be able to read them.

Label Your Pie

The options for data labels are different for
Pie charts. Your choices are more than None
and Show—you get to choose between various positions (Center, Inside End, Outside
End, Best Fit), and if you pick More Data
Labels Options, the Format Data Labels
dialog box (shown in Figure 11-29) allows
you to convert your data labels to a percentage, so that each slice is labeled with the
percentage that slice represents in reference
to the entire pie's value.

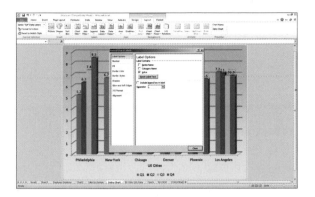

Figure 11-29
The Label Options tab within the Format Data Labels dialog box allows you to choose what information the labels will contain.

Tip

If you want it to be clear that your data represents dollars rather than units—so that if the label reads "8.5," people know that's millions of US dollars—convert your labels to Currency, using the Number category in the Format Data Labels dialog box. You can also make this kind of conversion for your value axis (through the Format Axis dialog box), so that the values on that vertical axis are shown with dollar signs ($).

Adding a Data Table

To add a data table, click the Data Table button and pick either Show Data Table or Show Data Table with Legend Keys. The former simply puts a grid on the chart with the chart's data in it, in columns and rows, matching the way the data is plotted in the chart. The latter ties the table data to the legend by repeating the legend colors in the table. Figure 11-30 shows the other options for formatting your table, available through the Format Data Table dialog box. You can open this dialog box by double-clicking the table once it's created, or by choosing More Data Table options from the Data Table button drop-down menu.

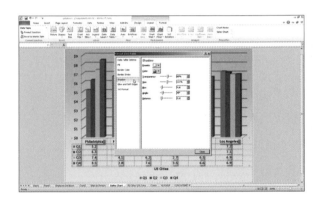

Figure 11-30
Customize your data table's placement, fill, or border. You can even give it a drop shadow.

Changing Chart Types

This is probably the trickiest thing you can do to an existing chart. Why? Because many times, the data you selected, with the original chart type in mind, isn't conducive to any other kind of chart. Or perhaps the formatting you've applied will conflict once the new chart type is applied. Lots of things can "go wrong," in that you won't love the chart you end up with after changing to a new type of chart. It's a relatively safe prospect if all you're doing is going from, say, a 2D Column chart to a 3D Column chart, or if you're changing to a Line chart with dots at each data point, instead of the one you have now with no dots. Changing from a Column or Bar chart to a Pie? It may be more trouble than simply making a new chart, because a Pie chart should only plot one data series, and your Column, Bar, or Line chart may have multiple data series in it.

If you're still game for a change in chart types, here's how it's done:

1. Click on the chart to activate it. This is necessary only if your chart is on a worksheet with data—if it's on a Chart Sheet (if you chose to place it on a new sheet when you created it or when you chose to move it), the chart is active whenever that sheet is active.

2. View the Design tab, and click the Change Chart Type button.

3. In the resulting Change Chart Type dialog box (shown in Figure 11-31), pick the type of chart you want from the list on the left, and then pick the exact chart within that type from the choices on the right.

4. Click OK to apply the new chart type.

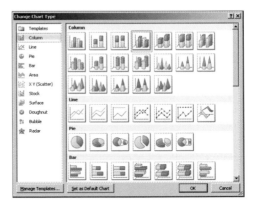

Figure 11-31
Pick a chart type, any chart type, that's a good match for the data you're plotting in the chart.

Tip

If your change in chart types creates problems in terms of new or changed elements in your chart, you can add or remove the legend (use the Layout tab's Legend button), add or remove data labels (also on the Layout tab), and tweak things like gridlines, titles, and the colors of your chart, as needed. If the chart type you've chosen has elements the previous type did not—such as grid-lines, which would not have been present in a Pie chart—you can format these new items to match the current formatting, which is preserved through the process of changing chart types.

Figure 11-32
Work with the Select Data Source dialog box to reset your chart's data to include additional cells, fewer cells, or an entirely new range of cells.

Adding/Removing Data to/from a Chart

If it turns out that your new chart type would be better served by more or less data being included, you can reset the chart data by using the Select Data button on the Design tab. Click this button and revisit your worksheet, as shown in Figure 11-32. Move the dialog box aside (or shrink it) and drag through the cells you want to now include in your chart. You can use the Ctrl key as you click or drag through cells to add to the existing selection, or start from scratch by dragging a new selection that replaces the existing one.

Be Sure to Update Your Legend

The Legend Entries and Axis Labels sections of the Select Data Source dialog box allow you to make sure your new/changed selection is properly reflected in the legend and within the chart's axes. Use the Add, Edit, and Remove buttons to update the legend, and click the Edit button to tweak the contents of the relevant axis (this option may vary depending on the type of chart you're now using).

Inserting

Illustrations

PICTURE YOURSELF AS A CHILD IN A CANDY STORE. Before you are bin after bin of colorful choices: licorice, chocolates, mints, hard candies, and soft candies. An endless array of goodies is available and you want them all. You take handfuls at a time and begin to eat. It doesn't take long before you realize exactly why your mother limited your sugar intake. As an adult you know that sometimes quality is better than quantity.

Excel, as with the other Microsoft Office applications, includes several tools you can use to add interest to what might otherwise be just a collection of numbers. These tools enable you to add pictures, shapes, and arrows, and even a set of professional-grade graphics, called SmartArt.

Remember, the power of Excel is the way in which it handles data. The ability to add graphic elements to your data is exciting, but newbies might find themselves adding so many illustrations that the data is overwhelmed. Illustrations should only be added to enhance your data.

Designing with Illustrations

IN EXCEL, AS WITH OTHER Microsoft Office applications, illustrations are any type of graphical content objects that you want to add to you file. These objects are found on the Ribbon's Insert tab (see Figure 12-1). You learned about charts in Chapter 11, "Generating Excel Charts," but there are many other types of graphic objects, including your own photographs and saved images as well as clipart drawings and photographs from Microsoft's collection.

You could also add a picture that has not been saved by copying it to the Microsoft Clipboard. With your mouse over the object, right-click to open a context menu. Select Copy to add the image to the Clipboard. In Excel, open the Clipboard by choosing the Home > Clipboard Dialog Box Launcher, and click the image to add it to your worksheet (as shown in Figure 12-2).

Figure 12-1
The Ribbon's Insert tab.

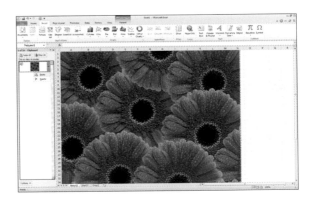

Figure 12-2
Adding a picture using the Clipboard.

Adding Saved Pictures

Microsoft defines pictures as any graphic content saved on your computer, which means that this category includes digital photographs as well as lineart or engineering drawings. To insert a picture, select the cell in which you want to place your picture and follow these steps:

1. Choose Insert > Illustrations > Picture. Excel opens the Insert Picture dialog box.

2. Select the desired image from your computer and click Insert.

3. Excel inserts the image you selected and opens the Ribbon to a new tab, Picture Tools Format.

Deselecting Your Picture

Once a picture is inserted, Excel selects the object so that you can immediately edit it. You can deselect the picture by clicking anywhere else on the worksheet.

Using Clipart

Microsoft Excel includes hundreds of clipart images, but thousands more are available if you have access to the Internet. The images stored as Microsoft clipart are free for you to use without restriction. Using a familiar search interface, you are sure to find a clipart image to suit any topic. Clipart images come in a variety of formats:

- ▶ **Illustrations:** Lineart drawings in color and black and white.

- ▶ **Photographs:** You can find digital photography on a variety of subjects.

- ▶ **Video:** This category includes any moving images, including animated .gif files.

- ▶ **Audio:** An audio file plays a sound, such as bells or clapping, when activated.

Choosing Insert > Illustrations > Clip Art from the Ribbon opens the Clip Art pane. The pane opens on the right side of your Excel worksheet and stays open until you close it (see Figure 12-3). To insert a clipart image, follow these steps:

1. Choose Insert > Illustrations > Clip Art. Excel opens the Clip Art pane.

2. In the Search For box, type a word or phrase that describes the image you want. The more specific you are, the fewer choices will be available. For example, typing *business* will find people, buildings, currency, and several other options. Typing *business telephone* will find office phones and people talking on the phone.

3. Click the Include Office.com content option if you have access to the Internet.

Figure 12-3
The Clip Art pane.

4. Click the arrow to the right of the Results Should Be box and select the appropriate file type from the drop-down menu (see Figure 12-4). If you are not sure what type of file you are looking for, click the All Media Types option.

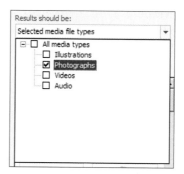

Figure 12-4
The Clip Art media types.

5. Click the Go button, or press Enter. Excel displays all of the images that match the search criteria.

6. Click the desired image, or click the arrow and choose Insert from the menu (see Figure 12-5). Excel inserts the image you selected and opens the Picture Tools Format tab.

Figure 12-5
The selected clipart image is inserted into your worksheet.

Formatting Illustrations

WHEN AN ILLUSTRATION is added to your worksheet, and whenever it is selected, Excel adds a new Picture Tools Format tab to the Ribbon (see Figure 12-6). The tools on this tab give you control over the appearance of the illustrations you've added. This tab contains four groups: Adjust, Picture Styles, Arrange, and Size. Each of these groups is described in the following sections.

Use Live Preview for a Quick Look

Excel's Live Preview makes formatting easy. With the illustration selected, as the mouse moves over formatting options, the formatting change will be applied temporarily. Once you've selected the option, the change will become permanent.

Figure 12-6
The Picture Tools Format tab.

Adjusting Illustrations

With the illustration selected, the tools on the Adjust group allow you to alter the image in the following ways.

▶ **Corrections:** Adjusts the brightness and contrast of the illustration. Additionally, this option can sharpen or soften the picture.

▶ **Color:** Changes the tone and saturation of the color on the picture. This option can also apply a color filter over the entire picture, as shown in Figure 12-7.

Figure 12-7
Applying a color filter over a picture.

▶ **Artistic Effects:** Applies an effect that transforms the image to appear as if it were created in some other medium. Some of these effects are chalk sketch (see Figure 12-8), pencil sketch, blur, light box, and several more.

▶ **Compress Pictures:** Reduces the file size of the image. Reducing the file size may reduce the quality of the image.

▶ **Change Picture:** Opens the Insert Picture dialog box, which allows you to choose a replacement for the existing picture. The new picture will be inserted into the same size and shape as the existing picture.

▶ **Reset Picture:** Restores the default settings for the picture and strips out any adjustments you've already made to the picture.

Figure 12-8
Applying the chalk sketch artistic effect.

Applying Picture Styles

The Picture Styles group has tools to change the shape of the picture, add a border, add the picture to a SmartArt graphic (see that section later in this chapter), and apply special effects to the shape and outline of the picture.

To apply these styles, select the picture, choose Picture Tools Format > Picture Styles from the Ribbon, and select the gallery from any button in this group. Although styles can only be applied one at a time, it is possible to select all of these style choices for a single picture.

For instance, the picture in Figure 12-9 has had the following styles applied:

- ▶ **Picture Style:** Rounded Diagonal Corner, White

- ▶ **Picture Border:** Purple

- ▶ **Picture Effects:** Reflection > Full Reflection, Touching and Glow > Purple 11pt Glow Accent Color 4, and Bevel > Angle and 3-D Rotation > Parallel > Off Axis 1 Right

Figure 12-9
Adding picture styles.

Arranging Illustrations

Once selected, an illustration can be moved, by dragging the picture to a new location, and resized, by dragging the sizing handles. The tools on the Arrange tab allow you to arrange pictures in relation to other objects on the worksheet.

- ▶ **Selection Pane:** As shown in Figure 12-10, clicking the Selection Pane button will open the Selection and Visibility pane to the right of the worksheet. In this pane, you can add a name for each object on your worksheet by clicking on the generic name (for example, Picture 13) and replacing the text with a more specific name. Clicking the picture name in the Selection and Visibility pane will select the picture in the worksheet. The more pictures you have in your worksheet, the more valuable this tool becomes.

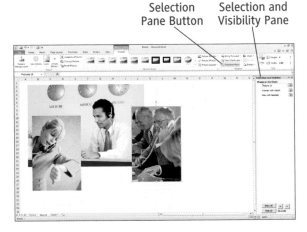

Figure 12-10
The Selection and Visibility pane.

- ▶ **Rotate:** This tool will rotate the selected image in one of several predefined options (see Figure 12-11). Compare the picture of the woman looking at her watch with the picture in Figure 12-10. The picture has been flipped horizontally so that she now faces the opposite direction.

- ▶ **Bring Forward:** This button moves a selected picture in front of other overlying pictures.

Figure 12-11
Rotating a picture.

▶ **Send Backward:** This button moves a selected picture behind other pictures.

▶ **Align:** With multiple pictures selected, this button will align the selected pictures in the desired manner. The pictures in Figure 12-12 have been aligned at the top of the pictures.

▶ **Group:** With multiple pictures selected, this button will group the pictures into a single picture object. Any further changes will be applied to the group as a whole. Clicking the button again allows you to ungroup the pictures.

Changing the Size

Besides dragging the picture handles to adjust the size of an image, you can use the Height and Width boxes in the Size group to manually change the size of the picture. This method is most useful if you need the illustration to be a specific size. As you type the new size in the appropriate box, Excel adjusts the size on the worksheet accordingly.

The cropping tool allows you to remove unwanted portions of an illustration. To crop an image:

1. Select the picture object you need to crop.

2. Choose Picture Tools Format > Size > Crop. Excels replaces the sizing handles with dark black cropping handles.

3. Drag the cropping handles to black out the portion of the picture that is not necessary (see Figure 12-13).

4. Click the Crop tool again to remove the unwanted portions of the picture.

Figure 12-12
Aligning pictures at the top.

Cropping Handles

Figure 12-13
Cropping a picture object.

Working with Shapes

NOT EVERYONE IS BLESSED with the ability to draw recognizable images. If you are one of those people, no one needs to find out because Excel contains a complete gallery of predefined shapes that can be included into your worksheet. You can draw arrows, boxes, circles, stars, callout bubbles, and flowchart objects (see Figure 12-14).

Figure 12-14
Predefined shapes are available from the Insert tab.

To insert one of these shapes into your worksheet, follow these steps:

1. Choose Insert > Illustrations > Shapes. Excels displays a gallery of available shapes.

2. Select the shape you want from the gallery. The mouse pointer changes to a cross.

3. Place the cross mouse pointer where you want to see the upper-left edge of the shape, and then drag the mouse diagonally down and to the right to draw the shape on your worksheet (see Figure 12-15).

4. If necessary, change the color and size of the shape using the tools on the Picture Tools Format tab.

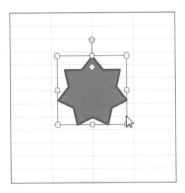

Figure 12-15
Inserting shapes.

Creating SmartArt

SMARTART OBJECTS ARE professionally designed graphics that combine shapes and text to show relationships, cycles, processes, and workflows. The graphics get their name because of the intelligence built into their design. As text is added into the SmartArt shapes, the text is automatically resized to fit the shape, and the text in all of the other shapes in the graphic are resized to match.

There are dozens of these SmartArt graphics included in Excel in seven categories, as described in Table 12-1. Several of these objects also allow you to add images to the selected graphic type.

To insert a SmartArt object into your worksheet, choose Insert > Illustrations > SmartArt from the Ribbon to open the Choose a SmartArt Graphic dialog box, as shown in Figure 12-16. Click a category from the pane on the left to see the graphic objects that best illustrate that type of relationship and then click on the object you want. Excel includes the object on your worksheet and adds two new tabs under a SmartArt Tools category (see Figure 12-17).

Table 12-1 SmartArt Graphic Categories

Categories	Purpose
List	Show non-sequential items
Process	Display steps that occur sequentially
Cycle	Demonstrate steps in a repeating, or continual, process
Hierarchy	Describe the relationship between two or more items, as in an organization chart
Relationship	Illustrate how items are connected
Matrix	Show how parts relate to a whole
Pyramid	Show proportional relationships with the largest component at either the top or the bottom of a pyramid

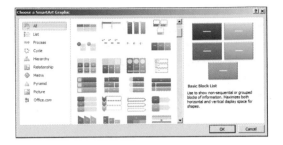

Figure 12-16
The gallery of SmartArt objects.

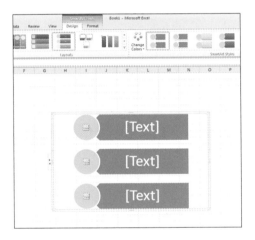

Figure 12-17
Inserting SmartArt objects.

Excel provides a number of opportunities to customize these objects:

▶ **Add text to your objects:** Choose SmartArt Tools Design > Create Graphic > Text Pane. Excel opens an editing pane to the left of the SmartArt graphic with the insertion point positioned at the first bullet (see Figure 12-18). Simply type your content into the bullet and press the down arrow, or click the next line, to move the insertion point.

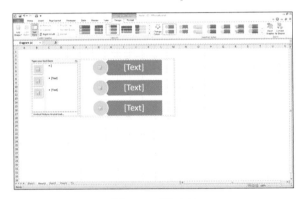

Figure 12-18
SmartArt Text Pane.

Tip

Pressing the Enter key after you type the SmartArt entry will add a new section to the graphic. Delete unwanted sections by selecting them and pressing Delete.

► **Change the color of your SmartArt objects:** Choose SmartArt Tools Design > SmartArt Styles > Change Colors and select a color option from the gallery (see Figure 12-19).

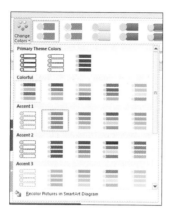

Figure 12-19
SmartArt color gallery.

► **Choose another SmartArt layout:** Choose SmartArt Tools Design > Layouts and open the Layouts gallery (see Figure 12-20). Click More Layouts to open the Choose a SmartArt Graphic dialog box. Select another layout from the options and Excel will convert your existing text and images to fit the new layout.

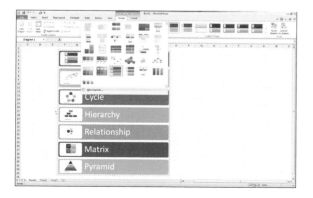

Figure 12-20
Replacing the SmartArt layout.

Adding Pictures to SmartArt

Imagine using a SmartArt graphic to record a list of related items. You've chosen a list graphic type and added the text to each shape, but you still don't feel like you've conveyed the full message. Now imagine how much more clear the difference between the items becomes if you could add pictures of each of the items (see Figure 12-21).

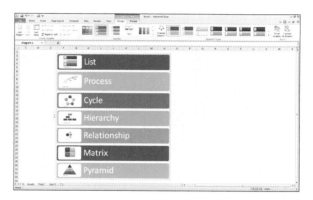

Figure 12-21
Adding pictures to SmartArt objects.

The Pictures category of the Choose a SmartArt Graphic dialog box contains several SmartArt graphics that include the option for adding a picture. You can add any image stored on your computer to these graphics. To add pictures to a SmartArt graphic, follow these steps:

1. Select your Picture SmartArt from the Choose a SmartArt Graphic dialog box and add the text as usual.

2. Double-click the picture icon on the SmartArt graphic. Excel opens the Insert Picture dialog box.

3. Select the picture you want to add and press Insert. Excel adds the picture to the SmartArt graphic.

Edit Your Image Before Adding

As pictures are added to SmartArt, Excel crops the picture to place the center of the image in the picture box. Use an image editor program, such as Paint or Photoshop, to add blank space around the image that will force the important portion of your image into the SmartArt graphic.

Changing SmartArt Shapes

SmartArt graphics come in a variety of shapes and sizes, but you may find that the predefined shape does not suit your content. You can use the Shapes tool you discovered earlier in this chapter to change the shape of one or all of the SmartArt graphics. Because different shapes can be applied to each graphic object, each object in the SmartArt graphic must be selected individually. To select more than one object at a time, hold the Ctrl key as you click each shape.

Select the objects you want to change and choose SmartArt Tools Format > Shapes > Change Shape to open a gallery of available shapes (see Figure 12-22). Choose a new shape from the gallery and Excel will update the SmartArt graphic to reflect that choice, as illustrated by Figure 12-23.

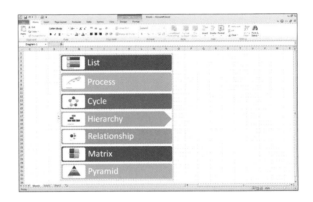

Figure 12-23
Shapes are applied to SmartArt graphics.

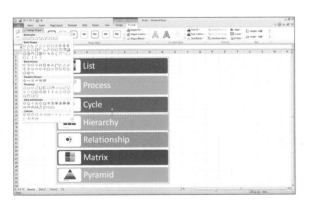

Figure 12-22
Changing the shape of SmartArt graphics.

Using Screenshots

A SCREENSHOT IS EXACTLY what it sounds like. It is a snapshot, or picture, of a screen open on your computer. Any window that has not been minimized is captured by Excel and available for you to use as an image in your worksheet. Screenshots are useful in recording information that might change. If you are collecting data on the traffic to your Website on a given day, for example, you may want to include a screenshot of the home page on that day so that you have a record of what content generated the traffic you are monitoring.

To include a screenshot, choose Insert > Illustrations > Screenshot. Select the screenshot you want from the drop-down menu of available windows (see Figure 12-24).

As demonstrated by Figure 12-25, Excel inserts the screenshot into your worksheet at the point of the active cell. Screenshot are images and can be edited using the formatting tools described earlier in this chapter.

Figure 12-25
Inserting a screenshot into Excel.

Figure 12-24
Excel captures an image of every open window on your computer.

Sometimes a screenshot captures more information than you need to include on a worksheet. In cases like this, Excel's screenshot feature includes a Screen Clipping tool at the bottom of the list of available windows. Clicking this tool will open the most recently visited window. Excel then dulls the screen and the mouse pointer changes to a cross. Drag the mouse over the portion of the screen you want to include in the screenshot (see Figure 12-26). When you release the mouse button, Excel inserts that portion of the screenshot into your worksheet.

Figure 12-26
Clipping a portion of a screenshot.

Caution

The Screenshot feature does not include a screenshot of the window you are actively working in. For example, if you are working in Excel and also have Word open, you will see a screenshot of your Word document, but not Excel.

Adding WordArt

WORDART IS A GALLERY of styles that apply special effects to text. More than just fonts and colors, WordArt actually makes a graphic element out of your text. For example, you can stretch your text to fit a predefined shape, such as an arc. You can also stretch the text similar to the text at the beginning of Star Wars, as shown in Figure 12-27.

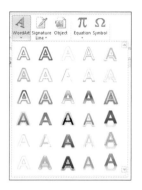

Figure 12-28
WordArt gallery.

Figure 12-27
A WordArt graphical element.

Follow these steps to add WordArt to your worksheet:

1. Choose Insert > Text > WordArt. Excel opens the WordArt gallery (see Figure 12-28).

2. Select one of the WordArt thumbnails that reflects the style you want to add to your worksheet. Excel adds a text box containing the words *Your Text Here* in the style you selected to the center of the worksheet.

3. With Excel's text selected, type your own text in the WordArt object. Excel replaces the *Your Text Here* text with your own text and adds a new tab, Drawing Tools Format.

4. With the WordArt selected, you can use the Drawing Tools Format > Shape Styles Dialog Box Launcher to make adjustments to the color, outline, and effects of your WordArt.

The Text Effects button applies a number of special effects, such as adding shadows, bevels, reflections, and transformation. The Drawing Tools Format > WordArt Styles > Text Effects > Transform tool can change the shape of the text in your WordArt graphic into anything from a wave to a triangle, or even a circle, as shown in Figure 12-29.

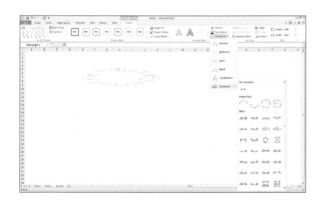

Figure 12-29
Transforming the WordArt shape.

By default, WordArt is inserted on a rectangular background, but you can change the background shape. Choose Drawing Tools Format > Insert Shapes > Edit Shape and select the background shape you want to see. Excel will modify the background shape of your WordArt, as shown in Figure 12-30, without changing the rest of the formatting.

Figure 12-30
Changing the shape of WordArt.

Caution

You will not see the background changes take effect unless your WordArt includes a background color.

Part IV
Using Excel Tools

13

Setting

Security Options

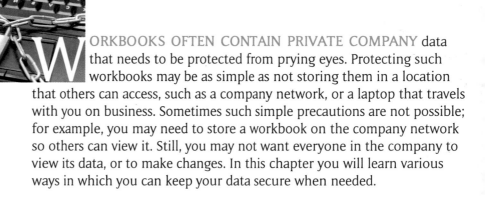

ORKBOOKS OFTEN CONTAIN PRIVATE COMPANY data that needs to be protected from prying eyes. Protecting such workbooks may be as simple as not storing them in a location that others can access, such as a company network, or a laptop that travels with you on business. Sometimes such simple precautions are not possible; for example, you may need to store a workbook on the company network so others can view it. Still, you may not want everyone in the company to view its data, or to make changes. In this chapter you will learn various ways in which you can keep your data secure when needed.

Inspecting for Private Information

WHETHER YOU ARE AWARE of it or not, your Excel workbooks contain more than just data. When a workbook is saved, Excel stores additional information with it, known as *metadata*. This metadata helps Excel to know certain things about the file and the people who have worked on it in the past, such as their name, company/department name, type of computer they use, and the name of the network server or hard disk where the workbook is stored. In addition, the metadata contains information about old versions of the workbook, hidden data, and any comments. Also, if you have ever e-mailed the document directly from Excel, your e-mail address may also be stored in the metadata.

Removing Private Info

You will not be able to remove personal data from a shared workbook, because it needs to retain that data in order to track who makes particular changes. So unshare the workbook first before removing private information.

If you share a workbook with someone else, you may not want to share all of this additional information. Use the Document Inspector to look for and remove such data before you share the workbook. Follow these steps:

1. Click the Save button on the Quick Access Toolbar to save any unsaved changes.

2. Click the File tab to display Backstage.

3. Select Info from the list on the left to display the Information options on the right.

4. Click the Check for Issues button and select Inspect Document from the pop-up menu. The Document Inspector dialog box, shown in Figure 13-1, appears.

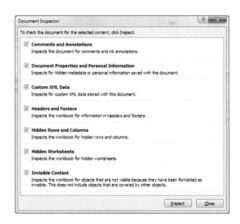

Figure 13-1
Look for data you might want to remove from a workbook before sharing it.

5. Select the checkboxes for the type of data you want to search for and possibly remove.

6. Click Inspect.

7. The Document Inspector looks for the type of data you selected, and then displays a list of the items it has found, as shown in Figure 13-2. To remove a particular type of data, such as the Document Properties and Personal Information, click that data's Remove All button.

8. Repeat Step 7 to remove the various data types you want.

9. When you're through removing data, click Close.

10. Save your workbook again by clicking the Save button on the Quick Access Toolbar.

Be Careful When Removing Hidden Data

If you remove hidden data, you might not be able to use Undo to get it back.

Figure 13-2
The Document Inspector reports on hidden data.

Hiding Data

IF YOUR WORKBOOK CONTAINS private company data or confidential information, you do not need to show it if you don't want to—you can hide it instead. In addition, if a workbook contains data that simply supports the main data, there's no need to bore people with it—hide it from view so the workbook's most important data remains the focus. In Chapter 6, "Managing Large Amounts of Excel Data," you learned how to hide rows and columns, and even a single cell's data. In this section, you learn how to hide an entire worksheet or workbook.

Tip

Hiding data does not prevent it from being seen by prying eyes. You must protect the worksheet or workbook to prevent users from simply redisplaying them. See the section "Protecting Data" for help.

Hiding Worksheets

When you hide a worksheet, its tab disappears. Now, if you rename your worksheets, it might not be obvious to your average user that a worksheet is secretly hidden. However, if you don't, a user might get suspicious that Sheet2 is hidden if he or she sees only two worksheets: Sheet1 and Sheet3. In any case, even though a worksheet is hidden, its data can still be referenced in formulas, elsewhere in the workbook.

To hide a worksheet, follow these steps:

1. Click the tab of the worksheet you want to hide. If you want to hide multiple sheets, press and hold Ctrl as you click each tab.

2. Click the Format button on the Home tab and point to Hide & Unhide from the pop-up menu.

3. Another pop-up menu appears; select Hide Sheet. The worksheet is immediately hidden from view.

Tip

You can right-click the selected worksheet tabs and choose Hide from the pop-up menu to quickly hide them.

If you want to prevent someone from unhiding your hidden sheets, you must protect the workbook—see the section "Protecting Data" for more information. Assuming the workbook is not protected, it's pretty easy to unhide a sheet assuming you know to even try. To unhide a sheet, click the Format button on the Home tab, point to Hide & Unhide, and select Unhide Sheet from the pop-up menu. The Unhide dialog box appears, as shown in Figure 13-3. You can also right-click any visible sheet tab and select Unhide from the pop-up menu to display the Unhide dialog box.

Figure 13-3
Select the sheet you want to unhide.

A list of all the hidden sheets appears in the Unhide dialog box. Select the sheet you want to display from the Unhide Sheet list and click OK. The hidden sheet magically reappears.

Hiding a Workbook

The main reason for hiding a workbook is to make it quickly disappear from the screen. For example, you might be working on a departmental budget worksheet that reveals you will only have three salespeople next year instead of five. Should someone from your department walk up while you're crunching numbers, it would be great if you could quickly hide the evidence that two people are about to be let go. With the click of one button, you can remove the worksheet from screen.

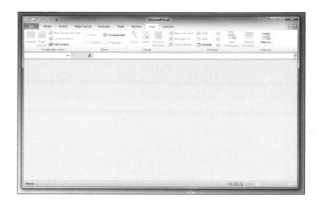

Figure 13-4
Hide a workbook quickly using the Hide button.

Tip

Hidden workbooks can be easily redisplayed by anyone who knows how. To prevent a workbook from being accessed by unauthorized personnel, you must protect it. See the section "Protecting Data" for help.

To hide the currently displayed workbook, click the Hide button on the View tab. The workbook is immediately removed from the screen, as shown in Figure 13-4. When a workbook is hidden, it remains open during your Excel work session. If you try to end your work session without redisplaying a hidden workbook, Excel will tap you on the shoulder and ask if you want to save it before it's closed. Click Save in the dialog box that appears to save the hidden workbook's data; if you don't want to end the session, click Cancel.

As you can see in Figure 13-4, there's nothing onscreen that obviously gives away the fact that a workbook is currently open but hidden. To unhide a workbook, click the Unhide button on the View tab. The Unhide dialog box appears, listing any hidden workbooks (see Figure 13-5). Select the workbook you want to redisplay from the Unhide Workbook list and click OK.

Figure 13-5
Unhide hidden workbooks when you are ready to work with them again.

Protecting Data

WORKBOOKS ARE MADE to be shared, and thus, Excel provides lots of ways in which you can easily do that. For example, you can share a workbook and track the individual changes everyone makes to it. You can later review those changes and accept or reject them as you want. See Chapter 14, "Collaborating with Others," for help. Another way that you can protect data is to simply lock it down, preventing anyone from changing it. You can lock down individual cells, a range of cells, or an entire worksheet in order to prevent anyone from changing its data. You can also protect a whole workbook, in order to prevent changes to its structure, such as adding worksheets or changing the workbook window's size. Finally, when needed, you can prevent unauthorized users from even opening a workbook at all.

Locking and Unlocking Cells

If your goal is to allow others to view data but to prevent them from messing it up by changing it, you must start by designating the cells you want to protect. You designate cells for protection by locking them down. After locking down cells, you turn on protection, which tells Excel to protect the data in all the locked cells. You can protect individual cells, ranges, or an entire worksheet in this way. You can also tell Excel to hide formulas. The formula result will still be shown, but not the formula itself—in other words, if someone clicks the cell, the formula is not displayed in the Formula bar.

By default, all cells in a worksheet are locked, which means that if you just turn on protection, no one will be able to change anything in the protected area. So you actually work kind of backwards, unlocking the cells you do not want to protect, and then turning on protection. Before you turn on protection, you can also hide formulas. Follow these steps to unlock the cells in a worksheet that you want to allow users to change, and to hide formulas as desired:

1. Select the cell or range you want to unlock.

2. Click the Format button on the Home tab and select Lock Cell from the pop-up menu to turn that option off.

3. Repeat Steps 1 and 2 to unlock as many cells as you want.

4. To hide a formula, click its result cell, and then click the Format button on the Home tab.

5. Select Format Cells from the pop-up menu. The Format Cells dialog box appears.

6. Click the Protection tab.

7. Select the Hidden checkbox and click OK.

8. Repeat Steps 4–7 to hide additional formulas. After hiding formulas and unlocking cells, you are ready to protect the data you've kept locked. To protect the locked cells, you must now turn on worksheet protection.

Tip

By default, objects are also locked when a worksheet is protected, but if you want to allow changes, you can. For example, to unlock a chart, click the chart and click the Format Selection button on the Format tab. The Format Chart Area dialog box appears; select Properties from the list on the left, deselect the Locked checkbox and click Close.

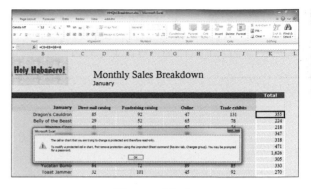

Figure 13-6
If a user attempts to change data in a cell that's locked, a warning message appears.

After locking cells and protecting a worksheet, users can view the data in locked cells, but not change it. If a user tries to change the data in a locked cell, a message pops up, indicating that the cell data is protected. (See Figure 13-6.) To avoid seeing a bunch of error messages, users can easily move from unlocked cell to unlocked cell by pressing Tab. By the way, a user can copy the data in locked cells, but he/she can't move it or delete it. In addition, data can't be copied over the top of the data in locked cells. If you've hidden formulas, then they disappear after your protect the worksheet (but not the formula results).

Unlocking Cells with Formulas

If you unlock a cell that contains a formula, an Error Options button appears next to the cell. It serves as a reminder that you might not want to allow other people to change your formulas. However, you can click the Error Options button and select Ignore Error to turn off the warning or Lock Cell to lock the formula cell.

Protecting a Worksheet

After unlocking the cells or objects you do not need to protect from changes, and indicating which formulas you want to hide, it's time to turn on worksheet protection so Excel can prevent data changes to the locked cells. Follow these steps:

1. Click the Format button on the Home tab and select Protect Sheet. You can also click the Protect Sheet button on the Review tab. The Protect Sheet dialog box appears, as shown in Figure 13-7.

Figure 13-7
Set options for the protected sheet.

2. To prevent unauthorized users from unpro-tecting the sheet, type a password in the Password to Unprotect Sheet box. Passwords are case-sensitive.

3. In the Allow All Users of This Worksheet To section, select the options you want to allow:

   - **Select Locked Cells:** Allows users to click on a locked cell (they still can't change its contents though).

   - **Select Unlocked Cells:** Allows users to click on unlocked cells, or to press Tab to move to one.

   - **Format Cells:** Allows users to apply for-matting or conditional formats to cells.

Using the Format Cells Option

If the Format Cells option is not enabled, and you applied conditional formats that should change because of a user entry, those formats will not change. For example, suppose you applied conditional formats to a range of cells that change to red if the net profits calculated in those cells become negative. If a user enters a value elsewhere in the sheet that results in a negative net profit for one of these cells, and you have not selected the Format Cells option here, the result cell will not turn red as you might expect.

   - **Format Columns:** Allows users to adjust column widths and hide columns.

   - **Format Rows:** Allows users to adjust row heights and hide rows.

   - **Insert Columns:** Allows users to insert new columns.

   - **Insert Rows:** Allows users to insert new rows.

   - **Insert Hyperlinks:** Allows users to add links.

   - **Delete Columns:** Allows users to remove columns.

   - **Delete Rows:** Allows users to remove rows.

   - **Sort:** Allows users to sort and filter unlocked cells.

   - **Use AutoFilter:** Allows users to change the settings on a filtered list.

   - **Use PivotTable Reports:** Allows users to manipulate PivotTable data and create new PivotTable reports.

   - **Edit Objects:** Allows users to make changes to charts, shapes, and other objects, and to add or edit comments. If this setting is turned off and a user changes data in an unlocked cell that affects a chart, the chart will change.

   - **Edit Scenarios:** Allows users to add and change scenarios.

4. Click OK.

5. If you entered a password in Step 2, the Confirm Password dialog box appears and you're prompted to confirm the password by retyping it. Do so and click OK. The work-sheet is immediately protected. You can repeat this process with other sheets if you want.

After protecting a worksheet, you may find it difficult to make all the changes that you, its creator, need to make. To remove worksheet protection, click the Format button on the Home tab and select Unprotect Sheet. You can also click the Unprotect Sheet button on the Review tab. If you password-protected the sheet, type your password in the dialog box that appears and click OK. The worksheet is no longer protected.

Protecting a Workbook

In addition to protecting worksheets from unauthorized changes, you can protect entire workbooks as well. When you protect a workbook in this manner, you protect its structure—preventing users from adding, deleting, hiding, or unhiding worksheets. You can also prevent users from resizing the workbook window. Here's how:

1. Click the Protect Workbook button on the Review tab. The Protect Structure and Windows dialog box appears, as seen in Figure 13-8.

Figure 13-8
Set options for the protected workbook.

2. Select the changes you want to prevent:

   • **Structure:** Prevents users from adding, deleting, hiding, or unhiding worksheets.

   • **Windows:** Prevents users from resizing the workbook window, although they can still scroll.

3. To prevent unauthorized users from unprotecting the sheet, type a password in the Password box. Passwords are case-sensitive.

4. Click OK.

5. If you entered a password in Step 3, the Confirm Password dialog box appears and you're prompted to confirm the password by retyping it. Do so and click OK. The workbook is immediately protected.

If you decide at some later date to remove the workbook protections (the workbook will no longer be shared, for example), just click the Protect Workbook button on the Review tab, enter the password if any, and click OK.

Preventing a Workbook from Being Opened

When the ultimate protection is needed, you can add a password to a workbook that prevents it from being opened by anyone who doesn't know the password. Follow these steps:

1. Click the File tab to display Backstage.

2. Select Info from the list on the left to display the Information options on the right.

3. Click the Protect Workbook button and select Encrypt With Password from the pop-up menu. The Encrypt Document dialog box appears. (See Figure 13-9.)

Figure 13-9
Protect your workbook with a password.

4. Type a password in the Password box. Passwords are case-sensitive.

5. Click OK.

6. The Confirm Password dialog box appears and you're prompted to confirm the password by retyping it. Type the same password you typed in Step 4 and click OK.

7. Save the workbook to save your changes.

The workbook remains open so you can continue to work on it. However, after you close it, when you open it again, you are prompted to enter your password, as shown in Figure 13-10. Do so and click OK. The workbook is opened and unless other protections are in place, you can make any changes you want.

Figure 13-10
You must enter a password to view this workbook.

Removing a Password

To remove a password from a workbook, after opening it, follow these same steps to open the Encrypt Document dialog box. Select the password and delete it, and then click OK. Save the workbook to save your changes.

Marking a Workbook as Final

IF YOU ARE THROUGH making changes to a workbook but still need to share its contents with others, you might want to make it "read-only". A read-only file is just that—available for reading (viewing), but not editing. With Excel, you make a workbook read-only by marking it as "final".

Marking a workbook as final only helps to prevent unwanted changes from your users. They can, if they are determined, remove the read-only status from the workbook and make changes anyway. Still, it's not an accidental thing, as you will see, so it's worth your time and trouble.

To mark a workbook as final, follow these steps:

1. Click the File tab to display Backstage.

2. Select Info from the list on the left to display the Information options on the right.

3. Click the Protect Workbook button and select Mark as Final from the pop-up menu.

4. Click OK to confirm your decision to mark the workbook as final.

5. A warning appears, telling you that the workbook has been marked as final. Click OK to continue.

6. Click the Home tab to view the worksheet. You can tell that the workbook has been successfully marked as "final" because a Marked as Final indicator now appears on the status bar, as shown in Figure 13-11.

7. Close it since you are done with it.

Marked as Final
Indicator

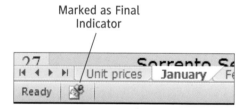

Figure 13-11
Mark your workbook as final to help
prevent further changes.

After you mark a workbook as final, it is ready to be shared. When a user opens the workbook, he or she will see a warning that indicates the workbook is read-only. The warning appears on the InfoBar, located just above the Formula bar, as shown in Figure 13-12. A user can view the workbook and print it as needed. The user can also override this warning, disable the Mark as Final status, and make changes anyway. To disable the Marked as Final status and enable editing, click the Edit Anyway button on the InfoBar.

Marked as Final
Warning

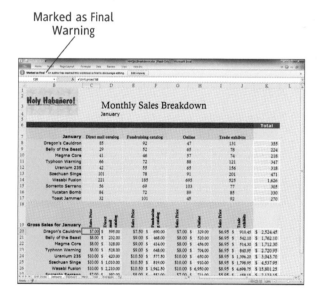

Figure 13-12
A warning appears in workbooks that
are marked as final.

Using Older Excel Versions

If a user opens a read-only 2010 Excel workbook in an earlier version of Excel, the read-only status is not retained and the user will not be prevented from making changes.

Mark as Final Is Removed

If a user overrides the warning, disables a workbook's final status, and later saves the workbook (whether or not the user made any changes), the workbook's Mark as Final status is permanently removed.

Collaborating
with Others

PICTURE YOURSELF COMPILING a large workbook, combining lots of data from a variety of sources, and working with one or more other people on the project. It would be very handy to be able to keep an eye on what's being added or changed over the life of the project, including knowing who made the changes and additions. Excel 2010 makes it really easy to do just that, providing several features for editing a workbook collaboratively—from literally marking all changes with the name of the contributor and the date and time of his or her contribution, to the use of comments to provide information about any cell in the workbook.

In addition to these collaborative tools, Excel also makes it simple to create rules, in the form of onscreen prompts that range from a nudge to a "stop right there!" approach, to help keep your workbook content consistent. From literally forcing users to enter only a certain type of data into particular ranges of cells to providing a gentle reminder to follow formatting rules for data entry, you can easily help your workbooks' users make their contributions cleaner and more useful.

Finally, to bring the collaborative concept full circle, Excel 2010 provides several ways to bring content from other applications into an Excel workbook, and also to export Excel content to other applications. This enables you to have consistency throughout various reports, databases, presentations, and documents, as well as within multiple Excel worksheets in one or more workbooks.

Considering Your Collaboration Options

WHENEVER MORE THAN ONE person is working on a single Excel worksheet or workbook, it's important to keep things straight—who added or changed the information, where they got the information, and whether the additions and changes are to be kept as they are, edited further, or removed entirely. Much of the process of collaborating on such a project is manual, in that you'll have to ask people to add or change the information that they're responsible for, someone will have to review what's been added or changed, and there will have to be meetings or some other communication between the collaborators, to make sure everything's going as planned.

For Excel's part, however, the process of tracking who did what and when it was done is entirely automatic—once you've turned on a feature called Track Changes. As shown in Figure 14-1, Track Changes is turned on via the Review tab's Track Changes command, through which you can control how Track Changes works—whose changes you want to track, which cells you want to monitor, and whether or not to keep changes a member of the team has made. But don't worry—while there are a lot of variables, Track Changes is really simple to use.

Track Changes Options

Track Changes Button

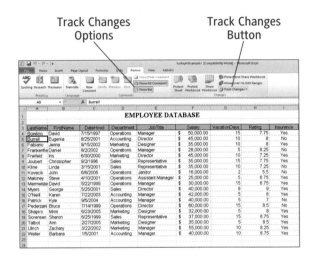

Figure 14-1
When collaborating on a worksheet, you'll spend a good deal of time in Excel 2010's Review tab.

Turning Track Changes On and Off

To turn Track Changes on, simply open the workbook you want to track, and from within any of its worksheets, click the Review tab on the Ribbon. As shown in Figure 14-2, the Track Changes command presents a menu, from which you can choose to Highlight Changes—this refers to the very process of tracking changes, which highlights those cells that are changed in any way after Track Changes is turned on.

It's Good to Share...Sometimes

When you turn Track Changes on, your workbook becomes shared. This means that anyone can open and edit it (which may be what you want), but anyone can also turn Track Changes off, which would cause you to lose all the information on the changes made to the workbook. To prevent this, click the Protect Shared Workbook command on the Review tab, and click the Sharing with Track Changes option within the resulting Protect Shared Workbook dialog box. Click OK to close the dialog box and confirm the protection, and later, if desired, click the Unprotect Shared Workbook command to turn this protection off. We'll discuss more about how to protect your workbooks from undesired viewing or editing later in this chapter.

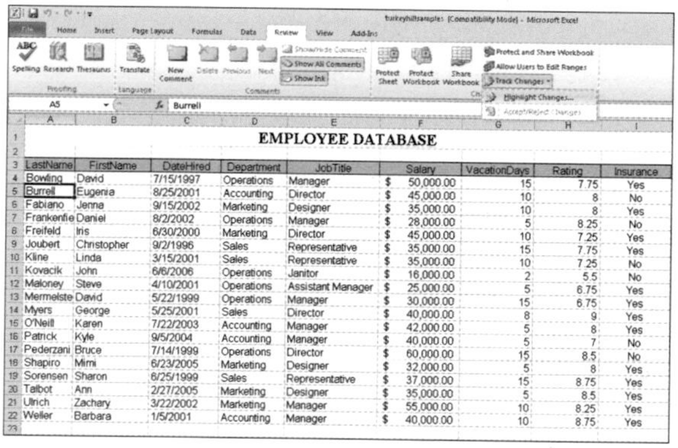

Figure 14-2
Choose to Highlight Changes from within the Track Changes command menu.

Figure 14-3
Set the When, Who, and Where for how your workbook's changes will be tracked.

After selecting Highlight Changes, the dialog box shown in Figure 14-3 appears. Click the checkbox next to Track Changes While Editing. This activates the rest of the dialog box, where you can choose from a series of options that determine exactly how Track Changes will work. You can, however, simply check the Track Changes While Editing checkbox, and click OK—the defaults (monitoring all cells in the workbook, made by everyone, from now until Track Changes is turned off) are just fine for most users.

And speaking of turning Track Changes off, to do so, just re-select Highlight Changes from the Review tab's Track Changes command drop-down menu, and in the dialog box shown in Figure 14-3, uncheck the Highlight Changes While Editing checkbox, and then click OK. Track Changes is now off, and any changes made while Track Changes was on are kept, but are no longer highlighted as changed, and you no longer have the ability to go through all changes and accept or reject them (I'll discuss how to do this later on in this chapter).

Caution

It's important for you to know how to turn off Track Changes, right at the beginning of this discussion, so that you aren't stuck working in Track Changes mode if you don't want to be. It's important to note, however, that if you turn off Track Changes without reviewing any changes made while it was on, you won't be able to tell what was changed and you won't be able to go back to the way things were before any particular change was made. Therefore, I don't recommend turning off Track Changes unless you literally don't care what changes were made and want to keep all of them or you've already done your review of all changes and kept the ones you want.

Choosing Which Changes to Track

As shown in the Highlight Changes dialog box in Figure 14-3, you can easily, and thoroughly, customize how Track Changes works. You don't need to make any selections from the following options, however, as the default settings were designed to meet the needs of most users and most situations.

If you do want to customize Track Changes, here are the settings you can use to do it:

▶ **When.** This option, which is checked (turned on) by default, allows you to specify which changes will be tracked—those made since the last time you saved, those changes that have not yet been reviewed, all changes (meaning no matter when they're made), or changes since a particular date. Note the ellipsis after the "Since Date..." option, which, if chosen, inserts the current date, but you can edit it as shown in Figure 14-4. All is the default setting.

Figure 14-4
If you choose "Since Date..."the system date is inserted by default, but you can edit it by retyping some or all of the values for the month, day, and/or year.

▶ **Who.** When you check this option, you can choose between Everyone and Everyone But Me. This is useful if you know you'll be continuing to work on the data, but are really only interested in the contributions of others on your team. Everyone is the default.

▶ **Where.** This option allows you to type a cell or range of cells into the field, or you can click the Collapse button at the right end of the field to shrink the dialog box. Once shrunken, as shown in Figure 14-5, you can click and drag through cells in your worksheet to specify a range of cells to be tracked. You can click any other worksheet in the workbook (note that the sheet name appears in the field if you do so), and once you've selected a range of cells to track, press Enter to display them in the dialog box, as shown in Figure 14-6.

Tracking the Whole Workbook

If you don't make any selection in the Where box, the entire workbook will be tracked—so you only need to specify a range if you want to restrict the tracking to that range of cells.

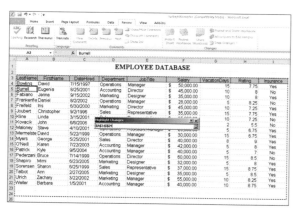

Figure 14-5
Shrink the dialog box to give yourself more elbow-room for selecting the cells you want to track.

Figure 14-6
Once you've picked the worksheet and range of cells within it to track, your selection appears in the dialog box, where you can tweak it as needed.

▶ **Highlight Changes Onscreen.** This option is turned on by default, and simply means that you want some kind of visual notification that Track Changes has detected a change to a cell or cells within the specified range. As shown in Figure 14-7, once a cell has been changed, a blue triangle appears in the upper-left corner of the cell, and if you mouse over the cell, a comment bubble pops up to indicate who made the change, when it was made, and what the change consisted of.

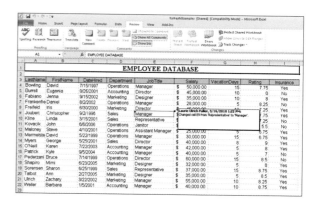

Figure 14-7
Mouse over a highlighted cell to find out what was done to change that cell's content.

Editing with Track Changes

While Track Changes is on, you don't have to do anything special when editing the worksheet—just work along as you would normally, adding, removing, and changing cell content. You'll notice, however, as shown in Figure 14-7, that whenever you edit a cell that's within the tracked range of cells, that a blue triangle appears in the upper-left corner of the cell. You don't need to do anything with that as you work, just know that as discussed, you can mouse over a cell and see the Track Changes information about what changes were made, by whom, and when.

If you find it distracting to have the triangles appear in the corners of edited cells while Track Changes is on—or if you fear your collaborators will find it distracting—you can turn off the highlighting, while still keeping Track Changes on.

1. With Track Changes already on, choose Track Changes from the Review tab on the Ribbon.

2. Select Highlight Changes from the drop-down menu.

3. In the resulting dialog box, turn off the checkbox next to the Highlight Changes On Screen option. Figure 14-8 shows the dialog box in place, with a range of cells selected behind it.

4. Click OK.

5. Track Changes remains on, but no highlighting will appear as you work.

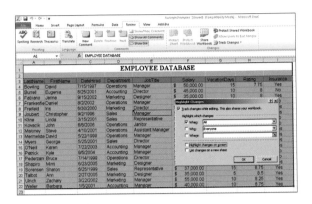

Figure 14-8
Highlighting tracked cells is an option
you can easily turn off.

Listing Tracked Changes in a New Sheet

Track Changes in Excel 2010 offers a powerful tool to enhance the collaborative process. The History sheet, shown in Figure 14-9, allows you to see every change made, including which cell was edited, who made the edit, what the previous content of that cell was and what it is now. Note that if a single user makes a series of changes to a single cell, only his or her last change will be listed—if several individuals make changes, however, all of those changes (the last one for each person) will be listed.

To create the History sheet for your workbook, follow these steps—it's assumed that Track Changes is on and has been on, and that edits have been made.

1. Save your workbook. Excel will only create a History sheet for saved changes, and you can save by pressing Ctrl+S, or choosing File > Save.

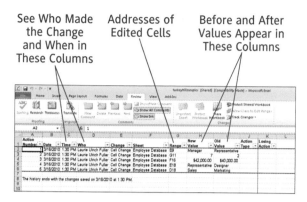

See Who Made the Change and When in These Columns

Addresses of Edited Cells

Before and After Values Appear in These Columns

Figure 14-9
The entire history of your collaborative work can be documented in a new sheet.

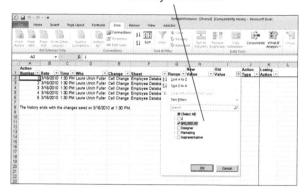

Filter Any Column in the History Worksheet

Figure 14-11
Your new History worksheet can be sorted and filtered to display and organize the data in any way you choose.

2. With your workbook saved, click the Review tab, and click the Track Changes command to display its drop-down menu.

3. Choose Highlight Changes. The Highlight Changes dialog box opens, as shown in Figure 14-10.

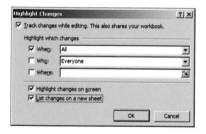

Figure 14-10
A newly available option appears in the Highlight Changes dialog box—to create a new sheet listing all changes made while Track Changes has been in use.

4. Check the box next to List Changes on a New Sheet.

5. Click OK. A new History worksheet appears, and is now the active worksheet, as shown in Figure 14-11.

To use the History sheet, review each sheet and cell that is listed. You can use it to see which changes you want to keep and which ones you might want to change again or reject, returning to the content prior to the collaborative process. If your History sheet has an abundance of data in it—row upon row of edited cells, some cells changed multiple times by multiple people—which might make it difficult to make decisions at a glance, you can use the Data tab's Sort and Filter commands (discussed in Chapters 7 and 8, respectively) to change the order in which the listed changes appear, and to distill the list of changes down to just the few you want to see—perhaps only those in a certain range of cells or performed by a certain person.

Redisplaying Your Changes

The History sheet does not remain after you save the workbook. If you need to see your listed changes again, you'll have to repeat Steps 4 and 5 in the previous procedure to display the current list of changes.

Accepting and Rejecting Collaborative Changes

The process of accepting and/or rejecting edits made by a team of contributors can be performed while Track Changes is still in use, or at the end of the collaborative process, just before turning Track Changes off. You can accept or reject changes on a weekly, daily, or hourly basis, at any interval that works for you. Once you've accepted or rejected a change, the cell/s are no longer highlighted (with that blue triangle you've seen so much in this chapter), and the cell will only be highlighted again if a change is made subsequent to the acceptance or rejection of its current content.

To accept or reject tracked changes, follow these steps:

1. In the workbook in which Track Changes is on, click the Review tab on the Excel Ribbon.

2. Click the Track Changes command, and choose Accept/Reject Changes from the drop-down menu, as shown in Figure 14-12.

Figure 14-12
Return to the Review tab to begin the process of accepting or rejecting the changes you and your team have made to the workbook.

3. In the resulting Select Changes to Accept or Reject dialog box, shown in Figure 14-13, choose which changes you want to deal with. Your choices are:

Figure 14-13
The Select Changes to Accept or Reject dialog box allows you to fine-tune your reviewing process.

- **When.** This is selected by default, and set to Not Yet Reviewed. You can also choose Since Date...from the drop-down menu for this option, and then either accept the automatically inserted system date, or edit that date to create a date value that works for your purposes.

- **Who.** This is not selected by default, and if you leave it off, the reviewing process that follows will allow you to review and then accept or reject everyone's changes. The choices are Everyone, Everyone But Me, and you (your name, or the name of the person under whose name Excel was installed, appears).

- **Where.** Also not selected by default, this setting allows you to confine your reviewing process to just some of the cells in your workbook. When not turned on, this setting will include all edited cells, on all worksheets in the workbook, in the reviewing process.

If you want to restrict the reviewing process to a certain sheet or range of cells, simply click in the Where field (or click the Collapse button at the far right end of the field to collapse the dialog box temporarily) and then move your mouse out onto the workbook to select a sheet and then select cells within that sheet. Once you've made your selection, expand the dialog box (if you collapsed it).

4. With your settings in place, click OK.

Tip

You can also make a sweeping decision and not view all the changes individually, by clicking Accept All or Reject All. You can also Close the dialog box without making any acceptances or rejections, at any point in the process.

5. In the resulting Accept or Reject Changes dialog box (shown in Figure 14-14), view the changes as they are displayed one at a time—clicking the Accept or Reject button to move through them individually.

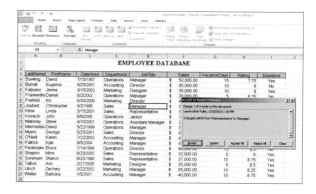

Figure 14-14
Review your changes, one at a time—or not.

6. To end the process before reviewing all the edited cells, click Close. Otherwise, if you accept or reject all the edits (one at a time or using the All-version buttons), the dialog box closes on its own.

You Can Review Some Changes Later

You can use this process to review just a few of the edited cells, by making Accept or Reject decisions one at a time and then clicking Close to leave the rest undecided (for now), and come back to them later. There's no requirement that you review and decide on all the changes just because you've started this process. As long as Track Changes remains on, your contributors' changes will continue to be tracked and highlighted, and you can review them at any time. If you decide to use the History sheet as your reviewing tool, when you're ready, you can use the previous steps to open the Accept or Reject Changes dialog box and then click Accept All or Reject All.

Using Comments in Collaboration

COMMENTS IN AN EXCEL workbook serve the same purpose as a whisper in your ear, providing some useful aside related to whatever you're looking at or discussing at the time. For example, if you're in a meeting and the person sitting next to you decides you'd benefit from having some quick piece of information relevant to the topic at hand, he or she might whisper it to you so as to provide the information without disrupting the meeting. Comments work the same way. If someone—you or a team member also contributing to the workbook's content—believes that there's some background or otherwise useful information about a particular cell that should be made available, a comment can be added to the cell, and viewed without disrupting use of the worksheet. Figure 14-15 shows a comment, displayed by moving your cursor over a cell into which someone has placed a comment.

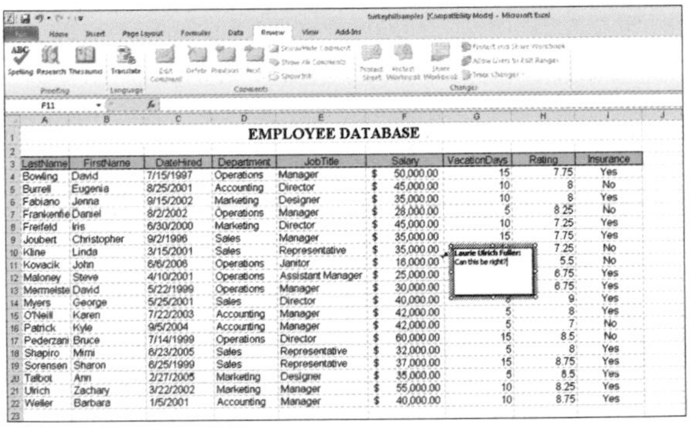

Adding Comments

To add a comment to your workbook, simply right-click on any cell, and choose Insert Comment. As shown in Figure 14-16, a small yellow box appears, with the user's name in it and a blinking cursor, awaiting the typed comment the user intends to add. It's that simple!

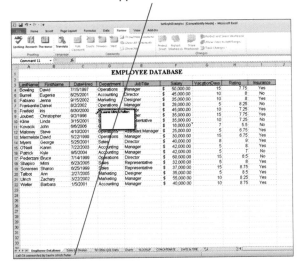

Figure 14-16
Insert your comment quickly and easily—from a word or two to entire paragraphs of text.

Figure 14-15
Other than temporarily obscuring adjacent cells while displayed, Comments can be a handy way of providing useful information about the content of a cell.

You can also use the Review tab's New Comment button to add a comment to any cell. Just click in the cell you want to comment on, and click the New Comment button. The same yellow box shown in Figure 14-16 appears, and you can type inside the box. When you've finished typing the comment, simply click anywhere outside it to complete the comment and continue working.

Tip

Although the user's name appears in the yellow box by default, that text can also be edited or removed entirely.

Editing and Deleting Comments

Once comments are added, regardless of your insertion method, you can edit them easily:

▶ **Click the Edit Comment button on the Review tab.** If you click on a cell with a comment associated with it, the New Comment button becomes an Edit Comment button, and clicking it activates your cursor in the yellow comment box for that cell. Just edit the text as you would any other text box, using Backspace or Delete as needed, and/or selecting and replacing text with your mouse and keyboard.

▶ **Right-click any cell with a comment, and choose Edit Comment from the pop-up menu, as shown in Figure 14-17.** Note that a floating formatting toolbar also appears, offering tools to change the font, size, color, and style of the text in the active cell.

The Comment Pertaining to Cell
F11 Can Now Be Edited

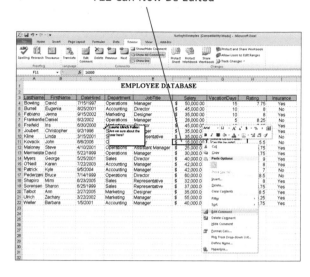

Figure 14-17
Choose to edit any comment using the pop-up menu.

To get rid of a comment you no longer want, click in the cell that has the unwanted comment and either click the Delete button in the Comments group of the Review tab, or right-click the cell and choose Delete Comment from the pop-up menu.

Tip

There is no "did you really want to do that?" prompt that appears, so make your comment deletions with care. You can use Undo to bring them back (click the Undo button on the Quick Access toolbar, or press Ctrl+Z), but if you don't catch the error or realize you needed to keep that comment until after you've ended your Excel session, you won't be able to bring the deleted comment back.

To do so, follow these steps to apply formatting to the comment text:

1. Find the cell with the comment you want to format.

2. Click the commented cell to activate it. The comment appears.

3. Click the Show/Hide Comment button on the Review tab. The comment for this cell is now displayed and won't disappear if you move away from the cell.

4. Move your mouse onto the comment box, and select the text you want to reformat.

5. Right-click your mouse in the selection.

6. Choose Format Comment from the pop-up menu, as shown in Figure 14-19.

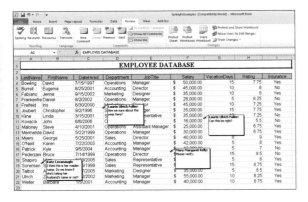

Figure 14-18
Part of the collaboration process can include viewing others' comments—and you can see them all at once, if you'd like to.

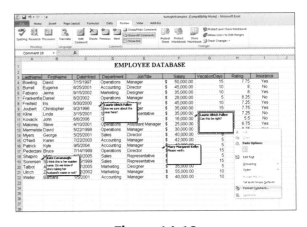

Figure 14-19
Right-click the selected comment text to access the Format Comment command.

Formatting Comments

Although most of the time, comments are just fine in the default font (Tahoma, 8 points) in the little yellow boxes, you may find that you want to add some emphasis to one or more words in a comment, or to make an entire comment stand out from the rest.

7. The Format Comment dialog box opens, as shown in Figure 14-20, through which you can choose a new font, font style, size, underline, color, and any special effects for the text in the comment box.

8. Once you like the preview and are sure that's what you want your comment text to look like, click OK.

9. Click the Show/Hide Comment button (on the Review tab) to toggle this fixed display of the current comment off. The comment disappears as soon as you move away from the cell to which it pertains.

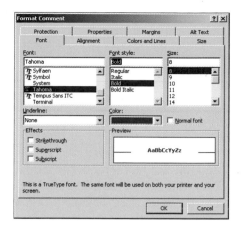

Figure 14-20
Looking just like the Format Cells dialog box Font tab, the Format Comment dialog box allows you to change the appearance of your comment text.

Validating Excel Worksheet Content

WHEN YOU'RE THE ONLY ONE populating an Excel worksheet with data, it's not too likely that the wrong data will be entered. You're not going to forget that the entries into the Date Hired column in an employees list have to include the year, or that only numeric content can be entered into the Price column in an inventory list. On the other hand, if you have other people helping you flesh out your worksheet, it can be really helpful to provide some guidance for them, so that the resulting content is accurate and reliable and the time saved by having helpers isn't canceled out by having to go back and fix their entries.

Excel makes it easy to provide this type of guidance, through Data Validation tools, found on the Data tab. As shown in Figure 14-21, the Data Tools group of the Data tab offers validation commands as well as a way to look for duplicate entries.

Data Validation
Button

Figure 14-21
Look to the Data tab's Data Tools group for help in creating consistency in the data entry process.

Setting Up Rules, Messages, and Alerts

You can set up rules for data entry at any time in the life of your workbook. In fact, most people don't realize they need these helpful features until there's a problem—usually through errors caused by someone not familiar with the data being responsible for entering it. Of course, optimally, the creation of rules for various ranges within a workbook is best done at the time that the worksheets are first set up, but if you're looking to promote more accuracy in an existing workbook, it's not too late. To invoke Excel's validation tools, follow these steps:

1. In the worksheet requiring validation, select the range of cells to which the validation rules should apply. This can be a single cell, a contiguous range, or multiple ranges (selected using the Ctrl key to add cells and ranges to a selection).

2. Click the Data tab and choose Data Validation from the Data Tools group of the Ribbon.

3. From the drop-down menu shown in Figure 14-22, select Data Validation.

Figure 14-22
Choose Data Validation to begin setting up your data entry rules.

4. The Data Validation dialog box opens, as shown in Figure 14-23.

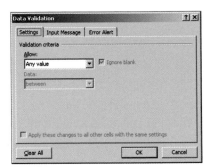

Figure 14-23
You can set up many levels and features for your validation rules, beginning with what kind of data will be allowed in the selected range of cells.

5. On the Settings tab, click the Allow drop-down menu and choose what kind of data will be allowed in the range of cells you selected in Step 1. Your choices range from Any Value to Custom, which requires that you type a value or select a cell that already contains the desired value that will be allowed.

6. Based on your choice in Step 5, using the Allow list, the next set of fields will vary, but typically includes a Data field, where you choose from options such as between, equal to, or greater than. Make a choice here, and move to the next field.

7. Enter the acceptable values, based on your choice in Step 6. As shown in Figure 14-24, when a Decimal is required, it must be between two numbers, so a minimum and a maximum must be entered.

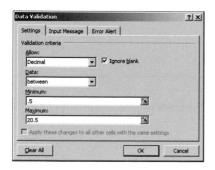

Figure 14-24
Control the acceptable values for the cells
you wish to validate.

8. Click OK. The rules for the selected range
are now in place, and you can test them by
making an entry that doesn't fit your requirements. Figure 14-25 shows the error message
that appears if you only use the Settings tab
and don't customize the rule beyond establishing allowed values/data types for a range
of cells.

Figure 14-25
A very stern default warning appears
when validation rules are violated.

As shown in the error message displayed in
Figure 14-25, Excel takes your validation rules
very seriously, and won't allow a breach of those
rules. The user who attempts to enter an invalid
value will be stopped and forced to retry or cancel. If the users choose Retry, the cell's contents
are selected, awaiting replacement, and the
users can try again. If users choose Cancel, the
cell is emptied or reverted to the previous entry,

if it was valid according to the established validation rules. It's up to the users to try again or
to move to another cell, perhaps one that's not
subject to validation rules.

If you want to customize the error message to be
more informative, you can easily do so. You can
also make the rules more flexible, allowing invalid
data to be entered, with a less rigid response from
Excel indicating that there's a problem with the
value entered. Here are your options and how to
use them:

▶ **Input Message.** In the Data Validation
dialog box (opened by choosing Data
Validation from the Data Validation drop-
down menu in the Data Tools group of
the Data tab), you can click the Input
Message tab and enter your own message,
including a title for the message title bar
and the body of the message, with as
much or as little guidance as you feel is
needed. Whatever message you type here
will appear whenever a cell in the selected
range is active—it won't wait for an error
to be made. Figure 14-26 provides an
example of the kind of message you
might use.

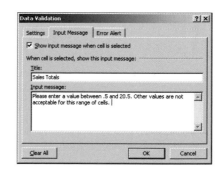

Figure 14-26
A gentle reminder that only numbers
between .5 and 20.5 are permitted in the
Sales Totals range is easy to set up.

► **Error Alert.** This type of message is a bit stronger than an Input Message, and instead of appearing before any entry is made in a selected cell, it only pops up if someone makes an entry that's in violation of the established validation rules for the cell in question. As shown in Figure 14-27, you can choose the style of alert (Stop, Warning, or Information) and then type the title and body of the error message.

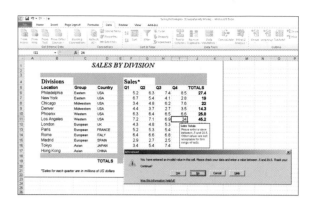

Figure 14-28
If you only want particular numbers in the selected range, an informative Warning such as this will help users mend their ways.

Figure 14-27
Users can be told to Stop, given a Warning, or simply provided with passive Information if you set up an Error Alert.

When you've created your Input Message and/or Error Alert (yes, you can do both), you can test them to see what the users will see when they use your workbook and attempt to make an entry in an area subject to validation rules. Figure 14-28 shows the error message that appears when an attempt to enter anything other than a value between .5 and 20.5 was made. Note that the gentle reminder set up in the Input Message tab also appears.

Turning Off Data Validation

You can turn off Data Validation at any time, by selecting the cells where you no longer want any rules to apply and then clicking the Clear All button in the Data Validation dialog box. This puts the Allow setting back to Any Value, which will end validation rules and also make any Error Alerts moot—nothing will trigger them. If you've set up an Input Message, however, you will have to use that tab in the Data Validation dialog box to turn off the message. Simply remove the check next to Show Input Message When Cell Is Selected.

Marking New Invalid Data

If you have data that's already entered prior to setting up validation rules and error messages, or if you've set your Error Alerts to a Warning or Information (which doesn't prevent invalid data from being entered), you can quickly mark all the cells containing invalid data. From the Data tab, choose Data Validation, and then choose Circle Invalid Data from the drop-down menu. All cells with invalid data will be marked, and you can edit them as desired. You can also choose Clear Invalidation Circles if you no longer want to see them.

Only City Is Checked, to Remove Duplicate Entries in the City Column Only

Figure 14-29
Don't repeat yourself—unless you want to. Let Excel look for and remove redundancies in your data.

Looking for Duplicate Entries

Got duplicates? Not sure? They can turn up frequently, especially when you have multiple people working on a worksheet, contributing content. You can make Excel look for and document them in a handy dialog box, giving you the opportunity to decide if they should stay or go. To use this handy feature, follow these steps:

1. Select the range of cells in which you want Excel to check for duplicates.

2. Click the Remove Duplicates button in the Data Tools group of the Data tab.

3. The Remove Duplicates dialog box opens, as shown in Figure 14-29, listing each column in the range of cells you selected.

4. Remove the checks next to any columns you don't want included in the removal of duplicates. If, for example, you want to allow them in all but the City column in a list of cities that includes State, Population, and other data about each city, remove the check next to the columns that contain duplicates that you want to allow.

Tip

Is Excel not seeing your column headings? Check the My Data Has Headers checkbox and Excel will assume the top row of your range contains column headings and will replace the generic Column A entries with whatever text appears at the top of each column.

283

5. Click OK to remove all duplicates from the selected columns.

6. View the results, displayed in a prompt indicating how many duplicates were removed and how many unique vales remain.

Importing and Exporting Your Excel Content

ONE OF THE GREAT THINGS about Microsoft Office—and there are many—is that it's really easy to share content between applications in the suite. It's also easy to take content from another non-Office application and bring it into an Office document, workbook, presentation, or database. Sharing in the other direction—from Office to a non-Office application—is usually pretty simple, too, thanks to the support Office provides for saving and exporting your Office creations (or portions thereof) in a variety of ways.

Using Word, PowerPoint, and Excel Together

To create consistency across your Office-created files, you'll probably need to bring content from a document or presentation into your Excel workbooks at some point. From graphics in a PowerPoint presentation to tables and text from a Word document, there's plenty of content that can easily become part of an Excel workbook, helping you to create a cohesive set of reports. You may also want to share Excel content with Word documents and PowerPoint presentations; the sharing can go both ways, quite easily.

The following examples, including instructions for making them happen will give you a good start on making all your Office files work effectively together:

▶ **Word tables.** These are perfect for use in Excel, assuming they're not populated with long paragraphs of text, that is, because they're already in a grid. To bring a Word table into your Excel worksheet, simply select the table (click the four-headed arrow, as shown in Figure 14-30 or right-click the table and choose Select, Table from the pop-up menu) and copy it to the Clipboard by pressing Ctrl+C. Then hop over to your Excel worksheet, click in the cell where the pasted content should begin (see Figure 14-31), and issue the Paste command (Ctrl+V). Thanks to the tabular structure, each cell in the Word table becomes an Excel worksheet cell. To go the other way, taking a block of cells from an Excel worksheet and adding it to a Word document as a table, simply select the range of cells in Excel, copy them to the Clipboard, and then go back to Word and Paste. It's really that simple!

Arrow Shows Presence of Word Table

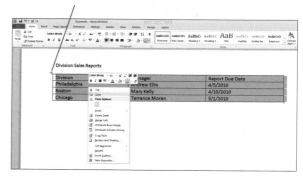

Figure 14-30
Select your Word table and copy it—it's ready to paste into an Excel worksheet in a matter of seconds.

Figure 14-31
Paste that table, and you've got instant worksheet content.

Tip

See that little Paste icon that appears (as shown in Figure 14-31) next to the pasted Word table content? It allows you to choose your Paste Options. You can choose to include the Word formatting that had been applied to the content while it was in the Word document (click the icon on the left for this option), or to just paste the content itself (icon on the right), with no formatting.

► **PowerPoint graphics.** Presentations are quite graphical—meaning they're usually driven by pictures, more than text. Well, a good presentation is, anyway, because a good presentation isn't filled with paragraphs and long bulleted lists. It makes its point with quick bursts of text ("Sales up in Third Quarter!") and then substantiates that with pictures—photos, clipart, and drawn shapes. To bring any graphic from PowerPoint (or Word, for that matter) into Excel, simply click on it to select it, copy it to the Clipboard (Ctrl+C) and then jump back to your worksheet in Excel and paste it (Ctrl+V). Graphics are placed above the spreadsheet (they float on top of it), so you can move and resize the graphics once you bring them into the worksheet, using the handles on the corners and sides. Figure 14-32 shows that process under way.

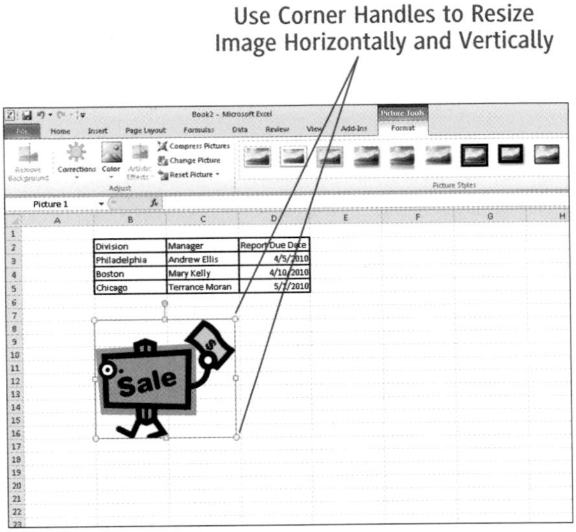

Use Corner Handles to Resize Image Horizontally and Vertically

Figure 14-32
Grab and drag from a corner handle to make your graphic larger or smaller, and maintain its width-to-height ratio at the same time.

Tip

What, no PowerPoint charts? Given that PowerPoint already fires up an Excel window when you create a PowerPoint chart, it makes more sense to copy that chart data into Excel and then use Excel's charting tools to make any chart you want shown in an Excel worksheet. To do so, double-click the chart in PowerPoint to open an Excel window displaying the data that made the chart, and copy that to the Clipboard. Then go back to your Excel worksheet and paste. You can then use Excel's charting tools (see Chapter 11 for the whole process) to make an Excel chart that can be instantly updated whenever the supporting data is changed.

▶ **Excel Charts.** It's easy to share an Excel chart with a PowerPoint presentation or a Word document. Select the chart you've made in Excel, and copy it to the Clipboard. Then go to the slide where you want it to appear in your PowerPoint presentation (or the page in your Word document), and paste it. If you edit the data in Excel—the data that was used to make the Excel chart, that is—you'll see it update not only the Excel chart but the pasted version in PowerPoint or Word. This is a great example of how this compatibility within the Office suite creates consistency—even if nobody will ever see the underlying Excel data that you painstakingly built into your workbook, they will see it through the parts of it used in the report you made in Word and the slide show you created in PowerPoint.

Tip

Access is a very rich, robust database application. If you're not already Access-savvy, it's a good idea to learn more about the application before attempting to use it build a database, which consists of more than just a single table that you bring in from an Excel worksheet. Access requires, for example, unique fields to facilitate some of its functionality. Note the ID field automatically created in Figure 14-35, for example. The copied Excel data (Figure 14-34) did not contain this field, but Access created it anyway, to satisfy its own need for a field containing unique records.

Using Access Tables and Excel Worksheets Together

Access tables are very much like Excel worksheets. They consist of a series of columns and rows, filled with cells containing text and numbers. The text in an Access table is usually spare, too—unlike a Word table, that might contain long paragraphs—because database text is usually limited to single words, short phrases, or very simple paragraphs, such as product descriptions in an inventory database. All this makes Access and Excel quite compatible, and it's simple to take an Access table and bring its content into an Excel worksheet and to go the other way, too—taking your Excel lists and populating an Access table with their records.

To take your Excel worksheet data and build an Access table, follow these steps:

1. Open your Excel worksheet and select the range of cells you want to add to the Access table. If you're planning to create a new Access table from the cells (as opposed to adding records to an existing table), be sure to select the headings, too, as shown in Figure 14-33.

2. Right-click the selected cells and choose Copy from the pop-up menu.

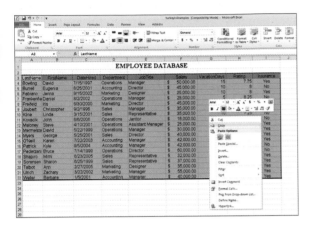

Figure 14-33
Select your Excel worksheet content,
readying it for the trip to Access.

3. Switch over to Access, and in your open database, click the Create tab, and then click the
Table button. A table, blank except for an ID
column, awaits data, as shown in Figure 14-34.

4. Click the Select All box (as indicated in
Figure 14-34) to select every cell in the
Access table.

Select All Box

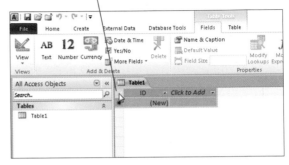

Figure 14-34
The Select All box selects all the records in the table,
even if there aren't any yet, as in this case.

5. Right-click any selected cell in the Access
table, and choose Paste from the pop-up
menu (you can also use the Paste command
in the Home tab). A prompt appears asking if
you're sure you want to paste the records, to
which you should reply by clicking the Yes
button. Your table is created, complete with
the headings (now field names) from your
Excel worksheet, as shown in Figure 14-35.

Figure 14-35
An instant Access table, courtesy of an
existing Excel worksheet.

To take your Access table and add it to an Excel worksheet, follow these steps:

1. Open your Access database, and then open the table that you want to use in your Excel worksheet.

2. Select the entire table, as shown in Figure 14-36. You can also select just a few rows or columns, as desired.

Figure 14-36
An Access table awaits copying and pasting into an Excel worksheet.

3. Copy the cells by choosing Copy from the Home tab, or right-click the selection and choose Copy from the pop-up menu.

4. Switch over to Excel, and click in the cell where the Access content should begin.

5. Press Ctrl + V (or click Paste from the Home tab). The table cells from Access now appear in your worksheet, as shown in Figure 14-37.

Once you paste your content, you'll probably need to widen certain columns to accommodate longer entries or adjust cell formatting—to format dates or numeric content properly, or to change the appearance of text. Figure 14-37 shows the raw content, with no such formatting applied yet. Note the text wrapping in cells, and the pound signs showing where numeric values can't fit within the width of the column. To find out more about the formatting process, review Chapter 5, "Making the Worksheet Look Good."

Paste Option Pop-Up

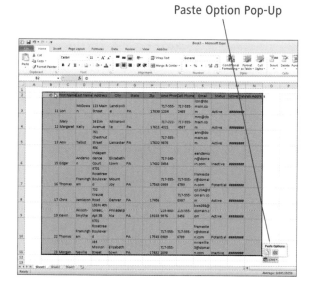

Figure 14-37
Access table content is an easy contribution to an Excel worksheet. You can ignore the Paste Option pop-up, as all formatting from Access (that's applicable in Excel) will come with it by default.

Using Your Excel Data in Other Applications

Excel, like the rest of the Office 2010 suite, makes it easy to share your work with other people, via a variety of applications. You can e-mail a worksheet to someone, you can add your worksheet to the Web for viewing globally, and you can export your worksheets and workbooks in file formats that people can view and print, even if they don't have Excel. All the tools for these forms of Excel outreach can be found on the File tab, using the Save & Send command, shown in Figure 14-38.

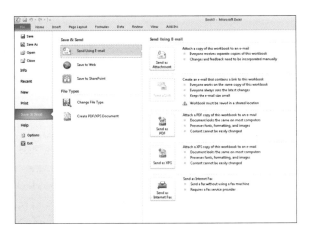

Figure 14-38
The Save & Send command offers you several choices for sharing your Excel workbook with one person or the whole world.

Depending on how you want to share your Excel workbook or worksheet with someone else, you'll make your choice from the Save & Send list. For each command in the list shown in Figure 14-38, the right side of the screen changes to show you the steps and/or options for using that command.

Here are some insights for using these commands:

▶ **Send Using E-Mail.** This command gives you five choices: Send as Attachment, Send a Link, Send as PDF, Send as XPS, and Send as Internet Fax. The icons for each, also shown in Figure 14-38, each either display more steps or actually do something when clicked. You'll have to interact with the steps as they proceed, giving your new file (PDF, XPS) a name, or addressing an e-mail message, but the procedures are simple.

▶ **Save to Web.** This feature requires a Windows Live ID. If you don't have one, clicking the Sign Up for Windows Live link shown in Figure 14-39 will allow you to register for one and continue the process of turning your workbook (or one or more of the worksheets in it) into Web content.

Figure 14-39
Begin the process of creating a workbook for the Web by signing in to Windows Live.

▶ **Save to SharePoint.** SharePoint is an online environment that provides centralized management of resources for organizations. If you don't have SharePoint installed or aren't a user within a SharePoint environment set up by someone else, you won't be able to use this feature. If you do have SharePoint access, click the Browse for a Location link (see Figure 14-40) and choose a spot to post your workbook. If you want to find out more about SharePoint, the Learn More About SharePoint link is a great place to start.

▶ **Change File Type.** This command gives you six workbook file types to choose from, and four non-Excel formats you can pick, too. Pick once by clicking the file type, and then click the Save As button to name and pick a location for your new file. Figure 14-41 displays your options for this Save & Send command.

Figure 14-41

Save your workbook for use by people with older versions of Excel or OpenOffice.

Figure 14-40

Got SharePoint? If so, you can share your Excel workbook with other SharePoint users in your organization.

▶ **Create PDF/XPS Document.** Choose this Save & Send command if you want to send your workbook to someone as a PDF (Portable Document Format file) to view through Adobe Acrobat (or Adobe Reader) or as an XPS (XML Paper Specification file), which can be viewed with Microsoft's XPS viewer, PageMark's viewer, or the Firefox browser, with an XPS viewer plug-in installed. PDF is more universally acceptable, as just about anyone you know will at least have Adobe Reader installed, and they'll then be able to open, view, and print your Excel-based PDF quite easily.

Using

PivotTables

PICTURE YOURSELF USING A LIST OF RECORDS—any list that you have stored in Excel, such as a name and address list, a list of products in inventory, or, as I'll use in the discussion throughout this chapter, a list of employees. Now picture yourself turning that list into a powerful, customizable report that you can use onscreen and/or print, that allows you to view the data from any number of useful perspectives, such as viewing only the employees in a given department, and adding the total salaries paid to them. If you can picture that—or better yet, picture a similar report based on *your* data—you're well on your way to understanding and using PivotTables in Excel 2010.

Creating a PivotTable

SO WHAT IS A PIVOTTABLE, ANYWAY?

The name doesn't really reveal too much, but if you think about what the word pivot means— "A person or thing on which something depends or turns; the central or crucial factor"—you're getting closer to the idea. A PivotTable is a tool by which you can turn your data and view it from any side or angle. Got a list of customers? A PivotTable allows you to quickly see only the people from a given state and to choose exactly the information that will be displayed about those customers. It even allows you to perform a mathematical function on that data, such as an average of their yearly sales. The State field (column) within that list therefore becomes the pivot point—the crucial factor on which everything turns in the report.

The process of creating a PivotTable is pretty simple. It all starts on the Insert tab, as shown in Figure 15-1, where you can see the PivotTable button highlighted. A quick click and the dialog box shown in Figure 15-2 appears, and that's where you'll get started.

PivotTable Button

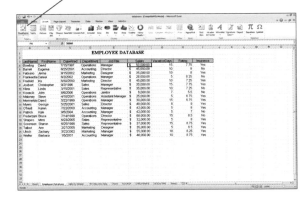

Figure 15-1
The Insert tab offers the PivotTable command.

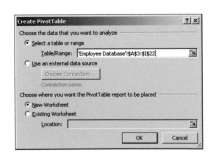

Figure 15-2
Choose which list will be the source of your PivotTable's data.

Preparing for PivotTables

A lot of the concepts covered in this chapter will remind you of the topics covered in Chapters 6, 7, and 8, which cover the ways Excel stores data. From creating and maintaining a list database to sorting and filtering it so you see the data in a way that's useful for your needs, these chapters should definitely be reviewed before you attempt to master PivotTables. If you haven't read them yet, go back and check them out now.

Choosing Your PivotTable Data

As shown in Figure 15-2, the first dialog box you see when you start making a PivotTable has some very specific questions:

▶ **Select a table or range.** This would normally be a worksheet that you already have open, which as shown in Figure 15-3, automatically includes all the records in the active sheet. Excel detects a list in the active worksheet and selects all the records in it—as well as the header row, where field names (column headings) appear. If you want to use another worksheet instead, click the sheet tab for the worksheet containing the data you want to work with, and then click and drag through that data. The range you select appears in the Table/Range box.

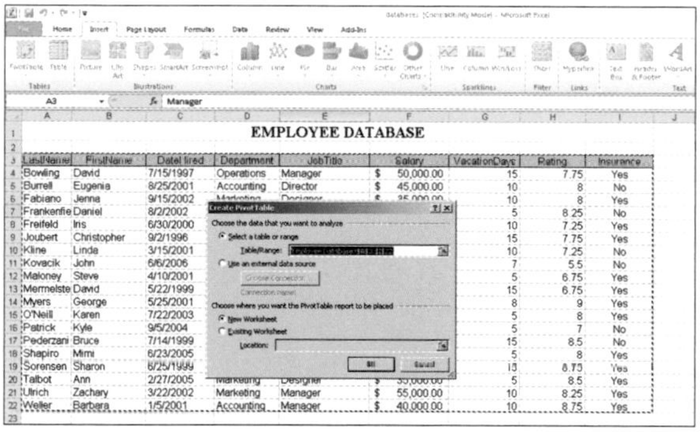

Figure 15-3
Excel's pretty intuitive—if your worksheet contains a list, the list is automatically considered to be the source of your PivotTable data.

▶ **Use an external data source.** This option opens an Existing Connections dialog box, through which you can tap into linked data from the open workbook, or use an MSN MoneyCentral database.

For Excel to automatically determine which list you want to use, you only have to activate one cell in that list before clicking the PivotTable button on the Insert tab. There is no need to select the entire range of cells containing data—in fact, the risk of your accidentally omitting one or more rows of your data or the header row in an attempt to manually select the data first makes it worth it to let Excel make its automatic decision as to the range containing your list!

▶ **Choose where you want the PivotTable report to be placed.** Your choices here are New Worksheet (this is the default, and usually your best bet, so you'll have lots of elbowroom for your PivotTable) or Existing Worksheet. If you opt for the latter, you will need to specify which worksheet should house your PivotTable-to-be. This can be done by clicking the sheet tab where the report should go, and once in that sheet, clicking in the cell where the report should begin. The sheet name and cell address appear in the Location box when you've made your selection.

Once you've told Excel which data you want to use for the PivotTable and where the PivotTable report should be placed, you're ready to start laying out the table, so click OK in the Create PivotTable dialog box, and you're on your way.

Setting Up Your PivotTable Layout

As shown in Figure 15-4, once you've confirmed the range containing your data and told Excel where to create the PivotTable, you're ready to begin laying out the table. As shown on the right side of the workspace in the PivotTable Field List, the empty table awaits your decisions as to which fields from your database to place in which parts of the table. The right side of the workspace also provides four boxes, one for each section of the table, into which you can place your fields to assemble the PivotTable. Here are the sections and how each one works within the table:

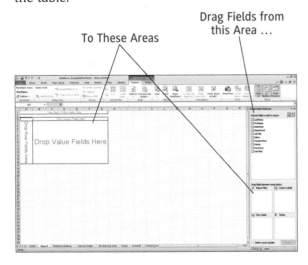

Figure 15-4
The main sections of the PivotTable are already laid out for you. When you drag the fields, the PivotTable will update with data as you complete the process.

▶ **Report Filter Fields (Report Filter)** are the fields that you'll be pivoting, or turning, your database on, to return to the concept of why these reports are called "PivotTables." If you want to see only employees from a particular department in the report, Department would be the Report Filter Field. If you want to see employees with a certain title, Job Title would be the field to place in this area.

▶ **Column Fields (Column Labels)** are the fields containing the data you want to see displayed horizontally for each record shown in the table. For example, if you chose to filter by Department, you could include Job Title in the Column Field area, so that for each department, a horizontal list of all the job titles within each department would appear.

▶ **Row Fields (Row Labels)** are also fields you want to see for each record shown via the Filter Fields. The difference is that these appear vertically. Continuing to use the Employee Database as an example, if you Filter by Department and put Job Title in the Column Fields, you could put Last Name in the Row fields, so that the PivotTable shown in Figure 15-6 would appear, listing each person, by job title, for the selected Department/s in the company.

▶ **Value Fields (Values)** are the fields containing numbers, like Salary (in this example) or, if you were dealing with a product database, the price of each item or the number of items in stock. You get to choose the calculation performed on the data placed here, and typically, people choose to Sum or Average the numbers.

To place the fields on these sections of the PivotTable, drag them, as shown in Figure 15-5, from the PivotTable Field List into the four section boxes in the lower-right side panel. As shown in the figure, the field name follows your mouse as you drag, and you just release your mouse when the box is hovering over the section where you want to drop it. As fields are added to these boxes, which represent sections in the table, a check appears in the box next to the field name, and the field name appears in bold type. Figure 15-6 shows the completed PivotTable, with Department in the Filter Fields section, Job Title in the Column Fields, Last Name in the Row Fields, and Salary in the Value Fields section.

Tip

If you want a chance to review which fields are dropped into which section before seeing the PivotTable created, click the Delay Layout Update checkbox at the bottom-right panel (beneath the four area boxes). Once you're ready to see your PivotTable created, click the Update button.

Tip

You can also drag the field names from the PivotTable Field List directly onto the table itself, dropping them into the sections that say "Drop _____ Fields Here." This causes the table to build as you drop the fields into it, allowing you to see your results immediately.

If you change your mind about a field you've added—either to the four area boxes in the right panel or to the table's Drop *x* Fields areas (where *x* is Row, Column, Filter, or Value)—you can remove any field simply by dragging it back out of the boxes/sections. Once removed, the field is no longer bold or checked in the PivotTable Field List, and you're free to drop it into a different box/section or to choose a different field for use in the table.

Drag Fields Here to   Checked Fields Are
Add to Table   in PivotTable

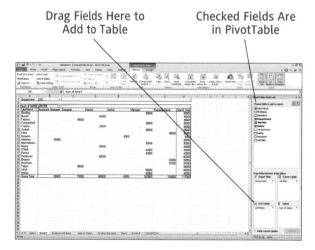

Figure 15-6
A completed PivotTable shows the salaries paid to each person in each Department, organized by Job Title. You drag fields into or out of the boxes in the lower-right to add them to or remove them from the PivotTable.

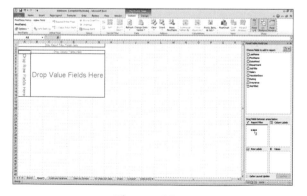

Figure 15-5
Drag and drop, field by field, to build your PivotTable.

Using the PivotTable Tools

ONCE YOUR PIVOTTABLE IS CREATED, you can use the PivotTable tools that appear on the ribbon (see Figure 15-7) to adjust its content and appearance. There are two tabs within this specialized ribbon—Options and Design—and while you don't have to tinker with any of them in order to create, use, and print a PivotTable, many of them are pretty handy.

Options Tab   Design Tab

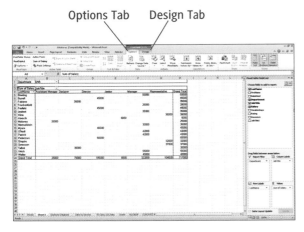

Figure 15-7
Use the PivotTable Tools tabs on the Ribbon to control the functioning and appearance of your PivotTable.

Starting with the Options tab, it's broken into nine sections:

▶ **PivotTable.** This section offers a list of the PivotTables in the active workbook, and if you click the Options drop-down menu, gives you choices for generating and viewing your PivotTable.

▶ **Active Field.** If you click on one of your Row, Column, Filter, or Value fields, all of the options in this section become available, enabling you to Expand and Collapse the data associated with that field, or access Field Settings. If you click that button, the dialog box shown in Figure 15-8 appears, offering you choices to apply to your report's subtotals (click the Custom option) and ways to print your PivotTable.

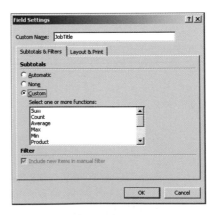

Figure 15-8
Use the Field Settings dialog box to control subtotaling, layout, and printing options.

► **Group.** This section of the ribbon offers Group and Ungroup commands for combining columns or rows within your PivotTable. Select the desired rows or columns you want to group and click Group Selection to give yourself another subset for filtering, sorting, and subtotaling. As shown in Figure 15-9, grouping the managerial positions—Director, Manager, and Assistant Manager—allows the report to show this level of employees separately from the others. If you want to put the grouped rows or columns back into the mix, select them again and click the Ungroup button.

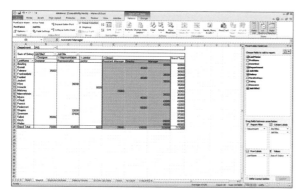

Figure 15-9
Make logical groupings of rows and columns of data in your table with Group and Ungroup.

Tip

You can use the Group Fields command to group numeric or date fields within the PivotTable. Select two or more such fields from your Values fields and then click the button to group them. Click it again to ungroup.

Tip

You can expand and collapse your groups by double-clicking the name (such as Group1). Double-click once, and you collapse it, double-click again to re-expand it. If you open a PivotTable and can't tell if a group within it is expanded or collapsed, check the group name for a blue button with either a plus (+) or a minus (−) sign. Plus means it's collapsed, minus means it's expanded.

► **Sort & Filter.** Use the buttons in this section to put your table in order from smallest to largest (A-Z) or largest to smallest (Z-A) or to open the Sort dialog box (shown in Figure 15-10) for more sorting variables. Be sure your active cell is in the column, row, or value area you want to sort before clicking the Sort button. The Insert Slicer command is less regularly used, but it expands filtering and cubing capabilities by allowing you to further break down a field by the data values within that field. You must be in Compatibility Mode for this tool to be available—which you achieve by opening files that were saved in Excel 97-2003 format (.xls).

Figure 15-10
Sort your PivotTable data up, down, left, and right with the Sort dialog box.

▶ **Data.** This section allows you to Refresh your PivotTable (which goes and checks the source data for changes since the PivotTable was made or opened) and/or to Change Data Source. If you opt for the latter, the Change PivotTable Data Source dialog box opens (see Figure 15-11), allowing you to type or select a different worksheet and/or range of cells to serve as the data that builds your PivotTable.

Figure 15-11
Pick a new source for your PivotTable's data.

▶ **Actions.** Use these three options (Clear, Select, and Move PivotTable) to remove data or filters, select any part of the table, exclusive of everything else, or to literally relocate your PivotTable to another worksheet in your workbook (or another workbook entirely). Each button has a drop-down menu, offering you choices for exactly what to Clear or Select, and to where to move your PivotTable.

▶ **Calculations.** In this section of the Options tab, you can Summarize your PivotTable values (choose a function to perform), display values in a variety of numeric formats (as percentages of the row, column, or grand total), or use the Fields, Items, & Sets command to create and edit calculated fields in your PivotTable. Each of the commands opens an associated dialog box.

▶ **Tools.** This section offers the PivotChart button (which you'll use later in this chapter), and access to OLAP (On Line Analytical Processing) tools and What If Analyses. These features go beyond the scope of this book, but you can find out more about them at Microsoft's Office 2010 Website at http://www.microsoft.com/ office/2010/en/excel/powerpivot/ default.aspx.

▶ **Show.** This last section simply lets you choose what you'll see in your PivotTable and the related workspace. All three buttons should be highlighted (indicating they're "on") by default, including display of the Fields List (on the right side of the workspace), +/− (Expand or Collapse) buttons, and Field Headers. The buttons all work as toggles—one click turns them off, another turns them on.

On the Design tab (shown in Figure 15-12), you can determine what you see in the PivotTable and how it looks. Here are your choices:

▶ **Layout.** Choose which parts of the PivotTable you want to see—Subtotals and Grand Totals—and from their drop-down menus, how they should look if they're displayed. The Report Layout option allows you to show your PivotTable in Compact, Outline, or Tabular format, and to choose how your item labels appear.

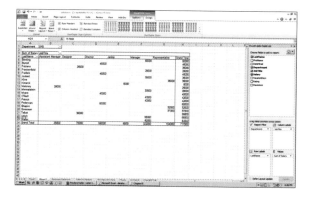

Figure 15-12
Your PivotTable Design options are all housed in the aptly named Design tab.

▶ **PivotTable Style Options.** Here, use the checkboxes to decide which things are included—Row Headers, Column Headers (both on by default), and whether or not to use Banded Rows and Columns. If you turn one or both of these on, the options in the next bullet point, PivotTable Styles, change to show banded options. *Bands* are colored rows and/or columns to help give your PivotTable a more graphical, colorful look.

▶ **PivotTable Styles.** Click on a button for any style that looks interesting—the use of colors, number of bands (colored rows/columns), and so on. Scroll through the list of buttons and test any that look interesting. Figure 15-13 shows one of the styles in place.

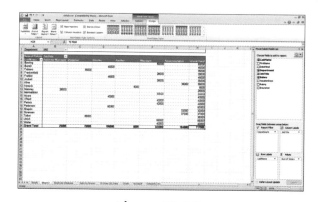

Figure 15-13
Colored bands in the top and bottom rows make this PivotTable more interesting to look at and help draw attention to the row and column labels.

Sorting and Filtering PivotTable Data

By default, all the records in your designated filter field are included in the PivotTable report—in this example, all departments were shown in Figure 15-6. Of course, it's easy to reduce that to show just one department or a selected group of departments, instead. You can also filter which job titles are shown, so that you see only certain jobs in certain departments. Figure 15-14 shows the report reduced to show only the Sales department, with only the sales reps' names and salaries totaled.

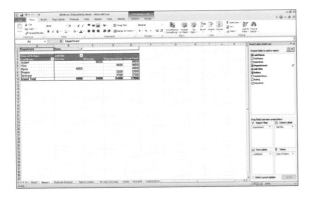

Figure 15-14
Distill the report down to just the one or two filter fields you're interested in, and then decide how much detail you want about each one.

Filtering PivotTable Fields

To filter a field, simply click the drop-down arrow next to it, and choose from the displayed list, as shown in Figure 15-15. The list will include all entries for that field, so in our case, filtering on Last Name wouldn't be the way to go—especially if there were hundreds of employees. Better to filter on Job Title, if you want to reduce the number of employees' and their salaries included for one or more departments. You can, of course, filter by the Report Filter field (Department, in this example), by making a single selection from the list. Turn on the Select Multiple Items checkbox to allow filtering for more than one entry in the list. To bring back the records that a previous filter has hidden, just redisplay the drop-down menu and choose All or Select All (the option will vary depending on whether it's a Report Filter or Column/Row Label field).

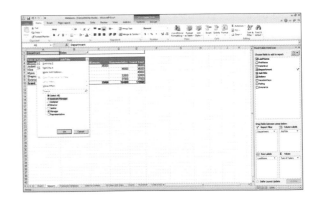

Figure 15-15
Click the drop-down arrow and choose your filter criteria.

Imagine All the Uses!

Need to imagine these concepts in use in some other kind of database? Imagine a list of towns and cities, with the name, state, population, median income, and median housing value included. You could place State in the Report Filter area, City in the Column Labels area, and drop Median Income into the Values box. The resulting report would allow you to view just one or a select group of states and all the cities listed, and have the median income averaged for the cities in the displayed state/s.

Click the Drop-Down Arrow

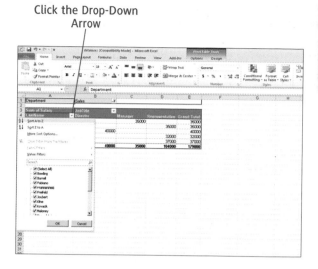

Figure 15-16
Pick which simple sort you want to perform on the records displayed. For example, click the drop-down arrow to see the options for display of the LastName field.

Changing Sort Order

For each part of the PivotTable—row or column fields, the main filter field, even fields added to the value section—it's easy to customize how the data for each field is displayed. As discussed previously, it's easy to choose which records to show, by simply clicking the drop-down triangle next to the field header (the field name) and picking which records you want to see. In that same drop-down menu, shown in Figure 15-16, you can also choose to sort the records in A to Z (ascending) or Z to A (descending) order, or to choose More Sort Options, which displays the dialog box shown in Figure 15-17.

Figure 15-17
Need more than a simple sort? Pick a field to sort by and a sort order for that field, or drag the records up or down within the field to put them in custom order.

Tip

If your PivotTable Field list (right side of the panel) ever disappears, click the Field List button in the Show section of the Insert ribbon tab to redisplay it. The Show section also offers buttons to show or hide PivotTable Buttons and Field Headers.

The Sort dialog box (whose title bar includes the name of the field you were in at the time you opened the dialog box, as shown in Figure 15-17), allows you to sort in the following ways:

▶ **Manual.** This first option is not on by default, but it can be handy if you don't want a traditional ascending or descending order sort. If you turn this option on, you are then free to drag records within the list (horizontal or vertical) of records for that field, creating a totally customized order. You might be ordering them by priority, preference, or some other quality that's not dictated by the first letter or a numerical value.

▶ **Ascending (A to Z).** This option allows you to click the drop-down arrow to choose a field to sort in ascending order.

▶ **Descending (Z to A).** This does the opposite with the field you select from the drop-down menu—it sorts it in descending order.

▶ **Summary.** This area simply describes the sort you've chosen.

▶ **More Options.** Click this button to display the dialog box shown in Figure 15-18, through which you can use AutoSort to automatically re-sort the report each time you update it with new data, or if you turn AutoSort off, you can sort by calculated field values. You will rarely, if ever, need these options, so you'd only ever open this dialog box to access the AutoSort option to turn it on or off.

Figure 15-18
Choose whether Excel will automatically sort your records each time the PivotTable is updated with new or changed data from your list.

Tip

Another way to quickly sort your PivotTable content—say a column of names or numbers—is to switch over to the Data tab on the ribbon, and use the A–Z or Z–A buttons in the Sort & Filter section of the ribbon. Just make sure one of the cells in the desired column is active, and then use the buttons to apply the sort. This can be faster than clicking a drop-down menu and then choosing a command from a menu, especially if you want to try sorting both ways—ascending and then descending—before deciding how you want the list ordered.

Updating a PivotTable Report

You know you can change the fields included in your report at any time, and you know you can move things around, so that what was once in a column is now in a row, or vice versa. That's easy. But what about making your report change to reflect changes in the data that was used to build it?

Picture yourself viewing a PivotTable report and thinking that it's totally up-to-date, only to find out later it wasn't, because while you were viewing it, someone else was adding or changing records. Or that the records you added to the database yourself weren't updated in the table. What to do? Well, first, you need to understand the relationship between the database and the PivotTable.

Just like charts, which you learned about in Chapter 11, "Generating Excel Charts," the PivotTable and the data on which it is based are automatically connected. Make a change in the data, and the chart—or in this case, the PivotTable—reflects that change. Now, if the change to the data just happened a moment ago, you will have to refresh the table to make Excel go back and check the database for changes. Otherwise, it won't check for changes until the table is closed and reopened. You can force this check to happen whenever you want to, however, and if changes are found, the requisite fields are updated in the table.

To make this refreshing change occur, simply go to the Data tab on your ribbon, and while you're in the PivotTable (by "in" I mean with any cell within the table selected), click the Refresh All button (see Figure 15-19) in the Connections section of the ribbon.

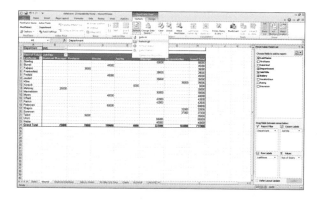

Figure 15-19
Click Refresh All to bring your PivotTable in synch with the database used to build it.

Formatting Your PivotTable

So your PivotTable is all set. You've got the right fields in the right sections, you've filtered and sorted it so that you're seeing the records you want to see in the order you want to see them. Now what? PivotTables in Excel 2010 are great, certainly—they make creating a report on your data simple and the reports themselves are much more useful than a sorted and filtered list. But what about the way the PivotTable looks? As shown in the figures throughout this chapter, PivotTables are pretty boring, visually, and if you or the people you expect to use the report are looking at a lot of data, you want to eliminate that "boring" look as quickly as possible.

To format the appearance of your PivotTable, you use the two different ribbons:

▶ **The Home tab offers formatting options** for changing the fonts, font sizes, colors, and fills applied to the cells in your PivotTable. For more information on using this tab and its Font, Alignment, and Styles sections (shown in Figure 15-20), review Chapter 5, "Making the Worksheet Look Good."

▶ **The PivotTable Tools section of the Ribbon** (activated whenever you're in a PivotTable) offers an Options and a Design tab. The Design tab, shown in Figure 15-21, offers layout options for choosing what you see in your PivotTable and how the rows and columns are structured.

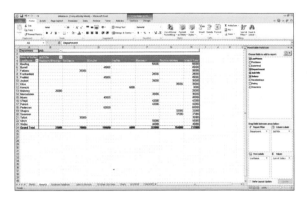

Figure 15-20
The familiar feel of "home" and many of the formatting tools you learned about in Chapter 5 can be used on your PivotTable.

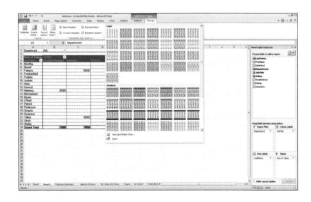

Figure 15-21
Use the PivotTable Tools' Design tab to apply preset PivotTable styles.

Creating a PivotChart

SO YOUR PIVOTTABLE isn't enough to create an easily digestible, here's-my-data-and-what's-important-about-it view of your rows and rows of information? Well, maybe a PivotChart will help complete the picture you'd hoped to paint.

As discussed in Chapter 11, charts are a powerful way to take lots of potentially boring or confusing numeric data and turn it into a picture—a picture that tells a simple story, like "Sales are up in the third quarter!" or "Our managerial salaries are quite high, compared to the rest of the staff." It stands to reason, therefore, that a PivotTable, which already helps distill your data down to the most important and dynamic pieces of information, would be even more powerful if it could also display your data as a picture.

As shown in Figure 15-22, a PivotChart showing the total salaries for each department in the sample company takes the PivotTable to another level. Not only do you see the amounts paid to each department's staff in the table, you see them in a comparative Column chart in the PivotChart. And unlike a static chart that only changes if the data that went into it changes, a PivotChart can be changed using the same filters and sorting tools that change the display in the PivotTable itself—even more flexibility!

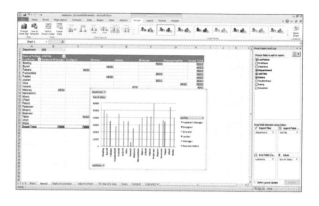

Figure 15-22
Paint an even simpler picture of your data with a PivotChart.

To create a PivotChart, of course you need an existing PivotTable. With any cell in that PivotTable active (to let Excel know which PivotTable you're using as the basis for your PivotChart), as soon as you click the PivotChart button (from the Tools section of the Options tab), the Insert Chart dialog box appears (see Figure 15-23). Use this dialog box to decide which kind of chart you want to create. Pick one and click OK.

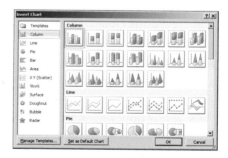

Figure 15-23
3D? Columns? A Pie chart? Pick the type of chart you want to build from your PivotTable data.

As soon as you click OK, the chart appears, as shown in Figure 15-24. Unlike a regular chart, the PivotChart has buttons for your Report Filter field/s, your Row Label field/s, and your Column Label field/s. Plotted within the chart is the data you added to the Values section of the PivotTable.

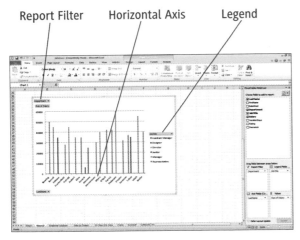

Figure 15-24
A PivotChart, based on your active PivotTable, is instantly created.

To continue developing your chart—changing its size and placement, formatting its bars, slices, lines, and other components, and dressing it up, you can refer to Chapter 11. There, you'll find out how to change the appearance of the chart itself, because despite being a PivotChart, it's still a chart—that you can edit to use the colors, fonts, and other graphical features you need to use in order to make it look as polished as the rest of your workbook. Remember, too, that your PivotChart can be copied and pasted into any Word document or PowerPoint presentation, so you'll need to make it look as good as possible.

That said, there are things about PivotCharts that require specific treatment. For example, using the buttons that list your Report Filter, Row, Column, and Value data.

How do you use them to change the PivotChart as easily as you can change the PivotTable?

▶ **Change the Report Filter field.** To do this, click the button that lists the current field by name. In Figure 15-25, you see "Department," and clicking that button displays a list of the Department field values you can choose from. Pick one or more, and distill the chart down to showing only data related to the Department/s you choose. Note that if you want to pick more than one item from the list of Departments, you must turn on the Select Multiple Items checkbox (as has been done in Figure 15-25).

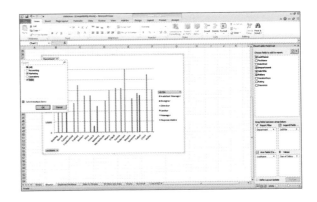

Figure 15-25
Want your PivotChart to show less data? Reduce the number of fields displayed through the Report Filter field.

▶ **Note the changes to the PivotTable fields list panel.** Instead of Column and Row label fields, you now have Legend and Axis fields. You still have Report Filter and Values (which are plotted along the vertical axis in a Column or Line chart), but because it's now a chart you're dealing with, the Row fields become the Axis fields and the Column fields become part of your Legend.

▶ **Change the focus of your PivotChart.** You can do this by making choices from the Legend drop-down menu (see Figure 15-26, where Job Title appears) or the Axis (LastName in this example) drop-down menu (see Figure 15-27). Once you make changes (choosing fewer or more items from the lists to include in the chart), the chart updates to show the requested data.

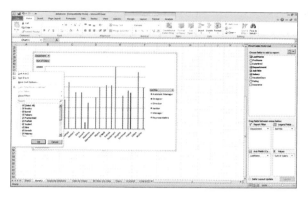

Figure 15-27
Reduce or expand the amount of data plotted along the X (horizontal) axis.

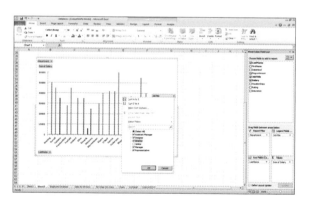

Figure 15-26
Choose which Legend data you want to include in your PivotChart.

PivotChart Data Changes when PivotTable Data Does

It's important to remember that whatever's in the PivotTable will be in the PivotChart. If you change, add, or remove fields in the PivotTable, the chart will update accordingly. This doesn't require any work on your part—as far as the chart is concerned—unless your changes create a problem in the easy or logical interpretation of the chart. For example, if you elected to do a Pie chart, adding multiple fields to the Row or Column fields could mean that there's too much data to plot in a single pie (as you learned in Chapter 11, Pie charts can plot only one data series at a time).

Consider Changing the Chart Type when Your Data Changes Significantly

Be prepared to change your chart type if you make significant changes to the PivotTable, and you can easily do that by clicking the Change Chart Type button (first button on the PivotChart Tools' Design tab). This will open a Change Chart Type dialog box, which is identical to the Insert Chart dialog box shown in Figure 15-23. Pick a chart type to change to, and click OK.

Most people choose to leave their PivotChart on the same worksheet as the PivotTable itself, but if your table and/or chart are large, you may choose to separate them onto individual sheets. To move your PivotChart to a new worksheet, simply create the sheet (click the Insert button on the Home tab and choose Insert Sheet from the menu) and then copy the PivotChart from its current location to that sheet. The connection between the PivotTable and its PivotChart will remain intact—regardless of which sheet the chart moves to.

Index

B

backgrounds
  applying images as, 122–123
  chart background, formatting, 227–229
  creating, 192
  deleting, 192
  Page Setup tools for, 189
  watermarks, inserting, 197
  for WordArt, 252
Backstage view, 8–9
bands in PivotTables, 301
Bar charts, 220–221
Begins With text, filtering for, 179
Below Average values, AutoFilter option for, 177
Between values, AutoFilter option for, 177
Bevel picture effect, 242
black and white charts, printing, 207
blank cells. *See* cells
block of cells. *See* cells
blur effect for images, 241
boldfacing text, 110
bookmarks for Web pages, 141
borders
  adding, 111–112
  formulas, colored borders for cells referenced by, 93
  images, adding to, 242
Borders menu, 111–112
Borders tool, 111–112
bottom alignment of text, 113
boxes, drawing, 244
brightness of images, adjusting, 241
bringing forward pictures, 242
Browsed Pages button, 141
Bubble charts, 221

C

calculated columns, 89
  errors, flagging, 89

calculations. *See also* **formulas; functions**
  automatic calculations, performing, 62
  in PivotTables, 300
  showing calculation steps, 93
  in Subtotal report fields, 163–166
Calibri font, 110
callout bubbles, drawing, 244
case-sensitivity
  of function names, 53
  for replacing data, 147
  for searching data, 145
cell addresses, 5
  absolute formula reference, creating, 47–48
  last cell, viewing, 11
  mixed formula reference, creating, 48–49
cell references
  in formulas, 36–37, 137
  in multiple worksheets, 137
  in other workbooks, 138
  #REF! error message, 85
cell rules
  creating, 117–120
  editing, 120
  highlighting rules, 118–119
  new rules, creating, 119–120
  Top/Bottom Rules command, 119
cells. *See also* **fonts; merged cells; range names;**
      range of cells; validating worksheet content
  active cell, 5
  blank cells
    accepting, 27
    searching for, 175–176
  block of cells
    deleting, 109
    inserting, 107–108
  deleting, 20–21, 109
    overlapping cells, content of, 108
  dependents, identifying, 96–98
  editing contents of, 19
  font size, changing, 104

F

field names, sorting data with, 160

files
    headers or footers, name and path in, 195
    workbook, changing file type in, 291

Fill Color tool, 111–112

filtering data, 169–181. *See also* **PivotTables**
    applying filters, 170–172
    blank cells, searching for, 175–176
    clearing filters, 171–172
        secondary filters, 174
    color, filtering by, 178
    comparison operators, filtering with, 180
    copying filtered data, 172–173
    date, filtering by, 177–178
    dynamic filters, 177–178
    formulas with filtered data, using, 181
    images, applying color filters on, 241
    multiple filters, applying, 174
    pasting filtered data, 172–173
    secondary filters, 174–175
    text, filtering, 179–180
    time, filtering by, 178
    values, filtering by, 176–177

final, marking workbook as, 264–265

Financial functions, 52
    working with, 66–68

find and replace, 144–147. *See also* **AutoFilter**
    blank cells, searching for, 175–176
    cell data, replacing, 146–147
    data, searching for, 144–146
    named ranges, finding, 25
    options
        for replacing data, 147
        for search, 145
    wildcards, 145–146

Find & Select button, 144

Fit All Columns on One Page scaling option, 187

Fit All Rows on One Page scaling option, 187

Fit Sheet on One Page scaling option, 187

flagging errors. *See* **formula errors**

flowchart objects, drawing, 244

focus
    of charts, 225–226
    of PivotCharts, 309–310

fonts
    applying, 110–111
    cell font size, changing, 104
    color, applying, 110–111
    for comments, 278
    for hyperlinks, 139
    for PivotTables, 306
    rows, changing font size affecting, 104

footers. *See* **headers and footers**

FORMAT argument with TEXT function, 72

Format button for changing column width, 103

Format Cell Alignment command, 113

Format Cells dialog box, 72, 113, 262
    for hiding cells, 154

Format Chart Area dialog box, 228
    Format tab, 228

Format Comment dialog box, 279

Format Data Labels dialog box, 232–233

Format Data Series dialog box, 226–227

Format Data Table dialog box, 233

Format Legend dialog box, 230

Format Major Gridlines dialog box, 228–229

Format Series dialog box
    Design tab, 227
    Format tab, 226

formatting
    cell content, 110–114
    cell rules, editing, 120
    comments, 278–279
    conditional formatting, 117–121
    finding formatting options, 145
    headers or footers, pictures for, 195
    images, 240–243
    numeric formatting, 115–117
    pasted data, 173
    PivotCharts, 308
    PivotTables, 306

Formula AutoComplete, 55–56

X–Y

XPS documents, creating, 291

Year argument, 75
YEAR function, 74

Z

zero, dividing by, 84
Zoom Slider, 149
    Full Screen view, removal in, 151
zooming in/out of worksheets, 148–149